SAMUEL DAVID LUZZATTO

Prolegomena to a Grammar
of the Hebrew Language

SAMUEL DAVID LUZZATTO

Prolegomena to a Grammar of the Hebrew Language

TRANSLATED, ANNOTATED,
AND WITH ADDITIONAL MATERIAL BY

AARON D. RUBIN

GORGIAS PRESS
2005

ISBN 1-59333-334-X

GORGIAS PRESS
46 Orris Ave., Piscataway, NJ 08854 USA
www.gorgiaspress.com

Printed and bound in the United States of America.

For my grandparents
SIDNEY AND EVELYN CHAIRMAN
with love

CONTENTS

ACKNOWLEDGEMENTS

This project would not have been possible without the outstanding Hebrew and Judaica collections of the Andover, Houghton, and Widener libraries of Harvard University. I would like to thank the staff of these libraries, including those of the Widener Judaica Division, for their assistance in obtaining materials from their collections.

It is my pleasure to thank Kimberly De Wall, who assisted with this project in a number of ways. Not only has she been a constant source of encouragement and moral support, but she has also been an excellent editor. In addition, when I was away from Cambridge, and unable to visit the Harvard Libraries, she was always willing to go in my place. Her research assistance was of enormous help, and for that I am very grateful.

For their generous help in translating Latin passages, from the *Prolegomeni* and from the secondary literature, I am indebted to Philip J. King, Daniel Berman, Philip Baldi, Paul Harvey, and Stephen Wheeler. For their help with difficult Italian passages, I must thank Valentina Cesco and Pierluigi Cuzzolin. My colleague Markus Asper also kindly came to my aid in matters classical and linguistic.

My sincere thanks go to Angel Sáenz-Badillos, who examined an earlier draft of this work and offered a number of valuable corrections and references, as well as to Geoffrey Khan and Jordan Penkower, for their expert assistance with various details.

I am grateful to George Kiraz and the Gorgias Press for allowing me the opportunity to publish this volume. Financial support for publication was made available by Penn State University, in part through the generosity of the Department of Classics and Ancient Mediterranean Studies (Gary Knoppers, Head) and the Jewish Studies Program (Brian Hesse, Director); my sincere thanks to them all.

I would like to thank my parents, Andrew and Louise (who bought me a copy of the *Prolegomeni* as a gift), my sister Jill, and my grandparents Sidney and Evelyn, for their unfailing love and support.

Finally, I would like to express my gratitude to Samuel David Luzzatto, whose work continues to teach and inspire.

TRANSLATOR'S PREFACE

The present work is an annotated translation of Samuel David Luzzatto's *Prolegomeni ad una grammatica ragionata della lingua ebraica*, which was published in Padua in 1836; the Italian original has never been reprinted, nor has it ever been fully translated. Luzzatto made it clear that these *Prolegomeni* were intended to serve as an introduction to a complete Hebrew grammar (see p. 3, below); his *Grammatica della lingua ebraica* appeared 1853–67.

The *Prolegomeni* is a remarkable work, which continues to possess great value for the modern scholar. The first part of the work is essentially a history of Hebrew scholarship, from the time of the earliest grammatical references in Rabbinic literature down to Luzzatto's own era. Though preceded by Hetzel's *Geschichte der hebräischen Sprache* (1776) and Gesenius's work of the same name (1815), both of which provide ample discussion of this topic, Luzzatto supersedes them in the scope of his survey. He includes both Christian and Jewish scholars, whereas the earlier two works focus almost exclusively on Christian Hebraists once their discussions move beyond the year 1500. In fact, Luzzatto's treatment of the history of Hebrew scholarship has, in some ways, yet to be surpassed. There have been several works that have treated particular periods of Hebrew scholarship in depth (for example, medieval Jewish grammarians or sixteenth-century Christian Hebraists), but no one has matched the scope and range of Luzzatto's concise survey. This is a major element of the book's present value and attraction.

The second part of the *Prolegomeni* deals with the history of the Hebrew language itself, including discussion of the Semitic languages and their internal classification, and discussion of the various phases of the Hebrew language. Luzzatto's ideas on the Semitic languages are clearly quite outdated; after all, at the time of his writing, Akkadian, Ugaritic, Eblaite, the Amarna letters, several Aramaic dialects, and the Modern South Arabian languages had yet to be discovered, the other Semitic languages were less well known, and the field of historical linguistics was still in its infancy. Many of the ideas put forth in this section of the *Prolegomeni* are now easily dismissible, most notably his notion that Aramaic is the parent language from which Hebrew descends. Yet within his discussion of the Semitic languages, in itself still interesting from a historical perspective, we find many worthy observations. Luzzatto's discussion of the different phases of Hebrew is significant, for Luzzatto was one of the first scholars to recognize the true nature of Rabbinic Hebrew as a living language (see especially §§ 82, 83, 89, below). Previously it had been almost universally believed that the Hebrew of the Mishnah and other Rabbinic texts was a creation of the sages, and not a living language spoken by the people. Luzzatto not only argued that this Hebrew was a true spoken language, but that it was worthy of the same critical study as Biblical Hebrew. Luzzatto also recognized the distinction between Pre- and Post-Exilic Biblical Hebrew, a division still endorsed today.

The third main section of the *Prolegomeni*, entitled "Fundamental Laws of the Grammatical Formation of Words," is an attempt to explain many phonological details of Hebrew and Aramaic. Though somewhat primitive in its linguistic execution, and though based on the incorrect notion that Hebrew has developed out of a primitive Aramaic, this section shows Luzzatto's natural brilliance as a linguist. Within the outdated ideas are once again insights that are of great value to the modern scholar.

Following these three main sections of the *Prolegomeni* are a series of appendices, some of which follow up on the phonological discussion of the previous section. Much more valuable are the discussions of the systems of Hebrew accentuation and pointing, a topic which is also discussed at length in the chapter on Hebrew scholarship. The history of these systems was not well understood in the time of Luzzatto, nor was their application. Luzzatto can be credited for reviving, or at least re-popularizing, the ideas of the gifted sixteenth-century grammarian Elijah Levita, who was the first to claim that the Hebrew vowel and accent signs were not ancient, but in fact dated to the first millennium of the common era. Luzzatto repeats and expands on the arguments of Levita. He also provides a detailed account of the use of the accentuation system, on which he further elaborated in the first fascicle of his *Grammatica della lingua ebrea* (pp. 47–75) and elsewhere. Finally, Luzzatto provides an explanation of the discrepancies in the use of the vowel points in various manuscripts, a most beneficial tool for anyone working with pointed manuscripts. Luzzatto's work thus illuminates both the use and the history of the Tiberian system of vocalization and accentuation, and has contributed greatly to our understanding of both.

In short, the *Prolegomeni* includes a wealth of valuable information on a variety of topics relating to Hebrew, which has for too long been inaccessible to modern scholars. It is hoped that this present translation will allow a greater number of scholars to appreciate the benefits of Luzzatto's work, as well as encourage further study (and translations) of his many other scholarly efforts.

SAMUEL DAVID LUZZATTO

Samuel David Luzzatto, also commonly known by his Hebrew acronym *Shadal* (שד״ל), was born in Trieste on August 22, 1800.[1] Though part of a well-known Italian family, which included several illustrious members both before and after his own time, Samuel David grew up in relative poverty. He was given a traditional Jewish education, much of it provided by his father Hezekiah, a turner by trade. At a young age, Luzzatto exhibited a remarkably keen talent for Hebrew language and textual study, as well as a highly critical eye. At just thirteen or fourteen, he independently concluded that the system of Hebrew diacritical marks that indicated vowels and accents could not be traced to antiquity as tradition held, and in fact began to write on the subject.

Due to an illness, Luzzatto was forced to quit school at age thirteen. He continued to study however, mainly with his father, who was himself well educated. The death of his mother in April, 1814, and the general financial situation of the family left Samuel with many responsibilities at home; however, he always maintained his studies. In fact, all attempts to teach him a trade were in vain, as learning was his only passion. For a two or three year period in his teens (ca. 1816–19) Luzzatto studied on a daily basis with his cousin Samuel Vita Lolli. In addition to becoming very close friends, they both benefited greatly from their scholarly exchanges. It was through Lolli that Luzzatto got to know and correspond with Isaac Samuel Reggio, a man who grew to be a great supporter of Luzzatto. In 1829, when Reggio founded the Rabbinical College of Padua (*Collegio Rabbinico di Padova*), he immediately hired Luzzatto as a professor. There he would remain until his death in 1865.

---

[1] For a detailed biography of SDL, see Morris B. Margolies, *Samuel David Luzzatto: Traditionalist Scholar* (New York, 1979).

Luzzatto's scholarly output was immense. Writing equally comfortably in Hebrew and Italian, he authored approximately forty books and a much greater number of articles.[2] His articles appeared in the leading Jewish academic journals of his day, most notably *Kerem Ḥemed* and *Bikkurei ha-Ittim*. There was hardly an area of Jewish scholarship in which he did not make an important contribution. In addition, he corresponded frequently with many of Europe's leading Jewish scholars, including Geiger, Zunz, Jost, Rapoport, Dukes, Steinschneider, and Letteris.[3]

Luzzatto's reputation was widespread even among his non-Jewish contemporaries. Wilhelm Gesenius, one of the greatest and most influential Hebraists of the nineteenth century, once referred to Luzzatto as the best Orientalist in Italy, and this while Luzzatto was only in his mid-thirties.[4] Much of his linguistic scholarship was scattered among his articles and letters, but he produced three major grammatical works, all written in Italian: the *Prolegomeni*, the above-mentioned grammar of Hebrew, and his grammar of Biblical and Talmudic Aramaic.[5] In addition, we should add to these three his Hebrew-language work *Ohev Ger*, or *Philoxenus* (Vienna, 1830; 2nd ed., Krakow, 1895), an important study of Targum Onkelos, which includes much discussion of linguistic issues. The final section of *Ohev Ger* includes a section devoted to Syriac, in which he briefly narrates its history and illustrates, with many examples, its value to the study of Jewish

---

[2] A detailed catalog of his work, totalling nearly five hundred pages, was compiled by his son Isaiah, *Catalogo Ragionato degli Scritti Sparsi di Samuele Davide Luzzatto* (Padua, 1881).

[3] Nearly seven hundred of his Hebrew letters—many containing valuable scholarly material—were published posthumously in the collection *Iggerot Shadal* (Przemyśl, 1882–91), collected by his son Isaiah and edited by E. Gräber. An additional collection of over seven hundred letters in Italian, French, and Latin was published by his sons as *Epistolario Italiano Francese Latino di Samuel David Luzzatto* (Padua, 1890).

[4] "Dieser ausgezeichnete und fleissige jüdische Gelehrte, den Gesenius den besten Orientalisten Italiens nennt…" This line appeared in an announcement of the publication of the *Prolegomeni* in the periodical *Allgemeine Zeitung des Judenthums* 86 (Leipzig, 19 October 1837, p. 344).

[5] *Elementi grammaticali del caldeo biblico e del dialetto talmudico babilonese* (Padua, 1865). An English translation of this work was made by J. S. Goldhammer (New York, 1876) and a German translation by M. S. Krüger (Breslau, 1873).

Aramaic dialects. In the *Prolegomeni*, he again introduces evidence from Syriac in order to shed light on the phonology, morphology, and semantics of Biblical and Targumic Aramaic, and even Hebrew. His use of Syriac is noteworthy, as Luzzatto was one of the first Jewish scholars to recognize its importance.[6]

Luzzatto's use of Syriac in his linguistic studies is a testament not only to his talent as a linguist, but also to his willingness to explore non-Jewish sources. It could be argued that it was precisely Luzzatto's familiarity with (and mastery of) both the Christian and Jewish scholarly worlds that made him such a unique and important scholar. The breadth of his knowledge and the sources with which he was familiar are evident in the first part of the *Prolegomeni*, which, as already stated above, is essentially unrivalled in content.

Luzzatto was also very interested in the medieval Hebrew poets and authors. His published works in the field include an edition of Judah ha-Levi's *Divan*, with commentary (Lyck, 1864). A number of other works, including Efodi's *Ma'aseh Efod* and Joseph ha-Cohen's *Emek ha-Bachah*, though ultimately credited to others, were published largely through the efforts of Luzzatto. His work on the medieval authors went a long way to opening up and promoting interest in the field. His expertise in this area, which provided him a much wider base from which to study Hebrew, is also evident in the *Prolegomeni*. It should be noted that Luzzatto was a poet himself, from the time he was a teenager.[7]

Finally, some mention should be made of Luzzatto's theology and philosophy. He was a traditionalist and a faithful defender of Orthodoxy, with little regard for the reforming tendencies of his time. He was adamant in his belief in the Mosaic authorship of the Torah, as well as in the unity of the book of Isaiah. At the same time, his faith did not stop him from critical scholarship. He refuted the Solomonic authorship of Ecclesiastes, for example. As already noted above, he broke with traditionalism in his stance regarding the antiquity of the Hebrew vowel and accent signs. He also felt free to amend the consonantal text of the Hebrew Bible (outside the

---

[6] Many would say he was the first, but Luzzatto himself in *Ohev Ger* (1895 edition, p. 93) states that Judah ben Zeev had already cited the value of Syriac in the introduction to his edition of Ben Sira (Breslau, 1798).

[7] Much of his poetry can be found in the collection entitled *Kinnor Na'im* (vol. 1, Vienna, 1825; vol. 2, Padua, 1879).

Pentateuch) when necessary—a somewhat radical idea at the time—not to mention the vocalization and accentuation.

He was a staunch opponent of the Kabbalah, and mysticism in general, which he saw as anathema to Judaism. He also objected to the fusion of Judaism with philosophy, and condemned scholars like Maimonides, Ibn Ezra, and especially Spinoza for doing so. He saw Judaism as diametrically opposed to "Atticism" (אטיציזמוס), that is, Hellenism, and rationalism. However, despite his strong opposition to philosophy and mysticism, it should be noted that he was very learned in both subjects, and was familiar with all of the principal Jewish, Greek, and Christian philosophers.

We see in Luzzatto a traditional and faithful Jew, and a supporter of the ideas that would become Zionism, who spent his life trying to find the perfect balance between his faith and his scholarship. The life's work of Samuel David Luzzatto can be summed up with the following statement of his: "Hebrew is my passion, and the revival of its literature the most beautiful dream of my life."[8]

PREVIOUS TRANSLATIONS OF THE *PROLEGOMENI*

Luzzatto's *Prolegomeni* was partially translated into English by Sabato Morais in 1896.[9] Morais made an admirable translation, but besides remaining relatively unknown, and being quite difficult to find, it suffers from several drawbacks. Most significantly, the translation is only partial, omitting the various appendices that make up about thirty-five percent of the original book (though he does provide a convenient summary of them) and occasionally omitting whole sections of the main text, in particular those which are essentially bibliographical lists (e.g., §§ 20, 27, 29). For the sake of brevity, Morais also omits Luzzatto's numerous footnotes, which are often very lengthy and full of fascinating insights; sporadically Morais does weave a part of a note into the main text. In addition, Morais omits many of

---

[8] "Enfin l'hébreu c'est ma passion, et la résurrection de sa littérature c'est le songe de toute ma vie." This comes from a letter to A. Geiger, found on p. 562 of SDL's *Epistolario* (see note 3, above).

[9] *Prolegomena to a Grammar of the Hebrew Language*, published as an appendix to *Proceedings of the Fifth Biennial Convention of the Jewish Theological Seminary Association* (1896). Biographical information on Morais can be found in the appendix to the present work.

Luzzatto's illustrative examples, again for the sake of brevity. Morais' own footnotes amount to but a handful.

Almost simultaneously, and by coincidence, the Italian scholar Vittorio (Yitshak Hayyim) Castiglioni,[10] made a partial translation of Luzzatto's *Prolegomeni* into Hebrew, which was published in two parts. The first part appeared in 1895,[11] and the second a year later.[12] Morais was able to see at least one of these just prior to the publication of his own translation, in the final two pages of which he praises that of Castiglioni. Castiglioni's translation is quite a faithful one, written in a very lucid Hebrew style that makes for undemanding reading. Unlike Morais, Castiglioni includes the original footnotes and does not abridge the denser paragraphs. On the other hand, he omits both the preface and part three (unlike Morais), as well as the appendices. Castiglioni's translations are very useful for their clarity of style, but much more so for the translator's valuable additions. At the end of part one, Castiglioni adds several pages (pp. 48–61) of valuable bibliographical data, listing roughly 140 works on Hebrew grammar that appeared subsequent to the publication of the original volume in 1836. Frequently inserted in the translation of part two (and clearly marked as additions) are his own lengthy footnotes, often citing more recent scholarly work.

THE PRESENT TRANSLATION

The present translation, in addition to being complete, has attempted to remain as faithful as possible to the original, both in form and content. I have retained Luzzatto's elevated and archaic style, even where this makes

---

[10] Biographical information on Vittorio Castiglioni can be found in the appendix.

[11] *Yad Shadal* (Krakow, 1895). Written in Trieste, this volume commemorates the erection of a monument over SDL's grave, on the thirtieth anniversary of his death. In addition to the translation itself (which bears the title *Mekor Dikduk ha-Ivri ve-Mahalach Shalmoto*), the volume includes sixteen pages in Italian relating to this event, namely a discussion of the monument erected, the text of the speeches of Castiglioni and others from the dedication ceremony, and a list of works which had appeared in honor of SDL's death.

[12] This translation, entitled *Toldot Leshon Ever* appeared in the journal *Otsar ha-Sifrut* 5 (1896), pp. 16–34.

reading somewhat awkward, with the aim of conveying to the reader the style in which the original was written. I follow Luzzatto's formatting more closely than Morais; that is to say, I provide Hebrew characters (and vocalization) only where in the original, and follow Luzzatto's use of transcription and translation. Luzzatto's use of capital letters, italics, abbreviation, and even punctuation is rather inconsistent; for the most part, I follow the original text in its inconsistency. It did seem useful to elaborate on (and correct) his bibliographical references, which is done so either in the footnotes or in square brackets [ ]. Brackets are also used for the insertion of words meant to elucidate certain passages, or, less often, to indicate the underlying Italian text where it seems particularly useful. All of Luzzatto's footnotes appear here in small print within the main body of text, designated—as Luzzatto did—with a number in parentheses: (1). The translator's notes appear as standard footnotes. Morais' own footnotes were rather few in number, but I make reference to most of them in my own.

TRANSCRIPTION

I have retained, more or less, Luzzatto's transcription system, with the necessary adaptations for English (vs. Italian) spelling conventions. The transcription of the Hebrew consonants are as follows: א '; ב *b*; ב *v*; ג, ג *g*; ד, ד *d*; ה *h*; ו *v*; ז *z*; ח *ḥ*; ט *t*; י *y*; כ *k*; כ *ch*; ל *l*; מ *m*; נ *n*; ס *s*; ע '; פ *p*; פ *f*; צ *ts*; ק *k*; ר *r*; שׁ *sh*; שׂ *s*; ת, ת *t*. Note that word-initial א and ע are not indicated.

Luzzatto used the Hebrew alphabet for Syriac and Arabic words. In order to remain faithful to the spirit of the original work, I have not altered this practice. I do not think that this hinders understanding of the Syriac or Arabic; in the rare case where I think it does, I have added a footnote with transcription.

REFERENCES

In the translator's footnotes, short titles have been used occasionally. The following abbreviations are used:

Encyclopaedia Judaica
> *Encyclopaedia Judaica*. 16 vols. 1971. Jerusalem: Keter.

Fürst, *BJ*
> Fürst, Julius. 1849–63. *Bibliotheca Judaica*. 2 vols. Leipzig: W. Engelmann. [Reprint, 1960, Hildesheim: Olms]

Gesenius-Kautzsch-Cowley
> Kautzch, E., ed. 1910. *Gesenius' Hebrew Grammar*. 2nd ed. Trans. A. E. Cowley. Oxford: Clarendon.

Hetzel, *Geschichte*
> Hetzel, Wilhelm. 1776. *Geschichte der hebräischen Sprache*. Halle: Carl Hermann Hemmerde.

Ibn Ezra, *Moznayim*
> Ibn Ezra, Abraham. 2002. *Sefer Moznayim*, ed. Lorenzo Jiménez Patón and Angel Sáenz-Badillos. Córdoba: Ediciones el Almendro.

Jastrow, *Dictionary*
> Jastrow, Marcus. 1903. *Dictionary of the Targumim, Talmud Bavli, Talmud Yerushalmi and Midrashic Literature*. New York: G. P. Putnam.

Jewish Encyclopedia
> *The Jewish Encyclopedia*. 12 vols. 1901–7. New York and London: Funk and Wagnalls.

Maman, *Philology*
> Maman, Aharon. 2004. *Comparative Philology in the Middle Ages*. Leiden: Brill.

Richler, *Hebrew Manuscripts*
> Richler, Binyamin, ed. 2001. *Hebrew Manuscripts in the Biblioteca Palatina in Parma*. Jerusalem: Jewish National and University Library.

Steinschneider, *BH*
  Steinschneider, Moritz. 1859. *Bibliographisches Handbuch zur hebräischen Sprachkunde.* Leipzig: Vogel. [Reprint, 1976, Hildesheim: Olms]

In addition to the above, the following other works on the history of the Hebrew language were consulted with profit, and are recommended to the reader as a starting point for further study:

Bacher, Wilhelm. 1892. *Die hebräische Sprachwissenschaft vom 10. zum 16. Jahrhundert.* Trier: S. Mayer. [Reprint, 1974, Amsterdam: Benjamins]

Bacher, Wilhelm. 1895. *Die Anfänge der hebräischen Grammatik.* Leipzig: F. A. Brockhaus. [Reprint, 1974, Amsterdam: Benjamins]

Chomsky, William. 1957. *Hebrew: The Eternal Language.* Philadelphia: Jewish Publication Society.

García-Jalón de la Lama, Santiago. 1998. *La gramática hebrea en Europa en el Siglo XVI: Guía de lectura de las obras impresas.* Salamanca: Universidad Pontificia de Salamanca.

Geiger, Ludwig. 1870. *Das Studium der hebräischen Sprache in Deutschland vom Ende des XV. bis zur Mitte des XVI. Jahrhunderts.* Breslau: Schletter'sche.

Gesenius, Wilhelm. 1815. *Geschichte der hebräischen Sprache und Schrift.* Leipzig: F. C. W. Vogel. [Reprint, 1973, Hildesheim: Olms]

Hirschfeld, Hartwig. 1926. *Literary History of Hebrew Grammarians and Lexicographers.* London: Oxford University Press.

Mierowsky, David. 1953. *Hebrew Grammar and Grammarians Throughout the Ages.* Johannesburg: D. Dainow.

Sáenz-Badillos, Angel. 1993. *A History of the Hebrew Language.* Trans. John Elwolde. Cambridge: Cambridge University Press.

Sáenz-Badillos, Angel and Judith Targaróna Borras. 1988. *Gramáticos hebreos de al-Andalus (Siglos X–XII): Filología y Biblia.* Cordoba: El Almendro.

PROLEGOMENI

AD UNA

GRAMMATICA RAGIONATA

DELLA

LINGUA EBRAICA

DI

SAMUEL DAVID LUZZATTO

DA TRIESTE

PROFESSORE DI LINGUA EBRAICA E CALDAICA, SACRA ESEGESI
TEOLOGIA DOGMATICA E MORALE, E STRORIA ISRAELITICA
NEL COLLEGIO RABBINICO DI PADOVA

PADOVA

Tipografia e Fonderia Cartallier

1836

AUTHOR'S PREFACE

The first step of human intellect, wherever it directed its speculations, was empirical; the second was rational; and every branch of knowledge was first History, then Science.

We began by observing, collecting phenomena, and distributing them into classes, following the most external analogy; thus we had Histories. Subsequently, it was discovered that some phenomena were the cause of certain others; then the known classifications were corrected according to more internal analogies; the causes of the phenomena were investigated more and more in depth, and thus we had Science.

The study of languages is also susceptible to these two methods, empirical and rational; and it necessarily must have begun with the former.

Living languages, as the object of a more practical rather than theoretical study, saw their cultivators stop for a long time at this first step; only very late and very slowly did they take care to move Grammars and Lexicons from the state of history to that of science.

Dead languages, as the exclusive property of Scholars, found sooner those who strove to investigate causes, and to weave from them rational and philosophical Grammars and Lexicons.

Just as familiarity with any language includes two kinds of knowledge: that of the words of the language, which is contained in the Dictionaries and Lexicons; and that of the inflections of those words, and the manner of connecting them in speech, which is contained in the Grammars; so also the philosophy of languages, or linguistic Rationalism, comprises two parts, analogous to this division, which we will call grammatical Rationalism and lexical Rationalism. It is evident that these two philosophies are never completely separated, but must go hand in hand.

In general, however, linguistic Rationalism can be of two types, inasmuch as the causes of the phenomena of a given language can be sought in the language itself, or in some other language from which we suppose it to have its origin, or at least derived some alterations or

1

developments. We will call these two manners of investigating the philosophy of languages: internal linguistic Rationalism, and external linguistic Rationalism. These two manners of linguistic philosophy cannot be separated: this is because every language must have its particular nature and its exclusive and characteristic ways, a fact which gives place to internal linguistic Rationalism; and every language is derived from another earlier one, or has received alterations and additions from other contemporary languages; or at least has given rise to other languages which serve to illustrate it; and this gives place to external Rationalism.

The Hebrew Language was very early on treated with a certain degree of Rationalism, both internal and external. Of the former, Judah ben Ḥayyuj may be considered the father; of the second, Judah Ben-Karish [ibn Quraish].

The non-Israelite Hebraists, after having translated and reorganized the theories of the [medieval Jewish] Hebrew Grammarians during the sixteenth century, began in the seventeenth to introduce the rational method into the study of the Hebrew language. Of the external linguistic Rationalism among the Christians, Ludwig de Dieu can be called the father; of the internal, Jacob Alting: and among the moderns, Albert Schultens of the former, and Georg Heinrich August Ewald of the latter.

After occupying myself in the years of my youth with a predilection for the internal Rationalism of the holy Language, about which I have published many things in various volumes of the Hebrew journal entitled BIKKUREI HA-ITTIM, concerning both the grammatical and lexicological parts of the language; I became aware in 1829 of the highly valuable works of modern Orientalists. The study of the works of the great Wilhelm Gesenius, Professor at Halle, in Prussia, was the reason that, with pleasure, my foot landed on the path of external Rationalism.

So when at the end of the same year 1829, I assumed the instruction of the Hebrew Language in this Rabbinical College (of Padua), I adopted as a guide for my grammatical lessons the widely acclaimed work *Lehrgebäude der hebräischen Sprache* of the same Gesenius;[1] and having contemporaneously to deal with the preparation of other courses required of me, exegetical, theological, and historical, I was content with adding here

---

[1] In SDL's *Autobiografia* (Padua, 1882, p. 65), he mentions acquiring this book in March of 1829, just before he left Trieste for Padua. He relates how this was the first complete book that he ever read in German.

and there some of my own discoveries and new thoughts to the views of the great Maestro, some of which had already been published in the above-mentioned journal, and some of which were the fruits of my research in the course of compiling these lessons.

But when, in subsequent years, after the first triennial cycle (the period fixed for the students of this Institute), I had occasion to go over these lessons, I had doubts about some of those theories that I had adopted from Gesenius. These doubts led to long investigations, and these enabled me to finally find in the Aramaic language explanations for some of the phenomena of Hebrew Grammar, clearer and more probable than those which were given by the above-praised Gesenius, who, following Schultens and Michaëlis, took them from Arabic. This led me to judge that Aramaic, ancient as it is, has to present better than Arabic the primitive image of the Hebrew Language, and contain the causes of its phenomena; and [my] external linguistic Rationalism, previously directed mainly towards Arabic, seemed to me with better reason turned towards Aramaic. This thought was all the more reaffirmed in my mind by successive daily meditations and observations, through which I found the rational part of Hebrew Grammar enriched by many illustrations not less satisfactory than important.

Such new principles obliged me to recast my lessons almost completely; and my Grammar, born imitative, became in large part original.

Eager to be able to profit from the advice of others, something so necessary to anyone who wishes to guard himself against the seduction of a new system, I judge it opportune that my Grammar should be preceded by another small work, which would expound these new principles; and to this object are devoted these present Prolegomena, in which (§§ 93–141) I expound and defend the fundamental Laws of the grammatical formation of words, those common to all languages first, then those particular to the primitive Hebrew, and finally those particular to the attested Hebrew.[2]

This contrivance has the additional advantage of separating from the body of the Grammar itself a hoard of discussions that would excessively complicate it, and render it irritating and ill-suited for beginners.

---

[2] So, these prolegomena are intended as a preface to an actual grammar of the Hebrew language. SDL's grammar was published many years later, in five fascicles, the fifth posthumously: *Grammatica della lingua ebrea* (Padua, 1853–67). It has never been reprinted.

In contemplation of these same two advantages, I add four Appendices (§§ 142–200), in which I expound several other new ideas, concerning various aspects of Hebrew Punctuation.

Before all of this I offer an outline of the History of the Hebrew Language (§§ 45–92), indispensable to the exposition and development of my fundamental Principle concerning the primitive Hebrew.

Before the History of the Hebrew Idiom, I put that of Hebrew Grammar, that is to say, an historical outline of the origins and milestones of the grammatical study of the Holy Language among Israelites and among Christians (§§ 1–44), in which the former, not without internal satisfaction, will see the copious number of Scholars from other nations, who have taken up study in their ancient Language [*Favella*]; and the latter will learn of the little-known merit of various Hebrew [Jewish] Grammarians from the last centuries, and will be convinced that the study of their own language, in the midst of quite unfavorable circumstances, never waned among the Israelites, at any time.

In addition to historical and bibliographical information, which in any discipline proves many a time necessary to students, and always worthwhile, there are found discussed in this History of Hebrew Grammar several questions of sacred Criticism, where Scholars will observe something new, which I submit, together with the rest, for their examination.

It remains to say a word about the importance, and also the amenity, of the study that is the subject of this work of mine; and it might seem all the more indispensable, since this same study is actually not the most appreciated and cultivated in our Italy.

But regarding such arguments on taste, compared to which there is nothing more variable, inconstant, and contradictory, I judge all discussion completely superfluous and unfruitful.

I wrote [this book] for the one who is a lover of these studies; and the method that I tried to follow in treating my subject is such that it may change in the mind of the young student any preconceived opinion against this very subject, and render it for him both interesting and amenable; and of this I have been assured by more than one experiment. I will be happy if the destiny of my efforts is to produce such an effect in many!

THE ORIGINS AND PROGRESSION
OF THE GRAMMAR
OF THE HEBREW LANGUAGE

I.

The theoretical study of the Hebrew language began around the year 900 of the common era, among the Israelites who were living under the Arabs, a nation in whose midst, in those tenebrous times, the sciences and letters felicitously flourished. Before then, the Hebrews, the better they (at least the Learned) had practical mastery of their language, the less they thought to study its theories, and to form a science of it. Extremely rare are the grammatical observations in the Talmud; for example in Tractate Yebamot (fol. 13[b]) one reads a definition of the local He. The book of Yetsira (ספר יצירה) contains the division of the alphabet into five classes, gutturals, palatals, etc.

II.

Hebrew Grammar was from the time of its founders modeled on the outline of Arabic Grammar.

Nevertheless, the Hebrew Grammarians, independently from the help they were able to draw from the enlightenment of the Arabs, found for themselves the road to uncovering the laws of the Language wondrously opened and paved by the great work of the Pointers [*Puntatori*]. Without the Pointing, the forming of the Grammar of a language already several centuries out of use would have been an impossible achievement: the zeal, the accuracy, and the supreme ingenuity of the Pointers rendered such an undertaking possible and easy.

Some scholars, it is true, have presumed that the Pointers even imitated the Arabs. Since, however, the latter have only three single vowel signs, whereas the Hebrews have a good twelve of them (1); the statement that these latter have imitated the former is true only to the extent that the example of the Arabs may have awakened in the mind of the Learned among the Hebrews the idea to also invent those signs which would indicate the vowels; never in the institution of these signs did the Pointers take anything from the Arabs.

Other reasons, however, render it a lot less credible that the idea to institute vowel points might have been suggested to the Hebrews by the Arabs. Since the vowels among the Arabs are certainly less ancient than Mohammed, they cannot have been invented before the middle of the seventh century of the common era. Quite the contrary, everything leads us to believe that the Hebrew Pointing is no later than sixth century, the epoch in which the Talmud was put into writing.

Since the supreme authority attributed to the Talmud by the Hebrews is well known; and the Pointing, as a little further below (§ 8) will be seen, is in more than one place in open opposition with it; such a thing the Pointers would not have dared to do, if they had lived several centuries after its compilation, that is to say after the authority of it was quite well stabilized and universalized. If such a contradiction to the Talmud had been dared by the Pointers, their work would certainly not have been so universally accepted and adopted, as it was, and almost more venerated than the Talmud itself.

(1)   These are the eight signs indicating the true vowels (§ 149), plus the four signs of the semi-vowels, namely the Schwa and the three compound Schwas.

III.

This consideration leads me to believe that those same Babylonian Scholars [*Dottori*], called Savoraim (רבנן סבוראי), who, around the sixth century, for fear that the oral law might fall into oblivion or be altered, determined to put it into writing, and wrote for the first time the Mishnah and the Talmud (1), which until then was only preserved by the memory of the students (2); they themselves, I say, resolved likewise to fix the reading of the sacred Text, and for such an operation they charged several among those Scholars, who devoted themselves more particularly to the study of scripture, and to the exact reading of the sacred text, Scholars who labeled themselves with the epithet of Karaim (§ 7), whose work, sanctioned by those same supremely authoritative Savoraic Scholars, could easily become accepted by the Israelites with respect, and religiously venerated, not any differently than the other parts of the oral law, received from the same hand.

Let me not be opposed by the judgment of Elijah Levita, the first supporter of the non-antiquity of the vowel Points, who, followed by the most respectable Orientalists, thinks the Pointers Tiberian, and therefore of Palestine, rather than of Babylonia or Persia.

Already [Solomon] Hanau (3) observed that Tiberians cannot have been the Pointers, since we know from the ancient Grammarians (4) that the Tiberians distinguished two sounds of the letter ר, as with the six letters בגד כפת (exactly as the author of the book of Yetsira, who seems Palestinian, says: שבע כפולות בגד כפרת, that is to say, seven letters have a double pronunciation, and they are בגד כפרת); which is in opposition to the system of pronunciation adopted by the Pointers.

Observing that the great and authoritative Academies endured in Babylonia until after the year 1000 of the common era, while in Palestine they ceased around 400, I judge that the Pointers must have been Babylonians, and that while there presumably lived in Palestine after the Talmudic times some men capable of such a work, they would never have enjoyed such credit and authority, for making it so that all the Israelites chose to read the sacred Text according to their Pointing; on the contrary, this could very easily succeed for the Savoraim, whose authority was unlimited among all the Israelites. The Masoretes, on the other hand, precisely for the servility of their work (see § 10), seem to me Palestinian rather than Babylonian.

(1) See Rashi on מציעה (fol. 33), and ערובין (fol. 62 verso), as well as the preface to the Commentary on the Mishnah called עץ חיים.

(2) In relation to this precaution of the ancient Hebrew scholars, a passage from Plato (towards the end of Phaedrus) is notable, where he introduces the Egyptian king Thamus, speaking with Theuth, the inventor of writing: "[275a] and now, since you are the father of writing, your affection for it has made you describe its effects as the opposite of what they really are. In fact, it will introduce forgetfulness into the soul of those who will learn it: they will not practice using their memory because they will put their trust in writing, which is external characters and depends on signs that belong to others, instead of trying to remember from the inside, completely on their own. You have not discovered a potion for remembering, but for reminding; you provide your students with the appearance of wisdom, not with its reality. Your invention

will enable them to hear many things without being properly taught, and they will imagine [275b] that they have come to know much while for the most part they will know nothing. And they will be difficult to get along with, since they will merely appear to be wise instead of really being so."[1]

(3)   Binyan Shelomo, fol. 32.

(4)   [David Kimḥi's] Michlol, foll. 108, 109.

IV.

Presuming this, it should not be hard to understand why the schismatic Hebrews, the so-called Karaites, adopted the pointed text of the Rabbinists. At the time of their schism, the promoter of which was Anan (ענן) [ben David], living in Babylonia around 750 (1), two centuries were already past since the sacred Text was pointed, and already the origins of the Pointing were obscure. The schismatics were able to believe the vowel signs to be of remote antiquity, or even contemporaneous with the language; this would not have been possible, if they had only been invented a few years earlier.

(1)   Here is not the place to refute [Jacob] Trigland [in *Diatribe de secta Karaeorum*, 1703], who supports the claim of antiquity of the Karaites. It should be sufficient to observe that they have no book nor any tradition from a time earlier than Anan (except for the genealogy of this same Anan, which, true or false as it may be, proves nothing); and every Sabbath they make mention, at the end of their honorific prayers, (printed in the Crimea in 1805) of the most distinguished men who flourished in the sect, praying well for their souls, naming various Scholars from the end of the tenth and eleventh centuries, but without mentioning anyone from prior to Anan, which in fact begins with the following words: Our God and God of our fathers, may he be merciful to our deceased and the deceased of all his people, the house of Israel. First and foremost to our Master, the Prince Anan, a man of God, the Exilarch [*Ecmalotarca*],[2] who opened the way of the Law, illuminated the children of the

---

[1] Translation by A. Nehamas and P. Woodruff, in *Plato: The Complete Works*, ed. J. Cooper (Indianapolis/Cambridge, 1997), pp. 551–52. SDL quotes this passage in Latin, but I have not reproduced this since the original language is Greek.

[2] SDL's unusual word *ecmalotarca* is a neologism from Greek αἰχμαλωσία 'captivity' (cf. αἰχμάλωτος 'captive') and ἀρχή 'chief'. I have found this word nowhere else.

Bible (the Karaites), turned many from sin and malfeasance, and led us on the right path.

אלהינו ואלהי אבותינו ירחם את מתינו ואת מתי כלל כל עמו
בית ישראל בראש ובתחלה לרבנו ענן הנשיא איש האלהים ראש
הגולה אשר פתח את דרך התורה והאיר עיני בני מקרא ורבים
השיב מעון ומעברה והדריכנו בדרך ישרה :

V.

Instead of admitting that the idea of the vowel Points had been suggested to the Hebrews by the example of the Arabs, I agree with [Johann] Jahn (Gramm. hebr. p. 19), that the Hebrews instituted them by the example of the Syrians. I am led to this by the analogy:

a) of the shape and the name of the Hebrew Zakef (בֹּ), of the Syrian Zekofo (בֹ);

b) of the shape and name of the Hebrew Schwa and the Syrian Shewoyo (:);

c) of the shape and value of the Hebrew Tsere and the Syrian Reboṣo (בֵ).

In fact, the Hebrew Tsere seems to me even to have an analogy with the name of the Syrian Reboṣo, in that the word צֵרֵי, which presents no satisfactory etymology, could well be an alteration of שְׂרֵי *put down, set down*, the near equivalent of רְבָצָא *lying down* (1).

I do not make mention of the analogy of the name of the Syrian פְּתָחָא with the פָּתַח of the Hebrews, because the Arabs also give their A the analogous name פַּתְחָא. See further § 180.

(1) Other alterations are met in the names of the Hebrew vowel points. Many ancients wrote שְׁבָא instead of שְׁוָא. The vowels שׁוּרֵק, חׄלֶם, חִירֶק, are all words distorted for the purpose of presenting in their first syllables which vowel is indicated by these words. [Judah] Ḥayyuj (or at least his translator) in the Tractate on quiescent letters [see below, § 12], writes always חֵלֶם, חֵרֶק, שֵׁרֶק, with two Seghols.

VI.

It will be claimed: The Hebrew Pointing cannot then go back as far as 500, since the Syriac [pointing] was, in the consensus of Scholars, invented by Jacob of Edessa, who, according to what Assemani relates (Bibliotheca orientalis, Vol. I. p. 468), died in 710; and in fact Jahn (Gramm., p. 443) affirms, the Hebrew vowel points are no more ancient than the eighth century.

However, I find poorly supported this common judgment, which makes Jacob of Edessa the author of the five vowel points of the Syrians.

Assemani, after having related the passage from Bar Hebraeus [*Abulfaragio*], where he says this Jacob to have refused the invitation made by a certain Paul of Antioch, who wanted to complete the Syriac Alphabet, adding those letters missing from it, he adds (ib., p. 478) that Jacob sent them nevertheless seven new forms, intended to express the vowels; the figures of which were seen, he says, by the same Bar Hebraeus. Now, if the vowels invented by Jacob of Edessa were the same that the Syrians made use of, would Assemani have referred the readers to see them in the inedited Work of Bar Hebraeus [*Bar-Ebreo*]?[3] To this can be added the discrepancy of the number, since the Syrians do not otherwise possess seven vowel points, but five, or, according to some ancient Grammarians, six (see §§ 175, 177); although some scholars among the Syrians distinguished seven vowels as far as their sound, there is no trace of seven different vowel signs or points (1). This leads one to think the five vowel points of the Syrians to be an invention prior to Jacob of Edessa, who imagined other forms unknown to us, and these were seven in number.[4] And so I find it much more probable that the Syriac Punctuation is more ancient than what is commonly said, since it is known from Saint Epiphanius (Assemani, ib., p. 351), that in his times, that is to say before 400, many Persians delighted in studying the language and literature of the

---

[3] Bar Hebraeus' grammatical treatise, *Ktābā d-Ṣemḥe*, has since been published, most recently by A. Moberg (*Les livres des splendeurs: La grande grammaire de Grégoire Barhebraeus.* Lund, 1922). Moberg also published a German translation (*Buch der Strahlen: Die grössere Grammatik des Barhebräus.* 2 vols. Leipzig, 1907–13).

[4] Jacob of Edessa's signs have since been discovered, so this statement has proven to be true. See J. B. Segal, *The Diacritical Point and Accents in Syriac* (London, 1953), pp. 40–44.

Syrians, and it is also known from Assemani (ib., pp. 204, 205) that the Syrians had in Edessa, a Mesopotamian city, various schools to which the Persian idolaters from the neighboring regions rushed to learn Syriac. Now, the need for vowels must have been deeply felt in these schools by the teachers who taught Syriac to foreigners, deprived of practical knowledge of that language; a need less felt as long as the Semitic languages were only studied by those who had practice in them from birth; and here is the highest probability in favor of the prominence of the Syriac Pointing.

Some among the numerous Hebrews from Persia and Mesopotamia, where flourished the Academies of Sura, Nehardea, Pumbedita, etc., may, if not in the capacity of students, have frequented the schools of the Syrians (2), and, observing the advantages of the Pointing, may have conceived the idea to invent such a system, apt to preserve in its integrity the pronunciation of the sacred Text.

(1) The great scholar Andrea Teofilo Hoffmann [Andreas Gottlieb Hoffmann] in his Grammatica Syriaca (Halle, 1827) wanted to avoid and elude this argument, asserting (p. 87) that Jacob of Edessa established seven vowel signs, however only five of these were put into use.—This is an assertion completely uncalled for. Assemani, in fact even Bar Hebraeus, would have said (if this were true) that Jacob sent to Paul the five vowel signs which were in use by the Syrians, and the other two which were not generally adopted.

(2) That various Scholars of the Talmud may have frequented some Christian schools, appears in the Talmud itself, Shabbat foll. 116, 152, and Avodah Zarah fol. 17.

VII.

The great complexity of the Hebrew Pointing need not be a point of surprise, nor need it be impossible that this work was done all at once, in a way that might lead one to suppose, along with many modern Scholars, that after having instituted, in imitation of the Arabs or the Syrians, a few vowel points, these were gradually added to, until the existing complicated system was formed (1). The surprise will cease, if one considers the extreme scrupulousness with which the ancient Scholars minutely attended to everything that concerns the Religion. If they were so engaged in the least important minutiae of the divine precepts, how much the more would they have been careful about the reading of the sacred books? And in fact, the

Talmud (Kiddushin fol. 30) attests that the ancient Scholars (סֹפְרִים) had numbered the verses, words, and letters of the various books of the sacred Scripture. The Mishnah (at the end of Avot [5:21]) wants the second five years of childhood [i.e., ages five to ten] dedicated to the study of scripture. A great honor, at the time of the Talmudists, was the epithet of Kara (קרא), Karai (קריי), or Karoi (קראוי) (Lev. Rabba, Parshah 30), for which the Talmud gives the following definition (Kiddushin fol. 49) דקרי אורייתא נביאי וכתיבי בדיוקא *who reads the Pentateuch, Prophets, and Hagiographia exactly* (2). R. Joḥanan (at the end of Megillah) condemns he who reads the Scripture without chanting; and from another Talmudic passage (Ḥagigah fol. 6), it appears that already in the time of the Talmudists a certain number of accents, more or less distinct, were in use for chanting, roughly analogous to the system of Accents that the Pointers later put in writing. And from all this, it is evident that even before the Pointers, the study of the reading and chanting of the sacred books, far from being neglected by the Rabbis, was cultivated with zeal and accuracy; therefore, all the vowel sounds and all of the accents, must be supposed as having been the object of scrupulous teaching, long before the Pointers, who only invented the signs with which the system of vocalization and accentuation already in oral use was committed to writing.

(1) The hypothesis that the Hebrew Pointing began with three single points, is completely unfounded. Judah ha-Levi is cited (Kuzari II, 80); but this [early eleventh-century] author, who wrote in Arabic, does not say more than that the Hebrew vowels can (like the Arabic) be divided into three, which are then subdivided into seven, the actual number of the Hebrew vowel points (§ 149). Ibn Ezra is also cited (in the beginning of צַחוֹת); but he says only that investigating the nature of the vowels, he found three of them, from which the other four can be composed [see § 171]. In support of the hypothesis of a primitive system of Pointing more simple than the existing one, the Masoretes are cited, who give names only to קָמָץ and פָּתַח. But the Masoretes do not fail to distinguish the other vowels with the signs אָי, אֹ, אוּ; and although the name of קמץ signifies for them the קמץ as well as the צרי, and the name of פתח indicates equally the פתח and the סגול, they nevertheless do not ever confuse the two vowels, so that recording a given number of words pointed with קמץ, one meets in some of these קמץ, and in others צרי; but the words of those recorded have all קמץ, or all צרי (See מסרת המסרת [of Elijah Levita] Broken Tables [= Third Part], discourse II). In the single case of פתח דספרא (See מסרת המסרת ib.) they have rightly confused פתח with

סגול, since both of these vowels usually change to קמץ in pause, and the same anomaly takes place then, when one or the other is preserved unchanged. [G. Heinrich] Ewald, who saw the Hebrew Pointing as original, and completely independent from that of the Arabs, supposes at the same time (Kritische Gramm. pp. 54, 57) that it became gradually more complicated, and in the beginning made use of only two points, one below, indicating the vowels *a, e, i*, and one above, indicating *o* and *u*; the first of these points was then transformed into חירק, צרי, סגול, פתח, and קמץ, below the letters, and the second into the חלם above the letter and the שורק inside the Waw. The שלש נקדות [Kibbuts] and the קמץ חטוף placed underneath the letters, render this hypothesis highly improbable.

(2) Likewise the Muslims, before the invention of the vowel signs, had some Scholars, called Mokri, whose duty was to teach the reading of the Koran. See [Barthélemy] d'Herbelot, Bibliothèque orientale, p. 87.

VIII.

In the manner, however, of the lapse of the centuries, emigration and persecution gave rise to various doubts and controversies in other parts of the oral tradition; so various uncertainties arose around the pronunciation of individual scriptural texts. Thus we see in the Talmud (Kiddushin fol. 30) that the Palestinians divided into three the ninth verse of chapter 19 of Exodus; that R. Ishmael (Avodah Zarah fol. 29) read דּוֹדֶיךָ in the second verse of the Song of Solomon, while R. Akiva read דּוֹדַיִךְ; that there was an argument (Ḥagigah fol. 6) over the syntactic relation of several words in one Text (Exodus 24:5), with the sole objective of knowing with which accents those words were supposed be read; and that five texts (Yoma fol. 52), according to others (Genesis Rabba, Parshah 80), six, are considered ambiguous, making it impossible to determine the correct accentuation.

Now, in this and in similar controversial passages, the Pointers decided according to their own exceedingly illuminated and sagacious reasoning. So, in Ecclesiastes 2:2, they pointed מְהֹלָל *mad*, though the Talmud (Shabbat fol. 30) interprets this text as if it were מְהֻלָּל *praised, praiseworthy*. In the text of Exodus 30:23, they adopted concerning the words וְקִנְּמָן־בֶּשֶׂם מַחֲצִיתוֹ the interpretation of the Jerusalem Talmud (Shekalim Ch. 6), against the judgment of the Babylonian Talmud (Keritot fol. 5). Vice versa, in the Prophet Obadiah, they join the word מִקָּטֹל with verse 9, whereas the Jerusalem Talmud (Peah ch. 1) joins it to verse 10; and in Exodus 19:9, they do not follow the practice of the Palestinians, who divided that verse into three. Many times they ignored the opinion of the Chaldean Targum, with regard to the vowels, as well as with regard to the accents; for example היה כאחד ממנו (Gen. 3:22), אֲמָתָהּ (Exodus 2:5).

In several places, however, the Pointers deliberately moved away from the natural sense of the sacred text, with the goal of disguising certain insolent metaphors, which the people might have misunderstood, and which may have been found scandalous. This prudent method, often used by the Chaldean translators, as I explained extensively in my אוהב גר, or Philoxenus (1), on Onkelos, was adopted by the Pointers, though more sparingly; as may also be seen in my Commentaries on Exodus 20:2, 20, Isaiah 1:12, 13, 6:2, Jeremiah 15:18, and Ezekiel 3:20. See also what I wrote on Isaiah 40:5 in the extracts of my Commentary published by the very celebrated Rosenmüller at the beginning of his Scholia on this prophet (2), as well as § 192c of the present Prolegomena (3).

(1) Vienna, 1830. See the analysis of this work in the Leipziger Literatur-Zeitung, February 1, 1832 [cols. 209–14]. See also Conversations-Lexicon der neuesten Zeit [und Literatur, 1832–34], vol. 3, p. 344.[5]

(2) Ern. Frid. Car. Rosenmüller, Scholia in Jesajae vaticinia in compendium redacta. Praemissae sunt. Sam. Davidis Luzzatto in Jesajae vaticinia animadversiones. Lipsiae, 1835.[6]

(3) This principle, namely, the preference of the public usefulness in the interpretation of Scripture, over the exegetic truth, is the crux of the oral law; and it is this which regulated the ancient Scholars in their decisions; it is the source and the key together of all the non-literal interpretations that have come down to us. This can be expressed by the following statement of Cicero (De inventione rhetorica, I. 38): Omnes leges ad commodum reipublicae

---

[5] The *Leipziger Literatur-Zeitung* contains a flattering, anonymous three-page review. On the other hand, the *Conversations-Lexicon*, s.v. "Orientalische Literatur," merely contains a list of recent publications. For *Ohev Ger*, it simply says, "Eine Beurtheilung des Textes des chaldaischen Übersetzers Onkelos lieferte Luzzatto in seinem rabbinisch geschriebenen Werke 'Oheb Ger' (Wien, 1830)."

[6] Luzzatto subsequently published his own commentary on Isaiah, along with an Italian translation, *Il Profeta Isaia* (Padua, 1855; 1867).

referre oportet, et eas ex utilitate communi, non ex scripti
est, interpretari.[7]

IX.

After the Pointers and before or contemporary with the first Grammarians,
were the famous Ben-Asher and Ben-Naphtali (1), from whom we have the
various readings (חלופי הקריאה) printed (but with less exactitude) at the
end of some Rabbinic Bibles (מקראות גדולות); which almost all deal with
the most minute and least important portions of the Pointing (2).

Kimḥi in his Commentary to the book of Judges (6:19)[8] makes
mention of a work entitled מחברת בן אשר, in which the word והמרק is
counted among the words with two Kametses. The Bomberg Rabbinic
Bible of 1517 contains at the end a very short Tractate on the Accents,
attributed to Ben-Asher,[9] who wrote in rhyming prose, obscure and not
very intelligible, and followed by various other grammatical and Masoretic
things, which may be a part of the work mentioned by Kimḥi; a part, I say,
since the passage Kimḥi cites is not found there (3).

(1) Everything about these two men—name, country, age, position—is uncertain
and obscure. [Abraham de] Balmes ([*Mikne Avram*] fol. d. 3) calls the first Moses
son of Asher (a name that was given to him also by R. Yom-tov [ben Abraham
Ishbili] in the מגדל עוז, Tractate ספר תורה Ch. 8),[10] and the second Jacob
son of Naphtali. Elijah Levita (מסרת המסרת third preface) calls the first

---

[7] "It is right, gentlemen of the jury, to relate all laws to the advantage of the
state and to interpret them with an eye to the public good and not according to
their literal expression." (Translation from H. M. Hubbell, *Cicero in Twenty-Eight
Volumes*, vol. 2 [Cambridge, 1949], p. 111).

[8] SDL has 6:9, but this is a mistake or misprint.

[9] This is the *Sefer Dikdukei ha-Te'amim*. An edition was edited by S. Baer and H.
Strack (Leipzig, 1879), and a critical edition was made by A. Dotan (Jerusalem,
1966–67).

[10] According to the *Jewish Encyclopedia*, s.v. "Shem-Tov ben Abraham ibn
Gaon," the work *Migdal Oz*, a commentary on Maimonides' *Yad* [= *Mishneh Torah*],
was falsely attributed to this R. Yom-Tov by some Rabbis, among them Gedaliah
ibn Yaḥya in his *Shalshelet ha-Kabbalah*. The true author was Shem-Tov ben
Abraham ibn Gaon.

Aaron son of Asher. R. Gedaliah [ibn Yaḥya] (שלשלת הקבלה), more positive and less critical than the others, calls them Aaron son of Moses from the tribe of Asher, and Moses son of David from the tribe of Naphtali. The ancients called them simply Ben-Asher and Ben-Naphtali. Elijah Levita makes them the heads of two Masoretic Academies, but the fact that they are simply called by the ancients only by the name of the father, renders such a rank less likely for these men.—As regards their homeland, Ben-Asher, at the end of the Rabbinic Bible of 1517, is called Tiberian. Ben Naphtali is regarded (as will be seen towards the end of this note) as Babylonian.—Their age, moreover, is fixed around the year 1000, and this after the same R. Gedaliah [ibn Yaḥya], who, after having finished speaking of the Geonim, of whom the last one, R. Hai [ben Sherira], died in 1038, adds, according to what he thinks, those two Scholars to have lived in that age.—Raymund Martin and [Gilbert] Génebrard made them, without any support, the authors of the Pointing. Louis Cappel[11] attributes to them the enlargement and development of the same [system]. In our times, the fine Jewish history scholar [Isaac Marcus] Jost made them simply the collators of the ancient Codices. I find the variations of Ben-Asher and Ben-Naphtali too few to believe that they are the authors or perfectors of the Pointing, and too uniform and systematic to believe they are simply the collators of the Codices. The authors of the Pointing would have had to disagree in things of greater importance; and the variations collected from the Codices would not have to follow any sort of order. I believe, therefore, these two men were two distinct Nakdanim, or Punctuators [*Punteggiatori*] and Correctors of the Bible (see § 147), who, observing in the already pointed Codices some slight discrepancies in the most minute details of the Pointing, removed them, following several principles adopted by them, and also introduced in the Pointing several slight modifications of their own will. In doing this, they took liberty rather more than was taken by successive Punctuators, and much more than the Masoretes (who did not claim for themselves the least authority); and precisely this makes me believe them to be prior to the Masoretes. Also Maimonides (ספר תורה Ch. 8)[12] attributes greater authority to Ben-Asher than to the Masoretes, who, he says, disagreed with the Codices that they took to oversee. The creditability of Ben-Asher, whose pointing was for the most part generally followed, prevailed; not exclusively, however. There is not, that I know of, any foundation for the assertion of

---

[11] SDL is referring either to Cappel's *Arcanum Punctationis Revelatum* (Leiden, 1624), in which he proves that the Hebrew pointing must date from after the Christian era, or his *Critica Sacra* (Paris, 1650), in which he proved that the consonantal text had not been transmitted without errors.

[12] *Sefer Torah* is a tractate in Maimonides' great *Mishneh Torah*.

Elijah Levita, blindly following many others, that the oriental and Babylonian Israelites followed the preference of Ben-Naphtali. It is from this assertion that many Scholars have inferred that Ben-Naphtali was Babylonian; a deduction equally baseless as the statement that serves as a basis for it.—After all, the variant readings of Ben-Asher and Ben-Naphtali do not have any relation with those of the Oriental and Occidental (חלופי קריאה בין מערבאי ומדנחאי), which, as the same Elijah observed, concern not the vowels and accents, but rather the letters themselves of the sacred Text, or at least to the marginal readings (קרי וכתיב), and none of which concern the Pentateuch.

(2) Among the variants of Ben-Asher and Ben-Naphtali, only one has so far produced a big difference of meaning. It is believed that in Psalm 62, verse 4, Ben-Asher read תְּרָצְחוּ *you will be killed*, while Ben-Naphtali read תְּרַצְּחוּ *you will kill*. I believe that both read *teratsehu* 'you will kill'; but that having found the צ without a dagesh (as indeed is seen in various editions), as happens not rarely with a letter pointed with שׁוא that was followed by a guttural letter (for example, יִקְחוּ, יִסְעוּ, יִשְׂאוּ, etc.), Ben-Asher pointed the ר with a קמץ (תְּרָצְחוּ), to indicate that the following שׁוא was mobile, while Ben-Naphtali preferred to leave ר with its original פתח; not differently from the form מאספיו (Isa. 62:9), where the ס is lacking דגש, [and where] the א is found as far back as the time of Kimhi (Michlol fol. 74) pointed in some books with קמץ, and in others with פתח.[13] See also § 194, note.

(3) The learned critic Jacob Ben-Ḥayyim, editor of the second Rabbinic Bible (1525), which was the first that contained the Masorah, recalls the article חלף of the final Masorah, the Tractate on the Accents of Ben-Asher, among those things already inserted at the end of the first Rabbinic Bible (1517), which he promised to improve on in the second edition edited by him. In effecting his promise, however, he instead reprinted the variants of Ben-Asher and Ben-Naphtali, and the other Masoretic items of the 1517 Bible; but he omitted that Tractate on the Accents, probably having found it obscure, and very inaccurate as well, since it was taken from a not very legible Codex, as the Editors attest to. He also omitted a passage concerning the pronunciation of several words used by a certain R. Pinḥas, called ראש ישיבה *Head of an Academy*; as also the presumed Masorah of Dosa son of Eliezer son of Afsoi concerning the number of verses in the whole Bible; a Masorah found in the last century in a Bible manuscript in the Bibliothèque du roi de France, and badly interpreted by [Étienne] Fourmont in the Mémoires de l'académie royale de France (see

---

[13] The reference in Kimhi can be found in the edition by W. Chomsky (New York, 1952), §24a, and is briefly discussed in his footnote 128.

Finetti, Tratt. della lingua ebraica, p. 30, and De Rossi, Mss. Codices, cod. 196),[14] who, believing to be indicated there the name of the Inventors of the Pointing, gave great credit to this discovery, due, as he says, to the manuscripts of the Roi de France; ignoring that that alleged Masorah was printed as far back as 1517. This Masorah then has all the appearances of an impostor.

X.

Probably after Ben-Asher and Ben-Naphtali were the Masoretes, who with extreme diligence, but not with equal depth of mind, observed the grammatical and orthographic phenomena in the sacred Scripture, with regards to the letters, vowels, and accents, scrupulously recording every anomaly, without, however, thinking to investigate the reasons for them (1).

(1) Elijah Levita, the first who revealed the Pointing to be posterior to the Talmud, that is to say 500 of the common Era, attributed this great work to the Masoretes. In such a way, he was at the same time a source of light and of error. Nothing is more absurd than the confusion of the Pointers with the Masoretes, that is to say men so greatly dissimilar in their intellectual strengths, and in the excellence of the works that were the effects of them. And still this error was and is generally followed by Scholars more distinguished in sound criticism, who are those that adopted the Elianic judgment regarding the non-antiquity of the Hebrew Pointing. However, the following are of help by facilitating the comprehension of the Masoretic jargon: the מסרת המסרת of Elijah Levita, the Tiberias of [Johannes] Buxtorf, and the סיג לתורה of the physician [Asher] Anshel Worms, Frankfurt am Main, 1766.

XI.

The first writers on Hebrew Grammar were: the Egyptian Saadiah Gaon (רבנן סעדיה גאון), who died in 942. Ibn Ezra (in the beginning of Moznayim) attributed to him three grammatical works (now lost):

---

[14] Bonifazio Finetti, *Trattato della lingua ebraica e sue affini* (Venice, 1756). Giovanni Bernardo De Rossi, *Mss. codices hebraici Biblioth* (3 vols., Parma, 1803). The books included in De Rossi's catalogue, then his own, are now owned by the Biblioteca Palatina in Parma. An excellent catalogue of this collection has recently been made by B. Richler; see Richler, *Hebrew Manuscripts*. The many codices that SDL cites from the De Rossi catalogue can all be found in that of Richler.

סֵפֶר הָאֶגְרוֹן,[15] in Hebrew, סֵפֶר לָשׁוֹן עִבְרִית and סֵפֶר צַחוֹת, in Arabic.[16] Rashi (Psalm 45:10) makes mention of a work entitled נִקּוּד (Pointing) by R. Saadiah. We cannot know for sure if this is identical with any of the three works cited by Ibn Ezra.

An anonymous Jerusalemite was the author, according to Ibn Ezra, of eight grammatical works, now lost.[17]

Adonim son of Tamim, a Babylonian, was the author of one work, as Ibn Ezra says, in mixed Hebrew and Arabic, and equally lost.

Adonim Levita of Fez, of whose writings we do not even know the names, is praised, however, by Ibn Ezra in the שָׂפָה בְרוּרָה. See Note 3 to the next section.[18]

Judah [ben David] Ḥayyuj, living around the year 1000, more on whom in the following paragraphs.

Samuel son of Ḥophni (בֶּן־חָפְנִי) Gaon, who died in 1034 (1).

Hai [ben Sherira] Gaon (רַבֵּנוּ הַאי), who died in 1038, the author of a lost מַאֲסֵף.[19]

Samuel [ha-]Nagid, who died in 1055, a disciple of Ḥayyuj, was the author of the lost סֵפֶר הָעֹשֶׁר, highly praised by Ibn Ezra, who in the

---

[15] Portions of this work have since been found and published with annotations by N. Allony, *Ha-Egron* (Jerusalem, 1969).

[16] These two titles probably refer to a single work, the *Sefer Tsaḥut Leshon ha-Ivrim*, also known as *Sefer Tsaḥut ha-Leshon ha-Ivrit* (see Ibn Ezra, *Moznayim*, p. 107 n. 20). A critical edition of the now-extant portions has been published by A. Dotan under the title *Or Rishon be-Ḥochmat ha-Lashon, The Dawn of Hebrew Linguistics* (2 vols., Jerusalem, 1997).

[17] This is Abu al-Faraj Harun. See Ibn Ezra, *Moznayim*, p. 208 n. 21.

[18] This Adonim Levita of Fez and Dunash ben Labrat, whom he mentions in note 2 to this section, are most likely the same person. Adonim is a Hebraized form of Dunash. So also, Adonim ben Tamim is synonmous with Dunash ibn Tamim.

[19] The Arabic title is *(Kitāb) al-Ḥawi*. Fragments have since been discovered and were published, in Judeo-Arabic and Hebrew, by A. Harkavy (*Divrei Yemei Yisra'el* 4, 1895/96, p. 3ff.; reprinted in a collection of his articles called *Ḥadashim Gam Yeshanim*, Jerusalem, 1969/70, p. 111ff.). Harkavy also has a very brief discussion in the journal *Mitspah* 1, 1885/86. Geniza fragments of this work have recently been published by A. Maman (*Tarbiz* 69 [2000], pp. 341–421), who is also preparing an edition of all known fragments; see further, Maman, *Philology*, pp. 371–72.

beginning of his יְסוֹד מוֹרָא attributes to him twenty-two grammatical works.[20]

Solomon [ibn] Gabirol, a famous Spanish poet, who died in 1070,[21] was the author of a grammatical poem of 400 distiches, of which the first 97 are preserved in the Imperial Library of Vienna in the Preface to the Lexicon of [Solomon ibn] Parḥon.[22] From the seventeenth verse of the preserved poem, Gabirol appears to have written it in his nineteenth year of age.

Jonah ibn Janaḥ, on whom see further in § 13 (2).

A profound Grammarian, as demonstrated in all of his Commentaries on the sacred Scripture, was R. Solomon (Rashi, also [erroneously; see § 17, n. 2] Yarḥi, died 1105), who, it seems, had never read the works of Ḥayyuj (3). Such were also his two grandsons, R. Samuel, known by the name of Rashbam (רשב"ם), and R. Jacob, known as Rabbenu Tam, who died in 1171 (4). The former shows this in his Commentary to the Pentateuch, and the latter in one of his Poems, containing the rules of the Accents (5).

(1) This famous Gaon, the father-in-law of R. Hai, is counted among the first Grammarians by R. Jonah [ibn Janaḥ] in the Preface of the רִקְמָה [see § 13], as reported in Richard Simon, Hist. crit. du vieux Testament, vol. 1, ch. 31.

---

[20] In actuality, the number twenty-two may refer to the number of sections in *Sefer ha-Osher*. The Arabic title of this work is *Kitāb al-Istiġnā*, and fragments of it have since been found in St. Petersburg. These were published by P. Kokovtsov in *Novye materialy dlia kharakteristiki Iekhudy Khaiiudzha, Samuila Nagida i niekotorykh drugikh predstavitelei evreiskoi filologicheskoi nauki v X, XI i XII viekie* (New material for the reference of Judah Ḥayyuj, Samuel Nagid, and some other representative Hebrew philologists of the X, XI, and XII centuries) (Petrograd, 1916), pp. 205–224; the Judeo-Arabic portions of this book (i.e., minus ca. 250 pages of Russian text) were reprinted, with additions to one text by N. Allony, under the Hebrew title *Mi-sifrei ha-balshanut ha-ivrit bi-ymei ha-benayim* (Jerusalem, 1969/70).

[21] The erroneous date of 1070 was commonly held at the time. More likely he died between 1057–59.

[22] This is Solomon ben Abraham ibn Parḥon's *Maḥberet he-Aruch*, written about 1160. See below, § 13, note 2. The fragment of the poem by Gabirol can be found in the collection of his poems edited by H. Bialik and Y. Ravnitzky (Tel Aviv, 1924; Vol. 1, pp. 173–80), and in the collection of his secular poems entitled *Shirei ha-Ḥol*, edited by H. Brody and J. Schirmann (Jerusalem, 1974, pp. 169–72).

(2) I omit Judah Ben-Karish [ibn Quraish], Menaḥem Ben-Saruk, and Dunash Ben-Labrat, since these were really Lexicographers rather than Grammarians. Regarding the first, however, see § 25, Note 1.

(3) It would be wrong to make Rashi responsible for the not at all literal interpretations scattered here and there in his Commentaries. None of these expositions is of his own invention, but they are all taken from the Talmud or Midrashim; collecting these things was a necessity of the time and place in which he was writing.

(4) Not in 1170, as De Rossi notes, against [Abraham ben Samuel] Zacuto,[23] who has him as dying in the year of creation 4930 [= 1169/70]. At the end of the work (little known to bibliographers) סדור רש"י, that I possess (deficient) in a membranous [vellum or parchment] manuscript written in 1282, the following note is read:

רש"י נאסף לעולמו בשנת ס"ה למאה תשיעי של אלף חמישי והייני
שנת תתס"ה לפרט וסימניך ששים וחמש שנה יחת אפרים מעם: ור'
תם בשנת ל"א למאה עשירי של אלף חמישי וסימניך ויאמר אלהים
אל יעקב:

"Rashi passed to the other life in the year 65 of the ninth century of the fifth millennium, that is to say, 4865, of which the text of Isaiah 7:8 can serve as a memorial (where we read the number 65); and Rabbenu Tam in the year 31 of the tenth century of the fifth millennium [= 1170/71], of which there is an anagram in the text of Genesis 35:1 (since אל = 31)."

(5) This composition of 45 strophes, of which the first is:

אֱלֹהִים לִי מָגֵן	Oh! my shield, eternal God,
בְּיָדִי צַר מַגֵּן	Let me conquer the enemy,
בְּהֵיטִיבִי נַגֵּן	Of the Accents and royals and servants,
מְלָכִים וּמְשָׁרְתִים	While I sing I alternate and vary.

and of which the acrostic, in addition to the alphabet, offers the words יעקב בר רבי מאיר חזק ואמץ לעד, is found (in addition to Codex De Rossi 563) in a membranous [vellum or parchment] manuscript owned by His Excellency Marco [Mordechai] Samuel Ghirondi, Head Rabbi of the Jewish Community of Padua. These verses are preceded by seven folios containing

---

[23] There is more than one well-known Zacuto, but SDL is probably referring to the historian Abraham ben Samuel and his work *Sefer ha-Yuḥasin* (written around 1500). In this passage, Castiglioni places "Moshe Zakut".

(under the title שערי נקוד) various grammatical rules, analogous to those of R. Moses Ḥazan (see § 15), an anonymous work, and possibly the work of the same R. Jacob [Rabbenu Tam], or of another ancient author not trained in the theories of Ḥayyuj. It will be indicated by me under the name anonymous שערי נקוד.

XII.

R. Judah [ben David] Ḥayyuj (1) of Fez, also known as Abba Zachariah, although preceded by various other grammarians, is with reason regarded as the father of Hebrew Grammar (2), because he, reforming the science (3), taught that Hebrew roots are triliteral; while Grammarians and Lexicographers that preceded him regarded quiescent and deficient roots as biliteral; a fact which enshrouded the oldest Grammars and Lexicons in obscurity and confusion, likewise, in some places, the Commentaries of the oldest interpreters; at the same time it filled the compositions of many distinguished Poets of those times with distorted words. Ḥayyuj developed his theories in two works, one concerning quiescent roots, and the other geminates. The first is called סֵ' אוֹתִיּוֹת הַסֵּתֶר וְהַמֶּשֶׁךְ, also סֵ' אוֹתִיּוֹת הַנּוֹחַ, סֵ' הַנּוֹחַ, or בַּעֲלֵי הָרִפְיוֹן;[24] the second as בַּעֲלֵי הַכֶּפֶל.[25] The first consists of 46 octavo folios, and is divided into three sections, of which the first, after various preliminary notions on the quiescent letters, treats all the verbs with a quiescent first radical, the second treats all the verbs which have a quiescent second radical, and the third treats those in which the third radical is quiescent. The second work, consisting of only 10 octavo folios, explains geminate verbs. Ḥayyuj also wrote סֵ' הַנִּקּוּד (Codices De Rossi 314, 396, 809),[26] סֵ' הָרִקְחָה (found at Oxford in the Bodleian Library)

---

[24] The Arabic title is *Kitāb al-Afʿāl Dhawāt Ḥuruf al-Līn* (The Book of Verbs Containing Weak Letters). Hebrew translations were made by Ibn Ezra and by Moses Gikatilla.

[25] The Arabic title is *Kitāb al-Afʿāl Dhawāt al-Mathalayn* (The Book of Verbs Containing Double Letters). Hebrew translations were made by Ibn Ezra and Moses Gikatilla. In the last two Hebrew titles given by SDL, בַּעֲלֵי may be a mistake or misprint for פָּעֳלֵי or פַּעֲלֵי.

[26] The Arabic title is *Kitāb al-Tanqīṭ* or *Kitāb al-Nuqaṭ* (The Book of Punctuation), and the Hebrew translation was made by Ibn Ezra. Regarding the three De Rossi codices cited by SDL, Richler, *Hebrew Manuscripts*, claims that they

dealing with syntax,[27] and a Lexicon. Ḥayyuj having written in Arabic, several of his works were in the same century translated into Hebrew by Moses Cohen [ibn] Gikatilla, a great grammarian and commentator, the author, according to Ibn Ezra, of a book entitled זְכָרִים וּנְקֵבוֹת. This translator added two annotations at the end of the Treatise on gemination, disagreeing with Ḥayyuj regarding the words מֹרֶךְ וְקָבְנוֹ.

(1)   Not Ḥiyyug. [Abraham ben Meir de] Balmes consistently writes חִיּוּג. The point over the Gimel was anciently used when one wanted the consonant to be pronounced soft, like the Italian G in the syllables Ge, Gi, and like the Jim of Arabic.

(2)   See R. Abram Ben-Dior [Abraham ben David ha-Levi], at the end of his Jewish history entitled ספר הקבלה, as well as [David] Kimḥi, in the preface to his Michlol.

(3)   As Ibn Ezra mentions in שָׂפָה בְרוּרָה, Adonim Levita [Dunash ben Labrat] was in part a forerunner of Ḥayyuj in the reform of Hebrew Grammar.

XIII.

In the tracks of Ḥayyuj, to the advantage of the science, followed:

Jonah ibn Janaḥ (1), also known as Abuwalid [Abu al-Walid], Merwan, or מרינוס, a doctor from Cordoba, author (according to Ibn Ezra, in the beginning of יְסוֹד מוֹרָא) of ten grammatical works, and of whom there is preserved in Paris and in Oxford a Grammar and a Lexicon entitled סֵפֶר הָרִקְמָה,[28] in which he here and there criticized Ḥayyuj, who was

---

all contain Moses ben Yom-Tov's *Darchei ha-Nikud* (see § 15).

[27] This title had long been corrupted from סֵפֶר הַקָּרְחָה (The Book of Baldness); the Arabic title is *Kitāb al-Nutaf* (The Book of Plucked Feathers). A critical edition of the extant portions of the Arabic version has recently been published by N. Basal (Tel Aviv, 2001).

[28] The original Arabic title of this work was *Kitāb al-Luma'*. It was translated into Hebrew by Judah ben Saul ibn Tibbon under the title *Sefer Ha-Rikmah*, in 1171. The Hebrew edition was first published by B. Goldberg and R. Kirchheim (Frankfurt am Main, 1856); the Arabic by J. Derenbourg (Paris, 1886). A more correct edition of the Hebrew version was published in a two-volume edition by M. Wilensky (Berlin, 1929–31; 2nd ed., Jerusalem, 1964).

defended by Samuel [ha-]Nagid, as [Solomon ibn] Parḥon mentions in the preface of his Lexicon;

Judah ben Bileam [ibn Balʻam], author of the טַעֲמֵי הַמִּקְרָא (published with Latin translation, Paris, 1565),[29] both in the eleventh century.

Ibn Ezra, a Spaniard, author of the סֵפֶר צָחוֹת, of the מֹאזְנֵי לְשׁוֹן הַקֹּדֶשׁ (Venice, 1546),[30] of the שָׂפָה בְרוּרָה (Constantinople, 1530),[31] and of the שְׂפַת יֶתֶר (Codex De Rossi 314),[32] around the middle of the twelfth century (2);

Joseph Kimḥi (קִמְחִי) of Narbonne, author of the סֵפֶר הַזִּכָּרוֹן (Codices De Rossi 396, 809), in the second half of the twelfth century; afterwards Moses and David Kimḥi, his two sons. Moses Kimḥi wrote the brief Compendium entitled מַהֲלַךְ שְׁבִילֵי הַדַּעַת (Pesaro 1508, Ortona 1519, etc.), as well as the lost book הַתַּחְבֹּשֶׁת (cited in Michlol foll. 83, 84); Balmes (in מקנה אברם, fol. g. 5) also attributes to him the inedited שֵׂכֶל טוֹב, which, however, [Johann von] Reuchlin, who possessed it [the manuscript], attributed to a certain Moses Zeyyag.[33] This work is preserved in the public Library of Durlach in the Grand Duchy of Baden bequeathed by the same Reuchlin. Around this time there lived another Moses, who wrote in Arabic the הוֹרָיִית הַקּוֹרֵא, translated into Hebrew by Menaḥem ben Nataniel (Codex De Rossi 764);[34] and perhaps also R. Elkanah, a

---

[29] The Arabic title is *Nuqaṭ al-Miqra* (Punctuation of the Bible). The Latin translation was made by Jean Mercier.

[30] This work is also known as *Moznayim*. A recent critical edition of this work, entitled *Sefer Moznayim*, was published by Lorenzo Jiménez Patón and Angel Sáenz-Badillos, with a Spanish translation (Córdoba, 2002).

[31] A new critical edition of this work, with a Spanish translation, was recently published by Enrique Ruiz and Angel Sáenz-Badillos (Córdoba, 2005).

[32] This work is better known now as the *Sefer Yesod Dikduk*.

[33] The authorship of Moses Kimḥi is accepted, and editions, with Kimḥi credited as the author, came out in 1894 (D. Castelli, *Révue des études juives* 28:212–27 and 29:100–10) and in 1920 (F. Javier de Ortueta y Murgoitio, *Moisés Kimḥi y su obra Sekel Tob* [Madrid]).

[34] The Hebrew version of *Horayat ha-Kore* has been edited by Giulio Busi (Frankfurt am Main, 1984). The original Arabic work (*Hidāyat al-Qāri*) has been attributed by some (as far back as the eleventh century) to Judah ibn Balʻam, but is now thought to have been written by Abu al-Faraj Harun; see pp. 18–22 in the

Spaniard, author of a key to the Grammar, מַפְתֵּחַ הַדִּקְדּוּק (Codex De Rossi 488).[35]

(1) Not Ganah. The Arabic name has Jim.

(2) He is portrayed as a philosopher grammarian in the Kuzari of Judah ha-Levi, roughly a contemporary of Ibn Ezra. It was his disciple Solomon Parhon (פַּרְחוֹן) who in 1161 wrote in Salerno an extremely valuable Lexicon, in addition to two grammatical works concerning Syntax and affixed particles (Codices De Rossi 764 and 1038). De Rossi published several extracts of the Lexicon of Parhon, under the title *Lexicon hebraicum selectum ex antiquo et inedito R. Parchonis Lexico* (Parma, 1805). He likewise gave several extracts of it (translated into Latin) in the Catalogue of his mss. for the above-indicated Codices 764 and 1038. [Wolf] Heidenheim in משפטי הטעמים (foll. 40–43) inserted a long excerpt from the preface of the same Lexicon.[36]

XIV.

David Kimhi, having written his מִכְלוֹל (1) and his Lexicon (שָׁרָשִׁים), with more clarity and method than all of his predecessors, eclipsed all of them, and [this] was the principal reason that the works of most of them were lost, or remained lesser known, and some remained untranslated from the Arabic in which they were written by their authors; this is also to be lamented, inasmuch as many of these ancients were superior to Kimhi in

---

edition of Busi. The same conclusion was made by Ilan Eldar in his *The Study of the Art of Correct Reading as Reflected in the Medieval Treatise Hidāyat al-Qāri* (Jerusalem, 1994; in Hebrew), pp. 40–43. As for the Hebrew translator, one manuscript names him as Menahem ben Nataniel, another cites him as Nataniel ben Meshullam (Busi, p. 23). In Codex De Rossi 764, Richler, *Hebrew Manuscripts*, claims that the piece entitled *Horayat ha-Kore* is actually Moses ben Yom-Tov's *Darchei ha-Nikud*; he is likely mistaken, though I have not seen the manuscript.

[35] The preface of this work was published by A. Berliner in *Festschrift zum siebzigsten Geburtstage David Hoffmann's*, ed. S. Eppenstein, M. Hildesheimer, and J. Wohlgemuth (Berlin, 1914), pp. 285–86. The work is also known from two other manuscripts, in the Russian State Library (MS Guenzburg 258) and in the Vatican (Biblioteca Apostolica ebr. 107).

[36] A modern edition of the Lexicon was edited by Solomon Gottlieb Stern (Pressburg, 1844; reprint, Jerusalem, 1969).

profundity and judgment, in particular [Ibn] Janaḥ (2). The esteem of
Kimḥi was also the reason for the loss or non-publication of the
grammatical writings of two Scholars who criticized his works, Samuel
Benvenasti [Benveniste] (around 1300), and Efodi, who in 1403 wrote his
valuable Grammar entitled מַעֲשֵׂה אֵפוֹד (3), in which (Chap. XI) he was
the first to explain the primitive nature (reciprocal, rather than passive) of
the verbal form נִפְעַל, a truth which was in our time newly discovered and
defended by Ewald. The Grammar of Efodi was translated into Latin by
Pagnini, but remained inedited.[37] Kimḥi was defended against the attacks of
Efodi by a certain Elisha son of Abram [ben Abraham], in a work entitled
מָגֵן דָּוִד (Constantinople, 1517). A certain Shabbatai, a German, defended
him against the objections of Elijah Levita, but this opuscule also remained
inedited (see Wolf, Bibl. hebr. Vol. 1, p. 1027).[38] A very important
circumstance in Kimḥi's life is related by him at the end of his Lexicon,—
his principal occupation was instructing boys in the study of Talmud.—
This pitiable fact, a testimony to the poverty of the time and place in which
our very famous Grammarian and Commentator lived, is his most firm
apology [of any shortcoming] (§ 43). David Kimḥi is also the author of the
Masoretic work עֵט סוֹפֵר, inedited, and possibly lost, cited by Elijah Levita
and by [Menaḥem] Lonzano.[39] Balmes ([Mikne Avram] fol. R. III) attributes
to the same Kimḥi the anonymous work known under the name
פֶּתַח דְּבָרַי, the words with which the book begins.[40]

(1)   Constantinople, 1532, and various reprints. It was translated into Latin by
      Pagnini (Paris, 1554). The edition of which I made use is that of Venice, 1545,
      in 268 folios.[41] Through the rule of proportion my citations were able to be
      approximately verified in every other printing. The Lexicon of Kimḥi was

---

[37] This was later published as *Maase Efod* (Vienna, 1865; reprint, Jerusalem,
1969/70), edited by J. Friedländer and J. Kohn, with Hebrew notes by SDL.

[38] Johann Christoph Wolf, *Bibliotheca Hebraea* (4 vols.; Hamburg and Leipzig,
1715–33).

[39] Subsequently published (Lyck, 1864; reprint Jerusalem, 1969/70).

[40] This work, a Hebrew grammar, was printed in Naples in 1492 (and thus is
important as a rare incunabula). The identity of its author remains uncertain.

[41] An English translation was made by William Chomsky, as *David Kimḥi's
Hebrew Grammar (Michlol)* (New York, 1952).

printed in Naples in 1490, and in 1491; in Constantinople in 1513; in Salonika without date, and several times in Venice.

(2) The renowned Badrashi [Jedaiah Bedersi] counts him (in his Ktav Hitnatselut כתב הנצלות) among the philosophers. He says of him thus, "Also the Grammarian R. Jonah ibn Janah, in the beginning of his grand work entitled Rikmah, states first many canons which, according to him, are necessary in the grammatical art, deducted by Logic, and some also by Physics. He brings into his work many interpretations of scriptural texts, intended to show them as conforming to reason." Gesenius (Handwörterbuch, 1834, p. XIV)[42] assigns to him the highest place among all of the Hebrew Interpreters and Commentators.

(3) The manuscript owned by me is of 270 octavo leaves, of which 42 are the preface. Regarding this work, see De Rossi, Mss. Codices, Cod. 800.

XV.

The author of the rules of Pointing (דַּרְכֵי הַנִּקּוּד) inserted at the end of the last volume of the Rabbinic Bible, who had the name Moses and was probably German, seems to have been prior to Kimhi (never making any mention of him, and citing only Hayyuj, Rashi, Ibn Ezra, and Parhon). Elijah Levita supposes him to be the so-named R. Moses Hazan (חזן) cited in the margins of some Bible manuscripts; and elsewhere, perhaps inadvertently, he calls him Moses Nakdan. He is commonly cited under this final name; I keep for him the epithet of Hazan, which in modern use means a Cantor, and public reader of the Bible.[43]

XVI.

Germany had various grammarians known by the epithet of Nakdan, on whom see § 147. Such was R. Samuel Nakdan, cited by the aforementioned

---

[42] Wilhelm Gesenius, *Hebräisches und chaldäisches Handwörterbuch über das Alte Testament* (4th ed., Leipzig, 1834).

[43] The author of this work was the English Rabbi Moses ben Yom-Tov of London, also called Moses Nakdan. This is presumably the same man referred to by SDL and Elijah Levita. A critical edition of his work *Darchei ha-Nikud ve-ha-Neginot* was published by D. S. Loewinger (*Ha-Tsofeh le-Hokhmat Yisra'el* 13:267–344, 1929 [1972]); Loewinger refers to the author as Moshe ha-Nakdan.

R. Moses [Ḥazan]. Such was R. Samson Nakdan, author of the חִבּוּר הַקוֹנִים (also שִׁמְשׁוֹנִי), and of the מַפְתֵּחַ הַדִּקְדּוּק (Codex De Rossi 389). And such was R. Jekuthiel [ha-]Cohen son of Judah, known by the abbreviation יהב"י, and also called R. Zalman Nakdan. He is the author of the עֵין הַקּוֹרֵא, containing grammatical notes on the Pentateuch; a work published [in 1818–21] by [Wolf] Heidenheim in his Pentateuch printed under the name חוּמָשׁ מְאוֹר עֵינַיִם.

XVII.

After Kimḥi, the following wrote grammatical works (in addition to those of Benvenasti [Benveniste] and Efodi cited above): the celebrated poet Immanuel [ben Solomon], a Roman, author of the אֶבֶן בֹּחַן (Codices De Rossi 396, 809);

Meir son of David [ben David], praised as an excellent grammarian by Efodi (Ch. 21), author of the lost work הַשָּׂגַת הַהַשָּׂגָה, against R. Jonah [ibn Janaḥ];

Joseph Ḥazan of Troyes, author of a grammatical work entitled סֵפֶר יְדִידוֹת, now lost, but cited in the מנחת יהודה on the Pentateuch, foll. 38, 78, 85 (1);[44]

Joseph Caspi, who, around 1300, wrote a commentary on the Grammar of Ibn Janaḥ (a commentary which has been lost), and who wrote a good Lexicon entitled שַׁרְשְׁרוֹת כֶּסֶף, existing in Rome and in Paris, and of which several lines can be read in [Johann Christoph] Wolf's *Bibliotheca Hebraea* (Vol. 1, p. 542);

Solomon Yarḥi (יַרְחִי), or [Latinized] Lunel, author of a short Compendium entitled לָשׁוֹן לִמּוּדִים, in which he is the first to fix the number of verbal patterns, or בִּנְיָנִים, at 7 (2);

Joseph Zarka (זרקא), who in 1429 composed the רַב פְּעָלִים (Codex De Rossi 511);

Messer Leon, Rabbi of Mantua, who in 1454 wrote the לִבְנַת הַסַּפִּיר, of 160 octavo leaves, a learned and rational work;

---

[44] There are several commentaries known as *Minḥat Yehudah*, but SDL is likely referring to the supercommentary compiled by Judah ben Eliezer, probably in Troyes, in the early fourteenth century (published in Livorno, 1783).

David [ben Solomon] ibn Yaḥya of Lisbon (died 1465), author of another לְשׁוֹן לִמוּדִים, printed in Constantinople in 1506 and 1542, and in Pesaro, without a year.[45] Moses ben [Shem-Tov ibn] Ḥabib, also of Lisbon, author of the פֶּרַח שׁוֹשָׁן (cited by Balmes), of the מַרְפֵּא לָשׁוֹן, and of the דַּרְכֵי נֹעַם (Venice, 1546).

Solomon Almoli, author of a certain הֲלִיכוֹת שֶׁבָא (Constantinople, 1519).

Abraham [ben Meir] de Balmes, of Lecce in the kingdom of Naples, a physician, who, at the request of the famous printer Daniel Bomberg, wrote the Hebrew and Latin מִקְנֶה אַבְרָם (Venice, 1523; reprinted in Hanau in 1594), a work full of erudition and [sound] criticism (see § 18, end). The author having died before the completion of this work, a certain Kalonymus son of David completed it,[46] adding to it the Tractate on the Accents, and finishing the Latin translation of it.

Menaḥem Tamar wrote in 1524, according to what [Giulio] Bartolocci reports,[47] a Grammar entitled רָאשֵׁי בְשָׂמִים.

The celebrated Karaite Commentator Aaron son of Joseph, known as Ha-Rishon, or, the first, wrote around 1300 a short grammar entitled כְּלִיל יֹפִי (Constantinople, 1581).

In the Karaite bibliography entitled אֹרַח צַדִּיקִים, printed together with דּוֹד מָרְדְּכַי in Vienna in 1830,[48] the following Grammars are found recorded: חֲנוֹךְ לַנַּעַר and רַךְ וָטוֹב, both by a certain Solomon [ben Aaron

---

[45] SDL's 'died 1465' is curious, and may be a misprint for 'born 1465', in which case he is confusing David ben Solomon (1440–1524), the author, with David ben Joseph (1465–1543), cousin of the author, who put out an abridged version of *Leshon Limmudim* in 1542.

[46] This fact, including the name of Kalonymus ben David, is stated at the beginning of this final chapter. The *Jewish Encyclopedia*, in various articles, mistakenly calls him Kalonymus ben Judah.

[47] Presumably in his *Bibliotheca Magna Rabbinica* (4 vols.; Rome, 1675–93).

[48] The *Oraḥ Tsaddikim*, a history of the Karaites with an important bibliographical compendium, was written by the Karaite scholar Simḥah Isaac Luzki (d. 1766). It is found on pp. 77–119 of the volume entitled *Dod Mordechai* (Vienna, 1830; reprint Jerusalem, 1966). On this latter work, see the entry for Mordechai of Nisan in the biographical appendix.

of] Troki; כְּלָלִים יָפִים עַל הַדִּקְדּוּק by Mordechai [ben Nisan], author of
the פּוֹרַת יוֹסֵף; דּוֹד מָרְדְּכַי by a certain Joseph [ben Samuel ben Isaac].

(1) This until-now unknown Writer was made known to me by the most learned
and wise Critic, Mr. Solomon Judah Rapoport of Lemberg, to whom the
bonds of profound esteem and true friendship have held me for many years.

(2) De Rossi, who in the Catalogue of his manuscript Codices (Cod. 800)
correctly notes that the Grammarian Yarḥi is not to be confused, as does
[Johann Christoph] Wolf, with the famous Commentator Rashi, should not
have to attributed this error to Balmes, who does not otherwise give the
Commentator the name Yarḥi, but Rashi, and then constantly calling Yarḥi our
Grammarian [Solomon Yarḥi]; there is no hint of a reason to attribute to him
[Balmes] the error of confusing these two scholars. Moreover, Balmes points
the Yod of רשׁי with חִירִק, namely רָשִׁי (see, e.g., folios p. 7, v. 5), signifying
with this that the Yod is an abbreviation of the name יִצְחָקִי Isaaci; he would
have written רָשִׁי, if that Yod had been intended as an indication of the word
Yarḥi.—Our Yarḥi makes mention several times of a certain Grammarian by
the name of Sar Shalom. A certain Moses Sar Shalom was the tutor of Balmes,
who names him in many places (e.g., in folios d. 1, f. 1, s. 3). These Sar
Shaloms seem to be two different people, since the tutor of Balmes, who died
a little before 1523 (see the following pp.), could hardly have been quoted by
Yarḥi, who (according to Balmes himself) was earlier than Messer Leon, who
was writing in 1454.

XVIII.

Surpassing all of the Grammarians subsequent to Kimḥi is the German
Elijah Levita (ר' אֵלִיָּה אַשְׁכְּנַזִי, ר' אֵלִיָּה הַלֵּוִי, ר' אֵלִיָּה בָּחוּר), born in
1472 in Neustadt,[49] near Nuremberg (1), and died in Venice in 1549. In
Rome, he taught the Hebrew language to the famous Cardinal Egidio da
Viterbo, by whom he was supported for thirteen years. He wrote many
grammatical works, which were mostly then translated into Latin (see below,
§ 20, notes 7, 10), and almost all reprinted many times. These are:

I.   Explanations to the מַהֲלָךְ of Moses Kimḥi;

II.   סֵפֶר הַבָּחוּר, a short Compendium of Grammar;

III. סֵפֶר הַהַרְכָּבָה, an alphabetical Tractate on anomalous words;

IV.   טוּב טַעַם, on the Accents;

---

[49] Probably in 1468 or 1469.

V. מָסֹרֶת הַמָּסֹרֶת, Key to the Masorah, a work which, more than all others, is original, both with regard to the learned and clear exposition of the language and the method of the Masoretes; and with regard to the critical thesis (in the third preface) in which he was the first to maintain and demonstrate that the sacred Text was not pointed before the year 500 of the vulgar Era (2);

VI. פֶּרֶק שִׁירָה or פִּרְקֵי אֵלִיָּהוּ, thirteen chapters in rhyming verse, containing the first rules of Grammar, which are followed by three chapters in prose;

VII. סֵפֶר הַזִּכְרֹונֹות, Masoretic observations, a work existing in manuscript in Paris, where the author had sent it to be printed;

VIII. נִימוּקִים, Notes to the Michlol and to the Dictionary of Kimhi.

In addition to these grammatical works, he wrote the שְׁמֹות דְּבָרִים or Nomenclator, a small German-Hebrew vocabulary; the תִּשְׁבִּי [= 712], containing an alphabetical explanation of 712 Rabbinical words; and finally the מְתֻרְגְּמָן, a Targumic dictionary. It is to the clearness and brevity of his method that this writer mainly owes his great fame, not unlike Kimhi, of whom he was almost always a follower; and this was the reason that the first non-Israelite Grammarians were all followers of Kimhi or Elijah. It is for this reason that [Sebastian] Münster, in the preface to one of his Grammars (3) condemns Balmes, as the perpetual opponent of the ancients. In fact, Balmes is not a blind follower of Kimhi, and his work is not the most appropriate for beginners, for whom the dogmatic style is more useful than the critical. It is sure, however, that the excessive deference to Kimhi and to Elijah Levita has slowed down, and not a little, the progress of the science of the Hebrew language; and it has also been the occasional cause of the invention of more than one erroneous system (for example, those of [Jacob] Alting and [Johann] Dantz); and the excessive credit of Elijah (as that of Kimhi, § 14) was the reason that many valuable works have been lost, or have not been printed; while to the contrary, Balmes has the merit of having preserved for us quite a few fragments of various inedited Grammars.

(1) Thus writes [Sebastian] Münster, in the Preface to the *Opus Grammaticum consummatum* [Basel, 1549], a contemporary and admirer of Elijah, with whom he also had correspondence by letter.

(2) This thesis was contested by R. Azariah [dei Rossi] (מָאוֹר עֵינַיִם Ch. 59) and by [Samuel] Archivolti (Chap. 26),[50] afterwards by the two Buxtorfs (Johann the Elder and his son, Johann), and by others; it was, however, victoriously maintained by Louis Cappel (*Arcanum punctationis revelatum*) and by others, and is today almost generally adopted by Scholars. In fact, neither the two Talmuds, nor the ancient Midrashim, ever make any mention at all of the vowel points or punctuation, as written things, but only of the accents and modulations in the reading and chanting. It is notable that one passage of the Midrash on Canticles (מִדְרָשׁ חָזִיתָ), where symbolically interpreting the text תּוֹרֵי זָהָב נַעֲשֶׂה־לָּךְ עִם נְקֻדּוֹת הַכָּסֶף [1:11], making it allusive to the writing of the Holy Book, these ancient Rabbis make the Points of silver refer not yet to the vowel Points or the Accents, as was to be expected, but rather to all the letters and lines. See also the same Midrash to the text 2:4, where the commentary מַתְּנוֹת כְּהֻנָּה says כִּי סִפְרֵיהֶם לֹא הָיוּ מְנֻקָּדִים ["For their books were not pointed"].[51] Off the point, Gesenius cites (Geschichte der hebr. Sprache und Schrift, p. 196), after Buxtorf, the Talmudic passage (Erubin fol. 53[a]) בְּנֵי יהודה דדייקי לישנא ומתנחי להו סימנים נתקיימה תורתן בידן,[52] interpreting סִימָנִים *vowel points*; and falsely he says that this word סִימָנִים was already declared by Rashi as נָקוּד *Pointing*, whereas he [Rashi] correctly explains the Talmudic sentence as relating not to Biblical study, but to that of traditional things, in which study the ancients made great use of סִימָנִים, that is to say, artificial vocabulary as memory aids; vocabulary of which the Talmud is full. The word נָקוּד Pointing is used rather by Rashi in Berachot (fol 62[a]), explaining the Talmudic expression מפני שמראה בה טעמי תורה,[53] a unique Talmudic passage, which would support the existence of the Accents at the time of the Talmudists. But Rashi offers two different interpretations of that expression *to show the Accents of the Law*, of which the first is: to show the written accents (בנקוד של ספר), and the second is: to show with gesticulations of the hand the various modulations of the voice in the chanting of the sacred Text. The second interpretation is supported by Rashi,

---

[50] This is chapter 26 of Archivolti's *Arugat ha-Bosem* (Venice, 1602).

[51] *Mattenot Kehunnah* is a very popular commentary on the Midrash Rabbah, written by Issachar Baerman ben Naphtali ha-Cohen (completed in 1584; first printed, Krakow, 1586–87).

[52] "Judeans who are exact in the language and place for themselves mnemonics retained their learning (lit., their Torah was confirmed in their hand)."

[53] "Because he points to [lit., shows] the accents of the Law with it." This quote is referring to why one should not use the right hand to wipe one's backside, one of several such reasons given in this text.

adding that he had seen such gesticulations used by Jews from the holy land.—
The passage from Megillah (fol. 22|a|):[54] אמר רב כל פסוק דלא פסקיה
משה אנן לא פסקינן ליה ושמואל אמר פסקינן ליה does not yet show
that according to the Talmudist Rav, the division of the verses had been put
down in writing by Moses, but only that the tradition of the division of the
verses goes back to Moses, and so the division and subdivision of the various
parts of the verses, and the relevant modulations of the voice, formed part of
the oral Law; an opinion that the same Rav holds also in Nedarim (fol. 37),
where he is contradicted (as he is here by Samuel) by R. Joḥanan.—The
Talmudic expressions מקרא סופרים הלכה למשה בסיני (Nedarim fol.
37) and יֵשׁ אֵם לַמִּקְרָא (Sanhedrin fol. 4 and elsewhere), prove that the
sacred Text at the time of the Talmudists was not pointed; otherwise they
would have said נְקוּד סוֹפְרִים and נִקּוּד and יֵשׁ אֵם לַנִּקּוּד. In the Midrash of
Exodus (שְׁמוֹת רַבָּא) one actually finds mentioned (Parshah 2) the accent
פְּסִיק. This, however, proves nothing in favor of the antiquity of the Accents,
that Midrash offering too many indications of its late age; regarding which see
the learned work of [Leopold] Zunz: Die gottesdienstlichen Vorträge der
Juden (Berlin, 1832), p. 256, where the Midrash of Exodus is judged to be five
centuries less ancient than that of Genesis; likewise [Solomon Judah] Rapoport
in the Biography of R. Nathan, Note 44.[55]—In conclusion, the antiquity of
the Pointing does not have support in Hebrew or Aramaic works from
antiquity recognized and admitted by sound criticism. See also the scholar
Moses Landau in the work Geist und Sprache der Hebräer, Prague 1822, pp.
13–36.—Saint Jerome then (in addition to never making mention of any
written vowels or accents) has a passage, from which it evidently appears that
the Hebrew Language was in his days entirely lacking of any vowel signs. He
says, in the Preface to the Book of Chronicles, that before beginning the
translation of that book, he wanted to read all of it in the company of a
Tiberian Hebrew scholar, in order to learn from him the pronunciation of the
names, which in the Greek and Latin versions were completely corrupt. He
would not have been forced to resort to this awkward situation if he had
found pointed books; and how would he not have found them if they had

---

[54] "Said the Rav: 'Any verse which Moses did not divide, we do not divide.'
And Samuel said: 'We (may) divide it.'"

[55] Originally published in the journal Bikkurei ha-Ittim (1829–30), this was
republished in Toldot Gedolei Yisra'el (Warsaw, 1904), then in Toldot (2 vols., Warsaw,
1913; reprint, Jerusalem, 1968/69). The biography of R. Nathan, Toldot Rabbenu
Natan Ish Romi, which forms the largest section of this latter work, appears on
pages 1–127 of the first volume of Toldot.

existed, he who knew how to find someone who, without the knowledge of his coreligionists, taught him the Hebrew language by night?

(3) This passage can be read in the Bibliotheca rabbinica of Buxtorf, article מקנה אברם, and in the Bibliotheca hebraea of [Johann Christoph] Wolf, Vol. 1, p. 70. It seems it must be found in the first edition of the בחור translated by Münster, since it is not read in any of the five Grammars by Münster (indicated further below, § 20, note 7) seen by me.

XIX.

Until around 1500, Hebrew Grammar occupied, almost exclusively, the minds of Israelites (1); at the beginning of the sixteenth century it began to be cultivated by the Christians. Johann Reuchlin or Reuchlinus, known by the Greek name Capnion, learned Hebrew from two Hebrews, first in Germany by Jacob Yeḥiel Loans, a physician of the Emperor and Chevalier; afterwards in Rome by the renowned physician, philosopher, and theologian Obadiah Sforno; and he published in Pforzheim in 1506, under the title of *Rudimenta hebraica*, a Lexicon and a brief Grammar (2). This work was (in addition to the tutelage of a number of ex-Jews, see § 20, Note 2) the main source from which Christian cultivators of the Hebrew language drew. Reuchlin also published in 1518 a Tractate *de Accentibus et Orthographia Linguae hebraicae* (3). The schism that began in Germany in 1517 greatly fostered the study of Hebrew among Christians, both sides having to make recourse to the original texts of the sacred Scripture. Luther wrote that he would not part with the knowledge of Hebrew that he had, whatever that may have been, for infinite millions of gold coins. The study of the Hebrew language having been introduced thus into theological studies, among the Catholics as well as the Protestants, Hebrew Grammars multiplied rapidly.

(1) The Hebrew language was, in the first centuries of the Church, studied by Origen and Saint Jerome. Around the middle of the thirteenth century, Saint Raymond of Pennaforte, General of the Dominicans, introduced to his Order the study of the Hebrew and Arabic languages, for the purpose of preaching among the Hebrews and the Moors. In 1311, the Council of Vienna decreed that these languages should be taught in the principal Universities. Nevertheless, before the sixteenth century, very rare among Christians by birth were those who knew Hebrew; as proof of which it is enough to know that Raymund Martin and Nicholas of Lyra, precisely for their skill in matters Hebrew, were by many Writers believed to be of Jewish birth. And indeed the

knowledge of the Hebrew language must have been very rarely preserved among the non-Israelites, since no Grammar and no Lexicon of it existed before 1500 in any of the languages of Europe. The first ones to make any attempt at a Hebrew grammar in the Latin language seem to have been Petrus Nigri, a Dominican, who in the second half of the fifteenth century wrote: *Rudimenta linguae hebraicae*, a work preserved in manuscript in Paris; and Conrad Pellicanus (the Teacher of [Sebastian] Münster), who published at Basel in 1503 a work entitled: *De modo legendi et intelligendi Hebraea*.[56] Reuchlin, however, in the preface to his Rudimenti [1506], claims not to have been in that work preceded by any Christian. The work of Negri could, since it is inedited, have been unknown to him. And Pellicanus, much younger than Reuchlin, even though he began his Hebrew studies without a teacher, was then a disciple of the very same [Reuchlin]; so he can indeed be said to have preceded him in the publication of the work, but not, however, that he was the first among the Christians who applied himself to spread among his own [people] the cognition of Hebrew. Reuchlin adds that he was determined to compose this work, seeing the Jews expelled by the Spanish and by several German regions, to be taken in by Muslims; with the result that it was feared that the Hebrew Language among the Christians, with grave damage to the sacred letters, was disappearing.[57]—If Francesco Sansovino were a more exact writer than he is, a Venetian patrician would be the first among the Christians who wrote a Hebrew Grammar. In the work entitled *Venezia città nobilissima e singolare* (Venice, 1581), he writes (fol. 246)[58] that under the *Doge* Cristoforo Moro, that is to say, from 1462 to 1471, the Venetian Lauro Quirino wrote an *Introductio ad linguam sanctam*. But this work is unknown to the investigators of Italian literature. [Girolamo] Tiraboschi makes no mention of it.[59] [Marco] Foscarini (*[Della] Letteratura veneziana*, Vol. 1, p. 342) says that it is not printed, and [Giovanni degli] Agostini (*Scrittori veniziani*, Vol. 1, p. 226) confesses that, except for Sansovino and his copyists, there is no one else who gives us an account of Quirino having even been instructed in the Hebrew language; this Sansovino then, according to the same Agostini (Preface, p. LV), made only a rough outline, full of anachronisms, ambiguities, and infinite imperfections.

(2) Reprinted, Basel, 1537, with additions by [Sebastian] Münster.

---

[56] This work was reissued with a preface by Eberhard Nestle (Tübingen, 1877).

[57] Previously, Christians would turn to Jews when they wanted to learn Hebrew.

[58] The material on page 246 of the 1581 edition can also be found on pp. 579–80 of the 1663 edition; this latter edition was reprinted in 1968 and 1998, and is thus more easily available. The 1581 edition is not rare, however.

[59] This must refer to Tiraboschi's *Storia della letteratura italiana* (Milan, 1833).

(3) Eternal gratitude is owed by the Hebrew nation, and by all those who love Hebrew literature, to this illustrious Scholar, for the zeal and resoluteness with which in his writings he opposed the burning of all the Rabbinic books, which, at the instigation of the ex-Jew [Johann] Pfefferkorn had been suggested to the Emperor Maxmillian by an Inquisitor, together with a Professor of Theology. See Bibliothèque universelle, Amsterdam, 1688, Vol. 8, p. 496,[60] or else Histoire des ouvrages des Savans, Rotterdam, 1688, Vol. 2, pp. 281–284.[61]

XX.

For a century, the Christian Grammarians only copied the Jewish Grammarians, and arranged their ancient teachings in a better system (1).

The following wrote in this period: Johann Böschsenstein, an ex-Jew (2), Alfonso de Zamora, an ex-Jew (3), Matteo Aurogallus (4), Santes Pagnini, from Lucca, a Dominican (5), Nicolas Clénard, of Flanders (6), Sebastian Münster, Professor at Heidelberg, then at Basel, and author of an *Horologiographia*, and of a voluminous *Cosmographia* (7), Paolo Paradiso, a Venetian ex-Jew, summoned to France by Francis I (8), Guillaume Postel, a Frenchman (9), Paul Fagius, a friend of Elijah Levita (10), David Kyber (11), Johann Isaac Levita, an ex-Jew (12), Jean Cinquarbres (13), Antoine Chevalier (14), Wigand Happel (15), Martin Martinez [de Cantalapiedra] (16), Cardinal [Roberto] Bellarmino (17), Marcus Marinus, of Brescia (18), Guglielmo Franchi, an ex-Jew (19), Joannes Drusius (20), and others.

(1) [Jacob] Alting, in the preface to his Grammar, after having mentioned R. David Kimḥi, writes thus: Cujus proinde viri vestigia presserunt linguae sanctae magistri, non Judaei modo, verum etiam Christiani, sic tamen ut hi lumen facilioris ordinis adhiberent, quaeque illi praecepta erudite congesserant ad leges methodi accuratius disponerent.[62]

---

[60] *Bibliothèque universelle et historique* (26 vols.; Amsterdam, 1686–1718).

[61] *Histoire des ouvrages des Savans*, ed. Henri Bosnage de Beauval (24 vols.; Rotterdam, 1687–1709).

[62] "Accordingly, the men followed in the footsteps of the master of the sacred language––not only Jews, but also Christians followed him—but nevertheless, in order that they might use the light of an easier order, whatever precepts they had collected in a learned way, they arranged more accurately for the laws of method." (translation Philip J. King and AR.)

(2) Elementale [introductorium in hebreas litteras teutonice et hebraice legendas], Augsburg, 1514. Hebr. Gramm. Institutiones, Wittenberg, 1518. Münster, in his preface to the Opus gramm. consummatum [see note 7 to this section], writes of him thus: Fuerunt et in exordio hujus nascentis studii alii quidam baptizati Judaei, qui privatim sed sine fructu docuerunt sacram linguam, carentes latinae linguae cognitione, inter quos et Johannem Buchsenstein numerandum censeo, qui levato multo aere a discipulis, nihil docuit. Testes sunt qui illum audierunt.[63]

(3) Introductio artis gramm. hebr. [1526]; Vocabularium primitivorum hebraicorum; in the Complutensian Polyglott [Bible], 1514; then separately in 1526.

(4) Compendium Gramm. hebr. et chaldaicae, Wittenberg, 1523 [1525], 1530 [1531].

(5) Institutiones Gramm. ling. hebraicae, Lyons, 1526, Paris, 1549, 1556. Abbreviatio Institutionum hebraicarum, Lyons, 1528 [and Paris, 1546]. Thesaurus linguae sanctae (Dictionary), Lyons, 1529. Paris, 1548, 1577, 1614.

(6) לוּחַ הַדִּקְדּוּק Tabula in Grammaticen hebraicam [hebraeam], Louvain, 1529, many reprints.

(7) ס' ההרכבה, translated into Latin, Basel, 1525; פרקי אליהו, translated, Basel, 1527. ס' הדקדוק Institutio elementaris, to which followed the Latin translation of ס' הבחור, Basel, 1532, 1537, 1543; Grammatica R. Moses Kimchi cum Commentis Eliae Levitae, Basel, 1536; טוב טעם and מסרת המסרת reprinted with a Latin compendium, Basel, 1539;[64] מלאכת הדקדוק השלם Opus grammaticum consummatum ex variis Elianis libris concinnatum, Basel, 1549 [first ed., 1540]; מקרי דרדקי Dictionarium hebraicum, Basel, 1525; ערוך Dictionarium chaldaicum, Basel, 1527; ס' השרשים Dictionarium hebraicum, Basel, 1535, 1539;

---

[63] "There were also in the beginning of this nascent study certain other baptized Jews, who taught the sacred language privately but fruitlessly, lacking knowledge of the Latin language, among whom I think Johann Böschsenstein is to be counted, who taught nothing, the [classroom] atmosphere being lightened considerably by his students. The witnesses are those who heard him." (translation Philip J. King, Paul Harvey, and AR.)

[64] For the works of Münster cited thus far, all of which are translations, see § 18 above, on Elijah Levita.

שלוש לשונות Dictionarium trilingue (Latin, Greek, and Hebrew), Basel, 1543 [first ed., 1530].

(8) De modo legendi hebraice, Paris [and Venice], 1534.

(9) De originibus, seu de hebraicae linguae et gentis antiquitate, deque variarum linguarum affinitate. Paris, 1538.

(10) Isagoge compendiaria in linguam hebraicam, Kostanz, 1543. He translated into Latin Elijah Levita's Tishbi (Isny, 1541), and likewise added the Latin translation for the שמות דברים, or Nomenclator of the same author (Isny, 1542) [see § 18, above].[65]

(11) יסוד הדקדוק De re grammatica hebraeae linguae; הגיון Meditationes grammaticae ex Threnis Hiermiae desumptae, Basel, 1552.

(12) לשון למודים Grammatica hebraea (4th ed.), Antwerp, 1564, and (5th ed.), 1570 [1st ed., Cologne, 1557].

(13) Hebr. ling. Institutiones, Paris, 1558 [1559].

(14) Gram. hebr., 1559.[66] Alphabetum hebraicum, 1565 [1566].

(15) Linguae sanctae canones grammatici. Basel, 1565 [1561].

(16) Institutiones in linguam sanctam [hebraicam et chaldaicam], Salamanca, 1571 [first ed., Paris, 1548].

(17) Institutiones ling. hebr., Rome, 1578, 1585, with many reprints.

(18) גן עדן Gramm. linguae sanctae (2nd ed.), Venice, 1585 [1st ed., Basel, 1580]. He also wrote a Lexicon תֵּבַת נֹחַ, Venice, 1593.

(19) שמש לשון הקדש Sole della lingua santa, Bergamo, 1591, 1599, 1603 [and 1657, 1800]; Alphabetum hebraicum, Rome, 1596.

(20) De litteris משה וכלב, 1599 [2nd ed.; 1st ed., 1589]. Gramm. hebraica [Grammatica linguae sanctae nova], 1612. He also wrote de recta lectione linguae sanctae [1609], as well as Alphabetum Ebraicum vetus [1587].

---

[65] Fagius also translated Levita's Meturgeman (Isny, 1541).

[66] This refers to the work entitled Rudimenta linguae hebraicae, published in Geneva, ca. 1560. The first edition is extremely rare, and the exact date of publication is disputed (see Steinschneider, BH, p. 34).

XXI.

In the first half of the seventeenth century, the Christian Grammarians began little by little to add some new observations, and shed new light on those of the ancient Hebrews, profiting especially from the languages kindred to Hebrew.

Johannes Buxtorf, Professor at Basel (died in 1629), after having in 1605 published the *Epitome Grammaticae hebraeae* (1), published in 1609 his *Thesaurus grammaticus linguae sanctae* (2), until today the most methodical and complete such work. The following wrote Grammars in this half-century period: Benedetto Biancuzzi (3), Francesco Mario [di] Calasio (4), George Mayr, a Frenchman (5), Wilhelm Schickard, Professor at Tübingen (6), Mr. G. [Georg] Faber (7) Thomas Erpenius, renowned Arabist, Professor at Leiden (8), John Row, an Englishman [Scotsman] (9), and others. Salomon Glass wrote the his excellent *Philologia sacra* (10), in which he greatly explains Hebrew Syntax, and the Rhetoric of the holy books. Ludwig de Dieu is the author of a Grammar of Hebrew, comparing it with the Chaldaic and Syriac languages (11). Mr. Caspar Ledebuhr, a Pomeranian, elucidated in his *Catena Scripturae* (12) the doctrine of the Accents. Johann Hottinger published a harmonic grammar of the Hebrew, Chaldean, Syriac, and Arabic languages, as well as a harmonic heptaglottic Lexicon (13). Andreas Sennert wrote a harmonic Hypotyposis of the Chaldean, Syriac, and Arabic languages with the Hebrew mother (Wittenberg, 1655); A Hundred Aphorisms of Hebrew Grammar (ib., 1656); and a hundred philological canons, concerning the Syntax and the Idioms of the Hebrew language (ib., 1665).[67]

(1)   Numerous reprints. The *Rudimenta Grammatica hebraicae ad usum Seminarii patavini*, Venice, 1681,[68] is in large part taken from this Epitome.

(2)   Many reprints. He wrote in addition to this a good Biblical Dictionary (*Lexicon hebraicum et chaldaicum*, Basel, 1607; eleventh edition, 1710), and a *Lexicon chaldaicum, talmudicum et rabbinicum*, published by his son (Basel, 1639). The

---

[67] *Hypotyposis harmonica linguarum Orientalium Chald., Syr. et Arab. cum matre Hebraea* (1st ed., Wittenberg, 1653; 2nd ed., 1655); *Aphorismi C succincti* (Wittenberg, 1656); *Centuria canonum philologicorum* (1st ed., Wittenberg, 1657; 3rd ed., 1665).

[68] The author (or editor) of this work was anonymous.

Buxtorf family produced four Scholars, who, for more than a century, held the chair of the Hebrew language at Basel.

(3) Institutiones in ling. sanctam hebr., Rome, 1608.

(4) דבר אלהים Canones generales ling. sanctae hebr., Rome, 1616.

(5) Institutiones ling. hebr. 1616, 1622, 1624, 1649.

(6) Horologium hebraium, 1623 [first published 1614], famous for its brevity, for which it was reprinted more than thirty times.

(7) Institutiones gram. hebr., Nuremberg, 1626.[69]

(8) Grammatica hebraica generalis, Leiden, 1627.

(9) Grammaticae hebraeae Compendiolum [= Hebraeae linguae institutiones compendiosissimae et facillimae], to which is attached a brief Vocabulary of a thousand words (Chilias hebraica), Glascow, 1644.

(10) Leipzig [Jena], 1623. Several reprints [in Leipzig].

(11) דקדוק לשונות הקדם Grammatica linguarum Orientalium Hebraeorum, Chaldaeorum et Syrorum inter se collatarum. Leiden, 1628. Frankfurt am Main, 1683.

(12) שלשלת המקרא, Leiden, 1647.

(13) Gram. quatuor ling. Hebr. Chald. Syr. et Arab. harmonica, Zurich, 1649;[70] Lexicon harmonicum heptaglotton, Frankfurt, 1661.[71]

XXII.

In the final half of the same seventeenth century, the Dutchman Jacob Alting, in order to satisfy the requests of his students, who asked him the

---

[69] This work is mentioned in other bibliographical works (e.g., Steinschneider, *BH*; Fürst, *BJ*), but I have been unable to locate a copy in any modern library catalogue. Steinschneider (p. 46) gives the title of this work as *Institutionum h. gr. libri iv.*

[70] This work was actually published in Heidelberg, 1659. A 1649 work was entitled *Thesaurus Philologicus, seu Clavis scripturae.*

[71] The second half of this note originally read: "Lexicon harmonicum heptaglotton, (a brief abridgement of the great work of Edmund Castell), Frankfurt, 1661." In the errata section, SDL instructed the reader to delete the words in parentheses.

reasons for various grammatical phenomena, made himself head of a new school [of thought], investigating the foundations and causes of the vowel changes that are present so frequently in the Hebrew language, and devising a hypothetical principle, called the *System of Moras* (see § 170), by which he derived all those changes with more ingenuity than truth. He espoused his new doctrine in the work *Fundamenta punctationis linguae sanctae* (1).

Alting's system, followed for a long time in Holland, was brought by Johann Andreas Dantz, with some slight alterations, into the German schools, where it also had a long life.

The Altingian system was also slightly modified by Alhardt de Raadt, who espoused it with mathematical method in an opuscule entitled סוגית הנקוד, *hoc est de Punctationis hebraicae natura Commentarius* (Leiden, 1671).

(1) Gröningen, 1654. Several reprints.

XXIII.

In 1666, Matthias Wasmuth published at Kiel his *Grammatica hebraea nova ac singulari facilitate, 50 regulis omnia et singula compendiose simul et absolutissime complexa*; as well as at Rostock in 1664 his *Institutio methodica Accentuationis hebraeae regulis 15*;[72] both valuable works, in which, however, the limited number of rules announced on the title page is rather misleading, these works being neither less long, nor less complicated than those of a similar type. Regarding the principle of Accentuation, Wasmuth reduced the Catena of Ledebuhr [see § 21] to a better method, and also added to it some observations of his own, but without removing all of the errors from it. The work of Wasmuth was reduced to better clarity by Philip Oesel, who published at Leiden the two works: *Introductio in accentuationem hebraeorum metricam*, 1714; *prosaicam*, 1715. Wasmuth's Grammar was abridged by Mr. Christian Reineccius, author also of two compendious Hebrew-Chaldaic Lexica (1).

Johannes Leusden is the author of a *Synopsis hebraica et chaldaica* (Utrecht, 1667). Christoph Cellarius wrote a Hebrew Grammar in synoptic tables, intended to make one learn the Hebrew language in twenty-four

---

[72] These two works make up parts one and two (of three), respectively, of Wasmuth's *Hebraismus facilitati et integrati suae restitutus* (Kiel, 1666).

hours (2). The Frenchman Jean Bouget composed a Hebrew Grammar and a Lexicon (3). Pierre Guarin, also a Frenchman, is the author of a Hebrew-Chaldaic Grammar (Paris, 1724[–26]), with an extensive Syntax; as well as of a Hebrew and Biblical-Chaldean Lexicon (ib., 1746).

(1) Gramm. hebraeo-chaldaica, Leipzig, 1704; 4th ed., 1741. Lexicon hebraeo-chaldaicum biblicum, ib., 1741 [2nd ed.; 1st ed., 1733]. Index memorialis, ib., Leipzig, 1735.

(2) Grammatica hebraica in tabulis synopticis, cum consilio 24 horis perdiscendi linguam sanctam, Zeitz, 1684.

(3) Grammaticae hebraeae Rudimenta, Rome, 1717; Lexicon hebraicum et chaldaico-biblicum, ib., 1737, three volumes in folio.

XXIV.

The above-mentioned [Johann] Dantz, a very learned Orientalist, and author of various works on Hebrew literature, put out in 1696 [1694] a Hebrew and Chaldaic Grammar, under the title מדקדק s. *Litterator ebraeo-chaldaeus*, and a Syntax, entitled מתורגמן s. *Interpres ebraeo-chaldaeus*; in addition to a Compendium of Hebrew-Chaldaic Grammar [1699], printed many times. This man of extremely keen intelligence disseminated in his grammatical writings new interpretations and derivations, quite ingenious, but not very sensible, and at times puerile and pedantic.

This same course, more ingenious than sensible, called by [Albert] Schultens *Via hebraizandi metaphysica*, was more or less followed by Valentin Ernst Löscher (1), Matthaeus Hiller (2), Friedrich Christian Koch (3), the brothers [Johann and Simon] Tympe (4), and most immoderately of all, Caspar Neumann, who claimed that each of the letters of the Hebrew alphabet had a special significance, the א, for example, signifying activity, motion, the ב, the cube (5).

(1) De causis ling. hebr., Frankfurt and Leipzig, 1706.

(2) Institutiones linguae sanctae, Tübingen, 1711.

(3) Grammatica hebr. philosophica, Jena, 1740.

(4) In the annotations by them, added to the Concordantiae Particularum by Christian Nold, Jena, 1734.[73]

(5) Genesis linguae sanctae, Nuremberg, 1696. Exodus ling. sanctae (in four parts), 1697–1700. Clavis domus Heber (in three parts), 1712–1715.

XXV.

Such errors were opposed by the Dutchman Albert Schultens (died in 1750), much to the benefit of the Hebrew language. But, as it usually happens that men do not know how to go from one extreme directly to a happy medium, but rather pass over to the other extreme; so Schultens, moving away from the metaphysical course, adopted a method hardly less fallacious, in fact, more dangerous, since that which is less arbitrary to the mind has more semblance of truth. Very learned in Arabic literature, he imagined with its help to be able to explain everything in the Hebrew language. Already Judah ben Karish [ibn Quraish] (בן קריש) (1), Jonah ibn Janaḥ (2), and other ancient Hebrews, as well as various Christian Scholars, had felicitously made use of the Arabic language to clarify the less obvious Hebrew words in the sacred Scripture. Schultens, and others following his example (among them, primarily J. D. Michaëlis), went beyond all fair limits, needlessly altering the meaning of the most common words; censured on this account by the most distinguished Orientalists of our day (3). Besides this, the use of Arabic was until then restricted to lexicography, that is to say, to the elucidation of the individual meaning of certain words; Schultens extended it to the grammatical realm. After various other works, he published at Leiden in 1737 his *Institutiones ad fundamenta linguae hebraeae*, which was subsequently abridged and reduced by Nicolaus Wilhelm Schroeder, professor at Gröningen (died in 1798), who in 1766 published

---

[73] The first edition of Nold's *Concordantiae Particularum Ebraeo Chaldaicarum* came out in 1679 (Copenhagen). In the revised 1734 edition, Johann Gottfried Tympe is responsible for the substantial annotations and corrections. Simon Benedict Tympe is also credited in this edition, though not equally to Johann; it seems he compiled the indexes, or at least some of the additional data. Appended to the 1734 edition is the short (ca. 20 pages) supplemental *Lexicon Particolarum Ebraicarum* (1718) by Johann David Michaëlis, as well as a second (only slightly longer) supplemental lexicon by Christian Körber (1712).

his Grammar (4), with the same title as that of Schultens; as well as in the same year by David Kocher (5).

Schultens, with a confidence that won over many, wanted (like several of the above-mentioned Germans, although in a very different way from them) to reduce the phenomena of Hebrew to analogy, that is to say, to find reason for everything, and remove all irregularities; for this objective three expedients were adopted by him. The first is to suppose many forms were in use in the Hebrew language that only present themselves rarely and in the guise of anomalies, which, however, are widely used and regular in the Arabic language. This method is not very secure, being that the Arabic language, as it is more modern than the Hebrew, certainly must have been modified and enriched after Biblical times, adopting various forms anciently unknown. The second is to change the natural derivation of words, doing open violence to the context and to good sense (6). The third, the most abrupt, consists of saying that a living language cares little for rules. This is certainly true in part, and it is precisely in consideration of this truth that the ancient Grammarians, whom Schultens enjoys ill-using, admitted to various anomalies in the sacred Text. More sincere than the Dutch grammarians, the Hebrews did not know this art of beginning with the magnificent boast of expecting to eliminate all irregularities, and ending with the admission that living languages care little for rules.

Non fumum ex fulgore, sed ex fumo dare lucem, was their thinking.[74]

This very learned, but not equally philosophical and critical, Orientalist, did not know how to free himself from some of the erroneous opinions of his predecessors, which are the Altingian system of Moras [see § 22, § 170], and the derivation of all Nouns and Particles from Verbs; to which he added his own doctrine on the segholate Forms (see § 121 *b*). The first has by now fallen into oblivion; the second, contested by [Karl] Aurivillius and by Jahn, and abandoned by Gesenius, has in large part, if not entirely, lost its influence; the third still prevails, and was embraced and taught in the past even by me; It was its lack of verisimilitude that put me on the path of those researches that gradually led me to the uncovering of my new principles regarding the primitive Hebrew (§ 58).

---

[74] "[He intends] not [to get] smoke out of a flash of lightning, but to give light from smoke." (Horace, *Ars Poetica*, 143), i.e., one should not deduce insignificant consequences from great things, but rather deduce important consequences from small things.

(1) An African, living (according to a learned observation by [Solomon] Rapoport) around 880 of the vulgar Era. He wrote, in Arabic, a work which he addressed in the form of a letter to the Israelite Community of Fez, in which he deals with the importance of the study of the Hebrew language, and explains many Biblical terms with the aid of Chaldaic and Arabic. This work is praised by Ibn Ezra under the name of סֵפֶר הַיַחַשׁ or אָב וָאֵם. It exists in manuscript in Arabic at Oxford, in the Bodleian Library. [John] Gagnier and [Christian Friedrich] Schnurrer obtained a copy of it, which is now in the hands of Gesenius. Schnurrer gave several extracts from it in Eichhorn's Bibliography of Biblical literature, Vol. III, p. 951ff.[75]

(2) See, for example, near the end of his Commentary on the Song of Solomon.

(3) See especially Gesenius, Handwörterbuch, 1834, pp. xxxiv–xxxv.

(4) Reprinted [1775,] 1778, 1784, Ulm, 1792 [and more].

(5) Rudimenta Gram. hebraeae secundum praecepta Alb. Schultensii.

(6) Thus he accounts for the word אֵיתָם (Psalm 19:14), in which the Yod is superfluous, interpreting it (p. 448) *I will be an orphan*; and he claims that the word חַמּוֹתִי (Isaiah 44:16), which should be accented on the penult, means not a past-tense *I got warm*, as the context requires, but *warming me*.

XXVI.

In the same eighteenth century, in Germany, the school at Halle in Prussia distinguished itself, boasting Christian Benedict Michaëlis, who died in 1764 (1); Johann Simonis, who died in 1768 (2); Johann David Michaëlis, son of the aforementioned Christian Benedict, born in 1717 at Halle, and died in Göttingen in 1791 (3), the introducer of the Schultensian method into Germany; Gottlieb Christian Storr, who died in Stuttgart in 1804 [1805] (4); Wilhelm Friedrich Hetzel (5); Johann Severin Vater (6), the first who arranged the Hebrew nouns in declensions, in the manner of Greek and Latin grammars; and finally, the still-living Wilhelm Gesenius, whose *Lehrgebäude der hebräischen Sprache* (Halle, 1817) by far surpasses the

---

[75] Johann Gottfried Eichhorn, *Allgemeine Bibliothek der biblischen Literatur* (10 vols.; Leipzig, 1787–1801). The extract referred to was published in the sixth fascicle of the third volume, 1792. The full text of the letter was published at Paris in 1857 by J. Bargès and D. B. Goldberg, and a modern critical edition was made by Dan Becker (Tel Aviv, 1984; in Hebrew).

Grammars of his predecessors, in every respect.[76] In 1834, he published the eleventh edition of his smaller grammar (*Hebräische Grammatik*). Attached to the Grammar was a Biblical anthology (*Lesebuch*), with notes and a Glossary, which has also been reproduced many times. In addition, he has an extremely valuable Hebrew and Chaldaic Lexicon, of which four editions are in German and one in Latin (1833); as well as a *Thesaurus philologicus criticus ling. hebr. et chald. veteris Testamenti*, not yet completed.[77]

(1) [Dissertationem philologicam I.] Lumina syriaca pro illustrando hebraismo sacro [Halle, 1756]. Dissertatio, qua soloecismus casuum ab hebraismo sacri codicis depellitur [Halle, 1739]. Dissertatio [inauguralis philologica], qua soloecismus generis a Syntaxi codicis hebraici depillitur [Halle, 1739], etc.

(2) Introductio Grammatico-critica in linguam hebraicam, 1753. Arcanum formarum nominum linguae hebraicae, 1735. Lexicon manuale hebraicum et chaldaicum, 1752, 1771,[78] reprinted with emendations and additions by [Johann Gottfried] Eichhorn, 1793, and by [Georg Benedikt] Winer, 1828. Onomasticon veteris Testamenti, 1741.

(3) Hebräische Grammatik, Halle, 1744 [1745]; 3rd ed., 1778, with a fine Appendix. Supplementa ad Lexica hebraica, Göttingen, 1785–1792.

(4) Observationes ad analogiam et syntaxim hebraicam pertinentes, Tübingen, 1779.

(5) Ausführliche hebräische Sprachlehre, Halle, 1777.

(6) Grammatik der hebr. Sprache, divided into two courses, Leipzig, 1797, 1807, 1816 [1814]. [1797 and 1814 = Hebräische Sprachlehre]

XXVII.

J. M. [Johann Michael] Dilherr wrote an *Atrium ling. sanctae hebraicae* (Nuremberg, 1759), and a *Peristylium linguae sanctae hebr.* (ib., 1760).[79] Dr. J. F.

---

[76] See the Author's Preface above, and the note of the translator therein.

[77] The *Thesaurus* was completed in 1853.

[78] Simonis' *Lexicon Manuale* was actually first published in 1756 (Halle). In 1752 (also Halle), there did appear Simonis' far shorter (72 pages, versus over 1000 in the Lexicon) *Dictionarium Veteris Testamenti Hebraeo-Chaldaicum*.

[79] SDL is mistakenly off by a century in the case of Dilherr, who lived from 1604–69. His *Atrium linguae sanctae Ebraicae* was published in 1659, and his *Peristylum*

[Johann Friedrich] Hirt, a follower of Dantz, published at Jena in 1771 the work *Syntagma observationum [philologico-criticarum] ad ling. sanctam [Veteris Testamenti] pertinentium*, in opposition mainly to the Schultensian doctrines; but he was perhaps the last one in Germany who supported the old metaphysical route.

Juvenalis Potschka is the author of a *Thesaurus linguae sanctae*, containing a Hebrew Phraseology and a Syntax (Bamberg, 1780). Karl Aurivillius in his *Dissertationes ad sacras literas et philologiam orientalem pertinentes* (Göttingen, 1790) has various good things relating to the science of the Hebrew language.[80] The famous Johann Jahn of Vienna wrote a Hebrew Grammar, first in German (1792, 1799), then in 1809 in Latin.

J. G. L. [Johann Gottfried Ludwig] Kosegarten published at Jena in 1829 *Linguae hebraicae Paradigmata*.

XXVIII.

Georg Heinrich August Ewald published at Göttingen in 1827 the work *Kritische Grammatik der hebräischen Sprache*, an original labor, full of new ideas, all ingenious, varied, and sensible.

Without having arrived at the uncovering of the nature and the laws of the primitive Hebrew, calling, in fact, in many places, the Aramaic language less ancient than the Hebrew, Ewald divined the Kamets to be in many words not original, but a substitute for Schwa.

It is up to posterity to judge the epithet of *Founder of the science of the Hebrew language*, which Ferdinand Hitzig gives to Ewald in dedicating to him his Isaiah [*Der Prophet Jesaja*] (Heidelberg, 1833).[81]

XXIX.

In Italy, in the eighteenth century, Hebrew Grammars were written by Giuseppe Pasini (1), Gennaro Sisti (2), Ignazio Calcio (3), Orazio Rota (4),

---

linguae sanctae Ebraicae in 1660, both in Nuremberg.

[80] This book has a preface by Johann David Michaëlis.

[81] The dedication page reads: "Dem neubegründer einer Wissenschaft hebräischer Sprache, und dadurch der Exegese des Alten Testamentes, G. H. A. Ewald in Göttingen widmet als Zeichen der Anerkennung vielfacher und grosser Verdienste diese Schrift."

and Raffael Mori (5). Standing out at the end of the same century was Tommaso Valperga Caluso, who introduced the theories of Alting and Schultens to the University of Turin, and whose *Prime lezioni di Grammatica ebraica* (6) is in its conciseness rather accurate and instructive. From the priest Bonifazio Finetti, we have the *Trattato della lingua ebraica e sue affini* (Venice, 1756).

The renowned Giovanni Bernardo De Rossi is the author of a *Synopsis institutionum hebraicarum* (Parma, 1807), and an *Introduzione allo studio della lingua ebrea* (ib., 1815). And finally, Pietro Erminio [Emilio] Tiboni, Professor in the Seminary of Brescia, published a Hebrew anthology [*Anthologia hebraica*], accompanied by a fine Glossary (Padua, 1833).

In Switzerland, in the current [nineteenth] century, J. E. [Jacob Elisée] Cellérier published his Elements of Heb. Gram. (7).

In France, Mr. Frank [Adolphe Franck], a member of the Asiatic society of Paris, published a work entitled: *Nouvelle methode de la langue hebraïque* [Paris, 1834].

In Avignon, a *Grammaire hebraïque* came out in 1819.[82]

In Holland, Taco Roorda, a Professor in Amsterdam, is the author of a very valuable *Grammatica hebraea*, in two volumes (Leiden, 1831, 1833).

In England, Samuel Lee (8) put out in London in 1827 the work *Lectures on Hebrew Grammar* (9).

(1)   Gram. lin. sanct. Institutio, 2nd edition, Padua, 1739 [1st ed., 1721].

(2)   Lingua santa da apprendersi anche in quattro lezioni, Venice, 1747.

(3)   Ling. sanct. rudimenta, Naples, 1753.

(4)   Gram. della lingua santa, Venice, 1775.

(5)   Grammatica ebr. ad uso del Seminario fiorentino, Florence, 1787.

(6)   Turin, 1805; and with a preface and emendations by the very learned [Vittorio] Amedeo Peyron, ib., 1826.

(7)   Élémens de la grammaire hebraïque, suivis des principes de la Syntaxe de Gesenius, Geneva, 2nd ed., 1824 [1st ed., 1820].

(8)   Roorda calls him *Anglum eruditissimum, qui, quamvis multa, ab aliis vere dicta, temere subvertit, nonnulla tamen recte observavit ac monuit.*[83]

---

[82] This work was anonymous, written by a professor at the seminary of Avignon.

(9) A more extensive catalogue of the very numerous Hebrew grammars would go beyond the limits of these Prolegomena. A copious index of Christian Grammarians prior to 1700 and of their works on the Hebrew language is found in the *Bibliotheca latino-hebraica* of [Carlo Giuseppe] Imbonati, pp. 538–546 [Rome, 1694], which in the *Bibliotheca hebraea* of [Johann Christoph] Wolf, Vol. 2, pp. 600–620, is continued until around 1720.[84]

XXX.

Finally, meriting discussion for its extravagance is the system of the Frenchman François Masclef, Canon of Amiens, who (1) taught the reading Hebrew words, and those of related languages, without making recourse to vowel points, and pronouncing every consonant with the vowel that accompanies it in the form of its name. So, the ב must constantly and exclusively be sounded *be*, the ג *gi*, the ד *da*, because *beth*, *gimel*, *daleth* are the names of these letters (2). The only exception allowed to this reading is when a consonant is followed by a vowel letter, which are the six letters אהוחיע, to which our Canon liked to attribute the following values: א = A, ה = E, ו = U, ח = open E, י = I, and ע = sharp and aspirate A. Syllables in O do not exist in Hebrew, Chaldaic, and Syriac (!!): the ק, the only Hebrew consonant whose name has the vowel O, is called by Masclef Kuf. This monstrous system, refuted by many, and now fallen into oblivion, found followers for a time, because of the facility that it promised in the study of the language, liberating the Grammar from the infinite rules relating to the Pointing. But if this system brings facility to he who studies, it also brings a thousand great difficulties to he who has studied; increasing terribly the homonyms and ambiguities, and leaving to the discernment of the reader to determine when a word, for example דבר (that should be pronounced, according to Masclef, *daber*), signifies *thing*, *pestilence*, *speak* (Imperative), *he spoke*, or *speaking*. Moreover, in this system the two forms פָּעַל and פָּעֵל are entirely removed, and confused with קַל; even though in the Participle, and

---

[83] "Most learned Englishman, who, although he boldly subverted many sayings by others, some he correctly observed and pointed out." (Translation Philip J. King and AR.)

[84] Other more extensive bibliographies of Hebrew grammars can be found in the *Jewish Encyclopedia*, s.v. "Hebrew Grammar," Hetzel, *Geschichte*, and especially in Steinschneider, *BH*.

in Chaldean also in the Infinitive, the non-identicalness of these conjugations appears not in the vowels alone, but in the consonants as well, since the forms פָּעַל and פִּעֵל employ a Mem in the Participle (מְפַקֵּד, מְפַקֵּד) that does not appear in the קל (פָּקַד), and in Chaldean the Infinitive of the קל has an initial Mem (מִקְטַל), while the פִּעֵל (corresponding to the פָּעַל) instead employs a final He (קַטָּלָה). Nevertheless, the two forms Qal and Piel have in very many verbs quite different meanings. The Chaldean, for example, and the Syrian express buying with the word זְבַן, and selling with the word זַבֵּן. And buying and selling, in the Masclefian doctrine, must be expressed with the same word!!

(1) Gramm. hebr. a punctis aliisque inventis massorethicis libera, Paris, 1716, 1750.

(2) This bizarre idea could have been suggested to Masclef by the Arabic Grammar of Antonio dell'Aquila (Rome, 1650),[85] where, to help beginners read Arabic without vowel points, it is given as a first rule (p. 21) to read with the vowel *a* the consonants whose name has this vowel; and to read with the vowel *e* those which have in their name *e*, otherwise *i*; adding to this the exception of the consonants followed by a quiescent letter, which determines the vowel which must accompany to preceding letter. But to this crude and fallacious rule the Arabic Grammarian adds various others, which in part correct the imperfections of it; concluding that everything must be subordinate to the use of the language.

XXXI.

The system of Masclef was, with slight modifications, reproduced by the priest Giovenale Sacchi, who in a *Dissertazione dell'antica lezione degli Ebrei* (Milan, 1786) claimed the letters אהוחיע to be vowels (א = A, ה = E, ו = U, ח = sharp E, י = I, and ע = O); adding, however, (unlike Masclef) that in the absence of all vowels an Alef should be inferred. So the word דבר would always be read *dabar*. This system was refuted by Father Giambattista Gallicciolii in a Dissertation of the same name as that of Sacchi (Venice, 1787).

---

[85] *Arabicae linguae novae, et methodicae institutiones* (Rome, 1650).

XXXII.

Among Israelites, after the death of Elijah Levita, [the study of] Grammar remained stationary for a century; for which the principal reason was certainly the capture of Grenada and the subsequent expulsion of the Moors and Hebrews from Spain (see § 43).

XXXIII.

The study of Hebrew, however, was never abandoned by the Israelites. Moses Provenzale, Rabbi in Mantua, wrote in his youth, in 1535, one hundred and six tercets containing the primary rules of grammar. The work was printed in Venice in 1597, under the title בְּשֵׁם קַדְמוֹן, the words with which the work begins. David Provenzale, brother of the preceding, also wrote a Hebrew Grammar, which remains inedited, entitled מִגְדַּל דָּוִד, mentioned by R. Azariah [dei Rossi] in his מְאוֹר עֵינַיִם.

Solomon ben Melech of Fez published at Constantinople in 1554 [1549] his מִכְלַל יֹפִי, a valuable grammatical Commentary on all the Scripture, taken mainly from the works of Kimhi. This work was reprinted at Salonika in 1567, then in Amsterdam in 1661 and 1668 [1684/85] (and in Vienna in 1818) with notes by Jacob Abendana.

In 1557, Immanuel [ben Jekuthiel] of Benevento published at Mantua his לִוְיַת חֵן, and the Paduan Rabbi Samuel Archivolti printed in 1602 his עֲרֻגַת הַבֹּשֶׂם. Both of these writers, if they do not have the merit of invention, have that of clarity and method.

XXXIV.

Jacob Levita [Jacob Levi ben Isaac Finzi] published at the age of twenty-three years the דִּבְרֵי אָגוּר, a short Compendium (Venice, 1605).

In 1618, R. Menahem Lonzano, a Levantine, published at Venice his שְׁתֵּי יָדוֹת, a volume containing various opuscules, among which the אוֹר תּוֹרָה (the first in the collection) and the הֲלִיכוֹת שְׁבָא (at fol. 80) show him to be a good Grammarian and sound critic.

The famous Menasseh ben Israel wrote in his youth a Grammar with the title שָׂפָה בְרוּרָה, which has remained inedited. Abraham son of

Raphael [de Lonzano] wrote a grammar entitled קִנְיַן אַבְרָהָם (Prague, 1623).[86] Solomon Jedidah [Jedidiah Solomon ben Abraham] Norzi, a Mantuan, finished in 1626 his גּוֹדֶר פֶּרֶץ, printed at Mantua in 1742, under the title מִנְחַת שַׁי. It contains valuable and instructive critical and grammatical notes on the entire Scripture. In the Preface (printed at Pisa in 1819 by the scholar Dr. Samuel Vita della Volta, a Mantuan), the author claims to have made use of sixty grammatical works.[87] Norzi added at the end of his work three Dissertations relating to several questions of orthoepy.

Grammatical and exegetical Notes on all the Scripture were published by Jacob Lombroso at Venice in 1639, Notes which were praised by Richard Simon.

Benedict [Baruch] Spinoza left among his posthumous works a Compendium of Hebrew Grammar, of 112 pages (Amsterdam, 1677), not lacking in new ideas: see [Albert] Schultens ([*Institutiones*,] p. 308) and [Friedrich Christian] Koch (Introductory Dissertation § 37).[88] Solomon [de] Oliveyra published in Portuguese a Hebrew and Chaldaic Grammar, and a Hebrew Lexicon with the title עֵץ חַיִּים (1). In 1693, Judah Löb Neumark published at Frankfurt am Main a valuable Grammar with the title שֹׁרֶשׁ יְהוּדָה (2); in the preface he says to have also written a Treatise on the Accents. Rabbi David Altaras (died in Venice in 1714) composed a short Compendium of Grammar [כְּלָלֵי הַדִּקְדּוּק], reprinted many times in the Bibles of Venice, Pisa, and Livorno. In 1718, Alexander Süsskind published at Köthen in the Duchy of Anhalt a Grammar entitled דֶּרֶךְ הַקֹּדֶשׁ, to which there is also a brief Treatise on the Accents written in German (in Hebrew characters), where he seems to have made use of the work of Wasmuth.

(1)   Livro da Gramm. heb. et chald., Amsterdam, 1689. Thesouro da lingua santa, ib., 1682.

(2)   See [Johann Christoph] Wolf, Bibl. hebr., Vol. 1, p. 444.

---

[86] This is a mistake; this grammar was published in Zolkiew, 1723.

[87] Norzi's introduction was published also by A. Jellinek (Vienna, 1876).

[88] SDL is referring to Koch's *Fundamenta linguae Hebraeae suis undique rationibus solide firmata, seu Grammatica Hebraea philosophica* (Jena, 1740). He cites a paragraph number only, since the introductory section of the book (entitled *Dissertatio Prolusoria*) has no page numbering.

XXXV.

Prior to Alting, Isaac son of Samuel Levita [Isaac ben Samuel ha-Levi], of Posen, published at Prague in 1628, under the title of שִׂיחַ יִצְחָק, the first annotated grammar of the Hebrew language. This work is in divided into text and commentary: the text contains with great conciseness and precision the empirical or historical part of the grammar, that is, the exposition of the laws and phenomena of the language; and the commentary contains the rational or philosophical part of it, that is to say, it lays out the reasons for the phenomena. Less systematic and more sensible than Alting, he take the motives of the Language not from an arbitrary law in the same language, but rather from the nature of human pronunciation. He wrote also the בְּרִית הַלֵּוִי concerning anomalous words, and another grammatical work entitled אֵלֶּה תּוֹלְדוֹת יִצְחָק; as well some Notes on the Michlol [of Kimḥi]; all these works remain inedited, and are perhaps lost.[89]

XXXVI.

This capable grammarian was the precursor among the Hebrews of still another more distinguished and meritorious. That is Solomon Cohen Hanau, author of the בִּנְיַן שְׁלֹמֹה שַׁעֲרֵי תוֹרָה (Frankfurt am Main, 1708), (Hamburg, 1718), יְסוֹד הַנִּקּוּד (Amsterdam, 1730), צֹהַר הַתֵּבָה ([Berlin, 1733;] 2nd ed., Dyhernfurth, 1787), שַׁעֲרֵי זִמְרָה (a posthumous work, Fürth, 1762), שַׁעֲרֵי תְּפִלָּה ([Jessnitz, 1725;] 2nd ed., Dyhernfurth, 1779), and קוּרֵי עַכָּבִישׁ, which is attached to קוֹרוֹת אֲרָזִים (Fürth, 1744), all works rich in completely new observations and theories (see § 194b, d). He deserves credit most of all for his שַׁעֲרֵי זִמְרָה, in which he sheds very clear light on the immensely complicated laws of the Accents, which he untangled with more precision and with more clarity and brevity than did [Caspar] Ledebuhr, [Matthias] Wasmuth, and [Philip] Oesel, whose works, written in Latin, were most probably unintelligible to him; as well as for his שַׁעֲרֵי תְּפִלָּה, in which he purged the Formulary of the Prayers from many

---

[89] *Brit ha-Levi* is mentioned on the title page of *Siah Yitsḥak* and is discussed in the introduction, as if it were intended to be included in the volume.

errors that it had incurred from the ignorance of copyists and editors (see § 86) (1).

This profound Grammarian had an utter plagiarist in Aloys [von] Sonnenfels, an ex-Jew, who in 1757 published in Vienna a Hebrew grammar in two languages, Latin and German, with the title אֶבֶן בֹּחַן, Lapis lydius, Prüfstein,[90] in which with great pomp he appropriated several of Hanau's new theories (2). [Hanau's] שַׁעֲרֵי תְּפִלָּה was bitterly attacked by Mordechai [Halberstadt of] Düsseldorf in a pamphlet of refutations (קונטרס השגות), written in 1738, and printed at Prague in 1784; and by Jacob Emden in his לוּחַ אֶרֶשׁ, published in Altona in 1769, after the death of Hanau. Hanau's doctrines were also combated harshly by Ruben Levita [Reuben ha-Levi Grishaber] in the עֲנַף עֵץ עָבוֹת (Fürth, 1744), and then (respectfully, however) on several conflicting points by the Rabbi Aaron Moses [ben Tsvi Hirsch] of Lemberg in his אֹהֶל מֹשֶׁה (Zolkiew, 1765), a clear and concise Grammar, containing some new views. This final [Grammarian] is also the author of a Compendium in verse, entitled הֲלָכָה לְמֹשֶׁה (Fürth, 1771).[91] Hanau was nevertheless followed by almost all subsequent Israelite Grammarians in Germany.

(1) I would like to transcribe what [Johann Christoph] Wolf writes of this Grammarian, unknown to modern Orientalists, in his *Bibl. hebr.* (Vol. 1, p. 1053): "R. Schelomo Salman ... scripsit סֵפֶר בִּנְיַן שְׁלֹמֹה *librum aedificii Salomonis*, h.e. Grammaticam Hebraicam Sacram ... quae tamen Judaeis se adeo non probavit ob antiquiores Grammaticos et Doctores, [Aben Esram, Kimchium, Eliam Levitam, Isaacum Abarbanelem & alios] liberius notatos, ut de eo flammis delendo cogitarent Rabbini Fracofurtenses, nisi mitiora aliorum consilia, & ipsius auctoris palinodia, obstitissent. [Distinctum est hoc aedificiuna in duodecim domos, quae in diversa abeunt conclavia, suis singula fenestris instructa.] Grammatica itaque est absoluta, nec elementaris tantum, sed simul exegetica & in primis ad interiorem Syntaxeos Hebraicae ac

---

[90] The book has two title pages. The first, in German, gives the title as אבן בוחן, *Prüfstein, oder Unterricht der Hebräischen Sprache*. The second, in Latin, has the title אבן בוחן, *Lapis Lydius, seu Institutiones Hebraicae Linguae*.

[91] The grammar in verse was entitled *Shirah Ḥadashah*. It was published together with *Halachah le-Moshe*, a detailed prose explanation of the former (Zolkiew, 1764; Fürth, 1771). According to Fürst, *BJ* (which was the source for the *Jewish Encyclopedia* article, "Lwow, Aaron Moses ben Zebi Hirsch"), he wrote another work entitled *Halachah le-Moshe*, containing novellae on the Talmud.

idiotismorum rationem manu ducens: digna quoque, quae a Christianis evolvatur. Fusiorem libri recensionem habes in Relationibus Innoxiis vernacula lingua editis an. 1713 p. 57 seqq."[92] As far as the retraction that Wolf has our author sing, it is certain that in the five of his works cited above, subsequent to בנין שלמה, he for the most part only repeats his same theories, continuing to censure the opinions of the ancient Grammarians, only with a less biting style.[93]

(2)   For example, the theory of the lenis vowel (from p. 108 to p. 137).

XXXVII.

Rabbi Jacob Bassan, who filled the position of Rabbi among the Spanish [Portuguese] Israelites, first in Amsterdam, then in Hamburg, published at Nuremberg in 1768, under the assumed name of Jacob Babani, the opuscule יְשָׁרֵשׁ יַעֲקֹב, containing his various grammatical observations on some erroneous readings in the Formulary of the Prayers.[94]

---

[92] "R. Solomon wrote *Sefer Binyan Shelomo* 'Book of the Edifice of Solomon'— which however did not prove agreeable to the Jews themselves regarding the ancient grammarians and scholars, Ibn Ezra, Kimḥi, Elijah Levita, Isaac Abravanel, and others noted freely—in order that the Rabbis of Frankfurt might think about this thing that was going to be destroyed by flames, if they had not put forth the more mild counsels of others, and [if not for] the retraction of the author himself. This edifice is divided into twelve houses, which are split into different rooms, each built with its own windows. The grammar, consequently, is complete, not only in the basics, but is also exegetical and especially leads by hand to the deeper study of Hebrew syntax and idioms—also worthy, which is being developed by the Christians. You have a more fixed recension of the book in Relationibus Innoxiis [*Unschuldige Nachrichten*], edited in the vernacular [German] language in the year 1713, p. 57 ff." (translation Philip J. King, Daniel Berman, and AR.) I have corrected SDL's transcription of the Latin slightly, based on the original text of Wolf.

[93] The Hebrew text of Hanau's retraction can be found in David Mierowsky, *Hebrew Grammar and Grammarians Throughout the Ages* (Johannesburg, 1953), pp. 207–8.

[94] Some scholars have attributed this to his son Abraham (cf. *Jewish Encyclopedia*, s.v. "Basan, Abraham"), though the *Encyclopaedia Judaica*, s.v. "Bassan, Abraham Hezekiah ben Jacob," reports that this is probably incorrect.

Benjamin Simeon Levita [ha-Levi] published at London in 1773 a Grammar entitled דַּעַת קְדוֹשִׁים. Solomon [ben Moses Chelm], a Rabbi in Lemberg, is the author of שַׁעֲרֵי נְעִימָה (Frankfurt an der Oder, 1776), a Treatise on the Accents of the poetic Books.[95]

XXXVIII.

The great [Moses] Mendelssohn, in the Preface (אוֹר לִנְתִיבָה, Berlin, 1783) of his Pentateuch (נְתִיבוֹת הַשָּׁלוֹם), spread—the first among the modern Israelites—the light of philosophy on various points of Hebrew Grammar, especially on the Syntax. He and Solomon Dubno, a Pole and a skillful Grammarian, his collaborator on the Commentary attached to his Pentateuch, applied in a learned and judicious way the doctrines of Hanau on the Accents to the Exegesis of the sacred Text. Dubno also wrote the תִּקּוּן סוֹפְרִים, attached to the above-mentioned Pentateuch, rich in grammatical illustrations.

XXXIX.

Isaac Satanow, a Pole, published at Berlin in 1773 a Compendium of Grammar, with the title שִׂפְתֵּי רְנָנוֹת; as well as a Hebrew-German Dictionary entitled שְׂפַת אֱמֶת ([Berlin, 1787;] 2nd edition, Prague, 1803), and the שָׂפָה אֶחָת, an annotated Dictionary of homonymous Hebrew terms [Berlin, 1784].

XL.

Naphtali Herz (also Hartwig) Wessely (born in Hamburg in 1725, and died there in 1805) applied profound study to distinguishing the meanings of synonymous terms, in the גַּן נָעוּל (Amsterdam, 1765, and Vienna, 1829), יַיִן לְבָנוֹן (Berlin, 1775), רוּחַ חֵן (ib., 1780), and in his Commentary to Leviticus inserted in Mendelssohn's Pentateuch; as did Solomon Pappenheim of Breslau (died in 1814) in the יְרִיעוֹת שְׁלֹמֹה (Part 1,

---

[95] The *Encyclopaedia Judaica* (s.v. "Chelm, Solomon ben Moses") mistakenly lists the publication date as 1766. Many subsequent reprints were published together with Judah ben Zeev's Hebrew grammar, *Talmud Leshon Ivri* (Vilna, 1830; 1856; 1883; 1912; Warsaw, 1875).

Dyhernfurth, 1784, Part 3, ib., 1811, Part 2, Rödelheim, 1831), and in the Lexicon חֵשֶׁק שְׁלֹמֹה, of which only the first fascicle appeared, containing the first two letters of the alphabet (Breslau, 1802).

XLI.

Moses Cohen Hechim [Höchheimer] published at Fürth in 1793 Kimḥi's Michlol, supplemented with illustrative notes.

Joel Löwe (called Bril) published at Berlin a Compendium of Hebrew Grammar in German, entitled עַמּוּדֵי הַלָּשׁוֹן (Berlin, 1794), in addition to various philological dissertations spread out in the fascicles of the מְאַסֵּף,[96] and in his excellent Commentary to the Psalter of Mendelssohn, reprinted many times.

Ḥayyim [ben Naphtali] Köslin published at Berlin his מַסְלוּל (Hamburg [1788], Brünn, 1796). See also § 86.

Judah Löwe Levita [Judah ben Moses Leib ha-Levi], a Pole, published in Lemberg in 1793 a short treatise on the Conjugation of verbs, entitled שָׂפָה לְנֶאֱמָנִים, containing several new observations.

The Polish Rabbi Judah Löwe Margolioth put out in 1796 the short work אִגֶּרֶת הַמְּלִיצָה וּמִשְׁפַּט לְשׁוֹן הַקֹּדֶשׁ.

The meritorious Judah Löwe ben Zeev, a Pole, first published at Breslau in 1796 his תַּלְמוּד לָשׁוֹן עִבְרִי, a Grammar more rich and profound than any other of the modern Israelites: it is the first that contains an extensive and well-organized Syntax. It was reprinted five times in Vienna. Ben Zeev is also the author of a Hebrew-German German-Hebrew Dictionary, entitled אוֹצַר הַשָּׁרָשִׁים (Vienna, 1807, 1816).

Judah Eliyakim [Eliyakim ben Abraham] of London published at Berlin the עֵין הַקּוֹרֵא and at Rödelheim the עֵין מִשְׁפָּט (both in 1803), both of them grammatical works.

---

[96] This was a monthly periodical which was published out of Berlin (1784–86, 1788–90, 1794–97, 1809–1811). Mendelssohn's commentary to his 1782 German translation of the Pentateuch, in which he praised the beauty of the Hebrew language, was the catalyst for the creation of *Ha-Me'assef,* the first sucessful Hebrew periodical and first organ of the Haskalah movement. Joel Löwe was one of the editors.

Moses Samuel Neumann published in 1808 a Compendium of Hebrew Grammar, entitled מַעְגַּל יֹשֶׁר ([Prague, 1808, 1816;] 3rd edition, Vienna, 1831).

In [1807–]1809, Shalom ha-Cohen [Shalom ben Jacob Cohen] published at Dessau in German his תּוֹרַת לָשׁוֹן עִבְרִית,[97] cited with praise by [Ernst] Rosenmüller in Jeremiah 22:21.[98] This Grammar was reprinted in 1816 in Vienna, and in the same year was reproduced in Prague, enlarged by the learned Wolf Mayer, who wholly recast it and notably improved it in the final edition of 1832.[99]

Solomon Löwisohn published at Prague his שִׂיחָה בְּעוֹלָם הַנְּשָׁמוֹת (1811), and his בֵּית הָאוֹסֵף (1812), valuable opuscules, containing various observations on language.

Also a distinguished Grammarian was Wolf Heidenheim, who died in 1831, and who in 1791 [at Offenbach] published the מֹאזְנַיִם of Ibn Ezra with his annotations, afterwards enriched the Pentateuch with philological notes entitled הֲבָנַת הַמִּקְרָא (Rödelheim, 1818–21), and philologically illustrated the holiday Prayers (מַחְזוֹר), which he translated into German [Rödelheim, 1800–5]; he is the author also of a Treatise on the laws of the Accents (מִשְׁפְּטֵי הַטְּעָמִים, Rödelheim, 1808).

The journal בִּכּוּרֵי הָעִתִּים (Vienna, 1820–31, 12 vols.) contains various grammatical and lexicological dissertations, many of which are mine (Vol. 6, pp. 25–35; Vol. 7, pp. 147–209; Vol. 8, pp. 86–166; Vol. 9, pp. 76–132).

XLII.

Italy, after the time of Archivolti and Norzi, can only boast the Dissertation קְרֹא מִקְרָא on some questions of Orthoepy, by Rabbi Menahem Navarra di Verona (1); the Hebrew Grammar of Rabbi Simone Calimani of

---

[97] This was first published in Berlin, 1802. The 1807–9 edition (Dessau) was expanded and improved.

[98] *Scholia in Vetus Testamentum*, Part VIII, vol. 1 (Leipzig, 1826), p. 535. Rosenmüller, after quoting an opinion of Cohen regarding a word in this verse, notes that it can be found in the grammar of this *doctus hebraeus* ('learned Jew'), and gives the reference (p. 53 [of part 1] of the 1807 edition). The praise does not extend beyond this.

[99] There were subsequent editions, the last being from 1850.

Venice (Venice, 1751; Pisa, 1815);[100] the annotated Hebrew and Italian Grammar of Samuel Romanelli of Mantua (Trieste, 1799) (2);[101] as well as the two elementary Compendiums of Rabbi Judah Briel of Mantua (שֵׁפֶר כְּלָלֵי הַדִּקְדּוּק, Mantua, 1730, and 1769), and of Rabbi Hananiah Cohen of Reggio, who died in Florence in 1834 (שַׁעֲרֵי לְשׁוֹן הַקֹּדֶשׁ, Venice, 1808), also the author of a Hebrew-Italian and Italian-Hebrew vocabulary, entitled מַעֲנֶה לָשׁוֹן (Reggio, 1812), and a collection of verbs from the Mishnaic language, entitled שָׂפָה אֶחָת (Reggio, 1822).

The Italian lawyer [Phillipe] Sarchi[102] published at Paris in 1828 his *Grammaire hebraïque raisonée et comparée* (3). He also wrote, in English, *An Essay on hebrew Poetry ancient and modern* (London, 1824) [as Philip Sarchi].

Mr. Samuel Vita Lo-ly [Lolli] of Gorizia, closely related to me by blood and by friendship, is the author of an inedited Grammar of the Hebrew language, in question and answer format.[103]

(1) It is inserted in the book פְּנֵי יִצְחָק (Mantua, 1744), foll. 23–27.

---

[100] *Grammatica ebrea spiegata in lingua italiana.*

[101] *Grammatica ragionata italiana ed ebraica.*

[102] There is some confusion as to Sarchi's first name. In SDL's index, he is listed as Samuel Sarchi. In some other sources (e.g., in modern library catalogues) he is credited as M. Sarchi. On the title page of his *Grammaire*, he is indeed called M. Sarchi, but this is simply to be read as Monsieur Sarchi; at the end of his dedication (p. vi), he signs as Phillipe Sarchi. His original name was Samuel Morpurgo (mistakenly given in the *Jewish Encylcopedia* [s.v. "Grammar, Hebrew"], as Samuel Marpurgo), but he changed it to Francesco Filippo Sarchi upon his move to Vienna in the 1780s and subsequent conversion to Catholicism. For more on his life, see Maddalena del Bianco Cotrozzi, "Samuel Morpurgo alias Francesco Filippo Sarchi, linguista e docente nella Vienna di fine settecento," in *We-Zo't le-Angelo: Raccolta di studi giudaici in memoria di Angelo Vivian*, ed. G. Busi (Bologna, 1993), pp. 199–229.

[103] Morais notes, "Ehud Lolli, Chief Rabbi of Padua, son of the late Samuel Vita, issued a valuable Hebrew grammar of his own in 1886." Morais is referring to his *Corso di grammatica della lingua ebraica* (Padua, 1878; Milan, 1886). Ehud Lolli, who also published a dictionary of Rabbinic Hebrew (Padua, 1867) and contributed to the *Jewish Encyclopedia*, was a student of SDL.

(2) Romanelli also wrote a Compendium of the most necessary rules of Hebrew
     Grammar for the use of beginners, inedited.

(3) The Author, in the Preface (p. xv), declares to have profited, in the compilation
     of the work, from the counsel and advice of the very learned Rabbi Chevalier
     Abraham [de] Cologna.[104] The latter, however, having left Paris to go to Trieste
     before the work was completed, found in it, to his great surprise and regret,
     several errors, which certainly would not have been introduced had he not left
     France before the completion of that Grammar. He pointed out to me, among
     the other erroneous statements, the one in which the characteristic דגשׁ of the
     פֿעַל is made (p. 102 and elsewhere) compensatory from a Nun.

XLIII.

Undertaking now to compare that which was done by the Israelites and by
the non-Israelites in the last three centuries on the theoretical study of the
Hebrew Language, the latter are perceived to have notably exceeded the
former. Whoever seeks to investigate the hidden reasons for this fact,
without stopping at its exterior aspects, will not have to be surprised at this.

The efforts of men regarding the study of a subject, and the progress
that they make in it, are usually proportionate to the need that they feel for
these studies, and the means that they have with which to dedicate
themselves to it with profit.

As to the means, the matter has no need of further explanation, since
it would be absurd that someone would do those things for which he lacks
suitable means of doing; that is to say, that he would do what he cannot.

As for the feeling of need, nothing is more true (and this is a truth too
often forsaken by Instructors) than the sentence that was the last written by
the famous Condillac, namely, that one usually learns very badly when one
studies before having felt the need of learning (1).[105]

Now the means that the Israelites have had to advance in the
theoretical study of their ancient language, especially in the last three
centuries, are far inferior to those possessed by the Christians.

The greatest advancements, since the revival of letters, that were made
in any branch of human knowledge were, as everyone knows, the work of

---

[104] Chevalier is his title. Sarchi (p. xv) calls him "M. de Cologna, chevalier de la
Couronne de Fer, actuellement Grand-Rabbin à Trieste."

[105] "On apprend d'ordinaire assez mal, lorsqu'on étudie avant d'avoir senti le
besoin d'apprendre." (*La Langue des Calculs*, p. 478).

those Scholars for whom public teaching of those disciplines was demanded by the Government; that is to say, those men who found themselves in the position to be able to dedicate themselves, by their talent, to a study that gave them a secure, and not meager, subsistence, and the means still to sustain those expenses that the perfection of the sciences demands.

Now the Israelites never had such persons, for whom the teaching of their language alone gave comfortable support. The Rabbis, the only ones among the Hebrews who drew a comfortable living from national studies (but not in all times, nor in all places), were always distracted by their incessant pastoral concerns from any literary occupation that was not closely related to their ministry. Teachers, moreover, because they could expect very scanty compensation for their efforts, had to teach not Biblical studies, but rather Talmud (as Kimḥi did); since [this was] the work that in past times (as long as the Hebrews enjoyed the right of autonomy, and the questions of *meum* and *tuum*[106] were decided according to the Talmudic laws) was of double importance for the Israelite people: namely, a religious importance and a judicial one.

[Solomon] Hanau, a profound grammarian, lived, as [Johann Christoph] Wolf relates, by going around the cities of Germany and Belgium and instructing young boys. Anyone can judge how much such conditions might be favorable to the progress of science (2), and whether they are comparable to those of the Christian Scholars, Professors of Hebrew language and sacred Scripture, stably and respectably paid by the State or by the Church.[107]

In addition, a great help in the perfection of the theoretical study of the Hebrew language is the knowledge of the related languages. The Hebrews, after the expulsion from Spain, have lost (in Europe at least) the opportunity to know Arabic. Syriac, moreover, was never known by them

---

[106] I.e., property rights.

[107] SDL probably overestimates a bit how well Christian Hebrew professors were paid. Johannes Buxtorf, for example, was forced to look for other work in the printing business in order to support his family; see Stephen G. Burnett, *From Christian Hebraism to Jewish Studies: Johannes Buxtorf (1564–1629) and Hebrew Learning in the Seventeenth Century* (Leiden, 1996). But SDL is certainly correct that those working as professors, teaching and working with Hebrew at the university level, certainly found more favorable conditions for producing grammatical works.

(3). Only the Biblical, Targumic, and Talmudic Chaldaic was left for them, of which they never had a Grammar,[108] feeling the difficulty of making one, rather than the utility.

All this makes it clear how the Hebrews lacked the necessary means for advancement in the science of their ancient language.

On the other hand, the need for theoretical study of the Hebrew language must have been much less felt by the Hebrews, who learned it, well or badly, practically from their infancy, than by the Christians, who wished to read the original Text of the sacred Scripture already at an advanced age.

This need was still less perceptible by the Israelites in the last three centuries than it was beforehand, due to the moral dejection of the entire nation brought on by its expulsion from Spain.

This fatal event damaged philological studies in two ways.

Firstly, the downcast spirits were afraid to stray from the judgments of the ancients, who were blindly venerated and almost worshipped by them. The pusillanimous mind sees with the eyes of others, resting on the knowledge of some notorious Scholar,

Di quel si pasce, e più oltre non chiede.[109]

No one ever dared to contradict Kimḥi; and having assumed that this teacher [*maestro*] was ignorant of nothing and was mistaken about nothing, who would ever feel a need to repeat the research and investigate further? We have already seen (§ 36 note 1) the scandal aroused by [Solomon] Hanau with his book criticizing the ancient Grammarians.

Secondly, the same disheartenment, inclining spirits toward allegorical and mystical interpretations, did not allow the need to be felt for deeper philological investigations. The anomalies were mysteries that were adored, and Kabbalistic doctrines gave reasons for everything. Grammatical explanations were not appreciated: the philologist seemed, and still seems to some, a profaner of sacred things, a sacrilegious person; or at least was pitied as a poor man with narrow views.

---

[108] As Morais notes, SDL later published such a grammar, *Elementi grammaticali del caldeo Biblico e del dialetto Talmudico babilonese* (Padua, 1865). This grammar was subsequently translated into German (Breslau, 1873), into English (New York, 1876), and (in part) into Hebrew (Saint-Petersburg, 1880).

[109] "On this they feed, and seek nothing more." Dante, *Purgatorio* XVI, 102.

(1) Langue des calculs, final lines.

(2) The author of the שֹׁרֶשׁ יְהוּדָה makes clear in the preface of the work this source of alienation from philological studies, making those who neglect them speak as follows:[110]

> מה לי להראות אוני וכחי בחכמת דקדוק ומסורת, והוא נעלמה
> ונסתרת, אין לי ממנה משכורת. אלך לי אל הר המורים, ללמוד
> פוסקים וטורים. אלך ואעבוד בדיני ממונות, ובריוח יהיו לי מזונות,
> אלך ואמסור נפשי לדרוש ברבים פשטים נאים וערבים, כדי שיפסקו
> לי צרכי מרובים, ומה לי ללמוד המקרא דבר שאינו עושה רושם,
> ואינו נחשב רק בקליפות השום :

(3) Nevertheless there was one Hebrew who served as an interpreter between the first Syrians who came to Europe, and Teseo Ambrogio, who was later the first who taught the Syriac language to Europeans. This was certainly Rabbi Giuseppe Gallo [Joseph ben Samuel Tsarfati] (whose father had been a physician of Pope Julius II), who, with the knowledge that he had of Biblical and Rabbinic Chaldean, translated for Teseo into Italian and into Latin the words that the Syrian Elia uttered in his own language, as the same Ambrogio relates on page 14 of his *Introductio in chaldaicum linguam* (Padua, 1539), and whose story can also be read in the Syriac grammar of [Andreas] Hoffmann (pp. 36, 37).[111] But for the Hebrews, motives that might cause them to study Syriac are not present, motives that are not lacking for the Christians, who must have had an interest in knowing the background of the Church of the East and in reading their ancient ecclesiastical writers.

---

[110] "What is in it for me to show my strength and power in the knowledge of grammar and Masorah, when it is so obscure, and I get no income from it? I will go to the Mount of teachers, to study Mishnah and Talmud. I will go and work in business, and with the profit I will have food. I will go and dedicate myself to interpreting pleasant and easy-to-swallow teachings for the masses, so that my many needs will be met. And why should I study Bible, a thing which does not make an impression, and is considered only as the skin of garlic?" This is presumably the *Shoresh Yehudah* of Judah Neumark (1693). The author includes several word plays and allusions in this short passage. For example, the phrase הר המורים *Mt. of Teachers* is a play on הר המוריה *Mt. Moriah*, and possibly also on מורים *rebels, disobeyers*.

[111] *Grammaticae syriacae libri III* (Halle, 1827).

In my *Philoxenus*,[112] I gave to my coreligionists some notes on this language and its character, with a sample of 125 words, and demonstrated the benefit that can be derived from it for the understanding of the Targumic and Talmudic language, and at times even the Biblical. I was at that time very far from imagining that this idiom could in itself contain the causes of a large part of the phenomena of Hebrew Grammar, and that it was a dialect of that most ancient language, which presents to us the primitive image of Hebrew (see § 58).

XLIV.

Taking into consideration all of these circumstances, it will be concluded, I hope, by every impartial judge, that the Hebrews of the last centuries are very deserving of compassion regarding the advancements that they have not made in the science of their language, and are deserving of praise and admiration for that progress which they have not failed to make in such unfavorable conditions.

If ever the present small volume, and the annotated Grammar which will follow it, will be so fortunate to bring to light some truth, and lead some steps towards advancing the science that is the subject of them, this also is attributed to the most favorable conditions of the present times: it is attributed to the foundation of this Rabbinical College [of Padua], in which the teaching of philology was assigned to me; and to the wisdom and kindness of the Emperor FRANCIS I, whose very wise Decree allowed the Israelites of these lands to imagine and support the foundation of such a new Establishment.[113]

May my efforts contribute to promoting among my coreligionists the study of the Hebrew Language, and reviving in the chests of the Israelites the ancient love for the national letters, which in various parts of Europe appears in recent times to have gracelessly lost its fervor and become notably lukewarm!

---

[112] *Ohev Ger, Philoxenus* (Vienna, 1830; 2nd ed., Krakow, 1895).

[113] The founder of the Rabbinical College of Padua, Isaac Samuel Reggio, had appealed to the Emperor for permission to establish the institution. His request was granted.

HISTORY OF THE HEBREW LANGUAGE

XLV.

The name of the Hebrew Language refers to the Language that was spoken in times past by the Hebrews, that is, the Language in which the original sacred Books of the Israelites are written (the Bible, the sacred Scripture, the Mikra), except for some chapters of Daniel and Ezra, and one verse of Jeremiah (10:11), which are written in Chaldean.

XLVI.

The name of the Hebrew language is not Biblical, nor was it in use by the ancient Rabbis, who, with more reason, meant by the title of עִבְרִית *Hebrew* the language and the writing from those lands which are on the other side of the Euphrates from Palestine, therefore known as עֵבֶר הַנָּהָר (Joshua 24:2) *countries across the river* (1). This denomination, introduced, apparently, by the Greeks, and in imitation of them by the historian Josephus Flavius writing in Greek, was introduced little by little also into the academic language of the Rabbis (2), and into the vulgar speech of the Israelites (3), and finally came to be more or less in use among the European Israelite writers (4).

(1) See the Babylonian Talmud, Shabbat fol. 115, and Megillah fol. 18; also, in Bereshit Rabba on Gen. 14:13, see the comment יְפֵה תֹּאַר.

(2) Babylonian Talmud, Gittin fol. 87. Jerusalem Talmud, Megillah ch. 1 § 9. Tosefta, Megillah ch. 2 § 1.

(3) Targum [*Parafrasi caldaica*] Esther 9:27.[1] Having been made for the comprehension of the population, the language of the Targums must have been, in some time and in some place, popular among the Israelites.

---

[1] This is 9:27 of the First Targum to Esther, where we find the phrase *rosham ivra'e* 'Hebrew characters'.

(4) Those who wrote their works in Arabic (as well as those who wrote in imitation of their philological works that they studied, even though they themselves wrote in Hebrew), adopted the denomination of the Hebrew language via the example of the Arabs. It was used rarely by the writers of the Middle Ages, who only or mainly dedicated themselves to Rabbinic studies, e.g., Rashi on Isaiah 66:3. Generally, they made use of the name עִבְרִי only where it served to distinguish the original Hebrew text from that of the Aramaic Targum, e.g., Gen. 49:24. So Tosafot to Berachot fol. 8.

XLVII.

The Hebrew Language has four other names among the Hebrews, of which only two are Biblical. These are:
  a) Language of Canaan [*Lingua di Canaan*]
  b) Judean Language [*Lingua giudaica*]
  c) Holy Language [*Lingua santa*]
  d) Assyrian language [*Lingua assiriaca*]

XLVIII.

The Language of Canaan, that is to say the Phoenician Language (שְׂפַת כְּנַעַן Isaiah 19:18), seems the most ancient and most natural denomination of the Hebrew language; a denomination taken from the country in which it was spoken since the most ancient times; as witnessed in the proper names of the Canaanites cities and people—not only from the time of Moses, but also from the time of Abraham—that are met in the Pentateuch, which are all, or nearly all, Hebrew in root and form; [witnessed] as well by the remains of the Phoenician language.

XLIX.

It was commonly called the Judean Language (יְהוּדִית) in Biblical times (1), at least after the division of the two kingdoms of Judah and Israel; the period after which the name Judeans [*Giudei*] was introduced.[2]

(1) 2 Kings 18:26, 28. Isaiah 36:11, 13. Nehemiah 13:24.

---

[2] Italian *Giudei* (singular, *Giudeo*) means both Judeans and Jews.

L.

Holy Language (לְשׁוֹן הַקֹּדֶשׁ) is the most common name in the Rabbinic writings, from the Mishnah onwards; a name that was given to the language after it ceased to be the only language spoken by the Hebrew nation; that is to say, ever since the Aramaic and Greek languages were naturalized in Judea, so that Hebrew no longer retained any special prerogative, except that of being the language of Religion, the language in which the sacred Books were written, in which the public prayers were recited, and in which the Scholars of the Laws used to give their ritual and moral teachings, and held their academic discussions.

LI.

Assyrian Language (אַשּׁוּרִית) is mentioned in the Mishnah (Megillah ch. 2 § 1). This denomination has wrongfully passed from the modern Hebrew writing system, the so-called כְּתָב אַשּׁוּרִי, to the Hebrew Language, which is usually written in the Assyrian alphabet.[3] The Talmudists express themselves with greater precision when they say אשורי יש לו כתב ואין לו לשון. עברי יש לו לשון ואין לו כתב (Jerusalem Talmud, Megillah ch. 1),[4] that is to say, that the Hebrews, having preserved the ancient Hebrew language, but not the ancient Hebrew script, for which they have substituted the Assyrian characters, resulted in the fact that Assyrian had (through the use of the Hebrews) a script, but not a language, and Hebrew had (among the same people) a language, but no script; also when they say (Babylonian Talmud, Sanhedrin, fol. 97b) מגילה כתובה אשורית ולשון הקדש *a parchment written in Assyrian characters, and in the holy language.*

---

[3] I.e., Hebrew square script, or Aramaic script. On the use of the term Assyrian to designate this script, see R. Steiner, "Why the Aramaic Script Was Called 'Assyrian' in Hebrew, Greek, and Demotic," *Orientalia* 62 (1989), pp. 80–82.

[4] "Assyrian has a script, but not a language. Hebrew has a language, but not a script."

LII.

The Hebrew Language belongs to the family of languages improperly known as Semitic (1), and which better are called triliteral languages (§ 53 a); these are:

a) Aramaic, which includes the Biblical Chaldean; the Targumic Chaldean, which is divided into Babylonian and Palestinian or Jerusalemite (2); the Syriac language; the Samaritan dialect; that of the Sabians [Mandeans];[5] and the Talmudic, which, like Targumic, is divided into Babylonian and Jerusalemite;

b) Hebrew (the ancient, i.e., the Biblical, and the *Seriore*,[6] or from later times, or Rabbinic), which also includes Phoenician and Punic;

c) Arabic, ancient and modern, and the Maltese language (3);

d) Ethiopic.

(1) As if they were each among the descendents of Shem; on the contrary, 1. the Canaanites descended not from Shem, but from Ham; 2. The Elamites or Persians, and the Assyrians, come from Shem, even though their languages are not analogous to those called Semitic.[7]

(2) I call *Babylonian* the Targums of the Pentateuch and the Prophets, known as Onkelos and Jonathan, whose language is identical; and *Palestinian* that of the Hagiographia and the two Targums of the Pentateuch, one known by the name יְרוּשַׁלְמִי (Jerusalemite) and the other by the name Jonathan, or Pseudo-Jonathan, the languages of which are notably similar. The epithet *Babylonian* was given to the Targum of Onkelos already by several ancient and very reliable Rabbis, namely by the author of the עָרוּךְ (in the articles אבוב and חלז), and by the writers of the notes to the Talmud known as תּוֹסָפוֹת

---

[5] Sabians (Italian *Zabii*) is another name for Mandeans, not to be confused with the Sabeans of the South Arabian kingdom of Sheba. Castiglioni has a long footnote (p. 18, note *zayin*), explaining the difference between Sabians/Mandeans and Sabeans. In the sixty years between the publication of SDL's Prolegomena and Castiglioni's translation, much information was brought to light on Mandaic (especially by Th. Nöldeke), as well as on the Sabean inscriptions of Southern Arabia (especially by J. Halévy).

[6] Morais translates *Seriore* as 'partaking of Syriac', certainly an erroneous translation. I would translate this simply as 'later'.

[7] Recall that the Assyrian language (i.e., Akkadian) had not yet been deciphered, so there was no reason to believe it was of Semitic stock.

(Tractate מְנָחוֹת, fol. 44).—And here I would like to submit for the appraisal of Scholars a conjecture of mine on the origin of the name Onkelos. It has already been observed by learned Israelite scholars that in speaking of this famous proselyte, the Babylonian Talmud consistently uses the name אנקלוס *Onkelos*, and the Jerusalem Talmud always uses the name עקילס *Aquila*. It has likewise been observed to be a strange thing and without [another] example that to express a Greek name, as is that of Aquila (Αχυλας), the Talmudists used the letter ע, unknown to the Greek language. All this leads me to the following hypothesis. The two words אנקלוס and עקילס express a single name, and this was pronounced neither Onkelos nor Akylas, but Ankylos, Αγχυλος, i.e., *curved, crooked*; the name possibly alluded originally to some physical imperfection. But in Palestine, where (more or less generally) both languages, Greek and Hebrew, were spoken, the name Ankylos, the meaning of which was known, was, with slight modification, reduced from the Greek, with the substitution of the Greek sounds *ankyl* by the Hebrew root with similar meaning עקל; then, allowing for the Greek desinence (as was done with פַּלְגָס, the name derived from פֶּלֶג *half*, and signifying *of the age between lamb and ram/ mutton*),[8] it was pronounced עקילס, from which then Αχυλας and Aquila. The Babylonians, on the other hand, who hardly heard Greek or Hebrew, preserved almost intact the original sound of the exotic name, whose meaning they did not know, and wrote אנקלוס, for אנקילוס or אנקולוס (*Ankylos*).

(3) See Giovanni Pietro Francesco Agius de Soldanis, Della lingua Punica presentamente usata dai Maltesi, Rome 1750; and Gesenius, Versuch über die maltesische Sprache, Leipzig 1810.

LIII.

These languages have in common the following properties, which render them notably distinct from the other Asiatic languages, as well as from the languages of Europe:

a) most of the words have a triliteral root, for which reason they can be called triliteral:

b) they almost always use only consonants to express the fundamental idea, which, by vowel mutation, is modified, but rarely changed; e.g., the forms *shamàr, shamòr, shemòr, shamùr, shomèr, shimmèr, shammèr, shummàr,* are all

---

[8] Jastrow, *Dictionary*, vocalizes this word as פַּלְגָס, and notes that the term can also be applied to a youth between boyhood and maturity.

in Hebrew from one common root, and all express the same fundamental idea *to guard* with various modifications of tense and mood; whereas in Latin, for example, the verbs *rego, rigo, rogo, rugo*, express ideas completely different from one another:

c) they make great use of guttural sounds (neither consonants or vowels) of various degrees of aspiration:

d) they do not have case, but they have a particular form for the Noun closely joined to another Noun which follows it:

e) they express the genitive and accusative of the personal pronouns with letters added to the end of the word (Suffixes):

f) they are written from right to left (except, however, Ethiopic):

g) they do not contain in their alphabets vowel letters, the lack of which is made up for by means of points or small lines, above or under the letters (1).

(1) The Ethiopians alter the form itself of each letter, according to the vowel whose pronunciation is desired; so each letter is susceptible to seven different forms. The Sabians [Mandeans][9] also modify the form of the consonants, attaching to them one of the three letters Alef, Vav, Yod. For the rest, it seems that property *b* of the triliteral languages was a reason that the inventors of their alphabets did not think to institute vowel letters. It is not, however, the case that they entirely neglected the vowel sounds: in fact, the first letter of the alphabet was destined to indicate them. The Alef has no sound, nor any degree of aspiration, like the other mutable letters, which were all originally consonants (Vav, Yod), or aspirates (He): the Alef alone is in its essence, however vague and indeterminate, a vowel sound. In vain there is usually attributed to it a faint degree of aspiration (unknown to the Hebrews, Arabs, and Syrians), comparing it to the smooth breathing of Greek, which (as Blomfield notes in his additions to Matthiae's Greek grammar § 19) is a mere invention of the Greeks, intended only to indicate the absence of a rough breathing.[10]

LIV.

The triliteral languages all have their remote origins in a common mother, now lost, which seems to have been in large part biliteral (formed from

---

[9] See translator's note to § 52.

[10] August Matthiae, *A Copious Greek Grammar*, trans. Edward Valentine Blomfield (Cambridge, 1818; 4th ed., London, 1832).

roots of two letters only) and monosyllabic (from words of one syllable), all natural and onomatopoetic, the first language of the human race, which probably was never written, but continued gradually taking shape and perfecting itself, until becoming artificial and triliteral.

LV.

That the triliteral roots are not primitive, but were, in large part at least, originally biliteral and monosyllabic, is gathered from the following phenomena, observable in all the triliteral roots, which, for the sake of brevity, will be observed here principally in the Hebrew Language.

a) Many quiescent or weak [*deficienti*] roots, which differ from each other only in one quiescent or weak letter, have the identical or nearly identical meaning; for example: טוֹב ,יָטַב; הָלַךְ ,יָלַךְ; בּוּז ,בָּזָה; פּוּחַ ,נָפַח; מוֹשׁ ,מָשַׁשׁ ,שׂוּם ,שִׂים ,קָבַב ,נָקַב; חָרָה ,חָרַר ,מוֹל ,מָל ,נָמַל; פּוּץ ,נָפַץ ,יָרַק, רָקַק ,יָקַשׁ ,נָקַשׁ ,שׁוּג ,שָׂגָה ,שָׁגַג ,נוֹד ,נָדָה ,נָדַד ,דוּם ,דָּמָה ,דָּמַם ,דּוּחַ ,דָּחָה, נָדַח ,צוּר ,יָצַר ,צָרַר ,שׂוּחַ ,יָשַׁח ,שָׁחָה ,שָׁחַח; דּוּן ,דָּכָא ,דָּכָה ,דָּכַךְ.

b) Some roots, not only quiescent and weak, but also some sound, similar in the first two letters and different in the third, express a single common fundamental idea. Such are the roots פָּצָה ,פָּצַע ,פָּצַח ,פָּצַם, all expressing the idea *opening with violence*; דָּחָה ,דָּחַף ,דָּחַק ,גָּב ,גָּבַהּ, גָּבַח ,גֶּבֶן ,גָּבַע *highness*; קָצָה ,קָצַץ ,קָצַב *knocking*, (with the kindred קָטַב ,קָטַף ,קָטַע ,חָטַב, קָצַע ,חָצַב), (Rabbinic, along with the kindred Chaldaic קָטַע) *cutting*; גָּלַח, גָּלַב *shaving*; קָשָׁה ,קָשַׁח *duress*; לָעַב ,לָעַג *derision*; חָפַר ,חָפַשׂ *investigation*; מָרָה ,מָרַד *disobedience*; עָצָה ,עָצַם ,עָצַר *closing* (1).

c) The identicalness of the fundamental idea is also observed in some roots which are identical in two root letters, without it being the first two, and without the third radical being quiescent or weak; for example, מָשַׁשׁ, גָּשַׁשׁ *to touch*; אָנַשׁ ,יָאַשׁ *to despair*; אָלַץ ,לָחַץ *to press*; הָדַף ,דָּחַף *to knock*; בָּרָה, בָּחַר ,בָּרַר *to choose*; סַם ,בָּשָׂם *drug, spice*. Likewise in Chaldean, the verb *to go out* is in some tenses סָלַק, in others נָסַק; and the verb *to go* is הוּךְ in some tenses, הָלַךְ in others.

d) Finally, many of the nouns, verbs, and particles that refer to the most common ideas and to the basic needs of a nascent society, are monosyllabic. Such are the nouns אוֹר *light*, אִישׁ *man, individual*, אֵשׁ *fire*, בּוֹר *well*, הַר *mountain*, טוֹב *good*, טִיט *mud*, יָד *hand*, יוֹם *day*, יָם *sea*, לֵב *heart*, סוּס *horse*, עִיר *city*, פֶּה *mouth*, צֹאן *small livestock*, קִיר *wall*, רֹאשׁ *head*, שֶׂה *lamb*, שׁוֹר

bull; the verbs בּוֹא *come, enter*, מוּת *die*, נוּס *flee*, סוּר *retreat*, קוּם *get up*, רוּץ *run*, שׁוּב *return*, שִׂים *put*; and the particles אוֹ *or*, אִם *if*, אַף, גַם *also*, זֶה *this*, כִּי *as*, לֹא *no*, עַד *until*, עִם *with*, פֹּה *here*, שָׁם *there*, etc.

(1)   This accounts for the etymology of the name of Noah (Gen. 5:29), which is in Hebrew נֹחַ, in the sacred Scripture derived from the form יְנַחֲמֵנוּ *he will console us*, a form belonging not to the root נוּחַ, but rather to נָחַם. The triliteral נָחַם is only the biliteral נַ, expressing the state of calmness, which with the addition of the final Mem came to express more specifically the calmness of the mind; that is to say, 1. the cessation of a moral sorrow, hence הִנָּחֵם *to be comforted, be given peace*, נִחַם *to console*; 2. the abandonment of a resolution, stopping thinking about what was first thought to do, hence הִנָּחֵם *to regret, repent*; 3. to calm one's anger by taking revenge, to take satisfaction (הִנָּחֵם Isaiah 1:24; הִתְנַחֵם Genesis 27:42). All these ideas were expressed originally in a confused way by the biliteral נַ, and Noah's father was able to say יְנִיחֵנוּ, and mean with this vocable taken from the root נַ the same idea that at the time of Moses was expressed with the form יְנַחֲמֵנוּ from the triliteral root נָחַם.

LVI.

The first language, having become triliteral, split up, with the division of human societies and nations, and according to the various climates and diverse characteristics of the various peoples, into the diverse aforementioned idioms, which derived from this [first language] their immediate origins. This happened because:

a) the words themselves were altered little by little in the mouths of the diverse peoples, depending on whether they, by effect of the climate or other circumstances, preferred harsh [*aspri*] or soft [*molli*] sounds, open or closed, aspirates or the sibilant letters, etc.

b) the language itself in different ways was perfected and enriched by the various peoples, according to the different levels and types of their cultures, at the point in which their respective dialects were fixed, becoming written languages.

LVII.

If we take the number of forms of the nouns (מִשְׁקָלִים) and of the verbs (בִּנְיָנִים), as well as the number of synonymous terms, as a standard and measure of the various degrees of perfection to which the different triliteral languages had reached, when they were fixed by means of writing, we find that Hebrew occupies the middle ground between the poverty of the Aramaic and the wealth of the Arabic (1).

(1) [Samuel] Bochart (Phaleg, book I, ch. 15) and Richard Simon (Histore critique du vieux Testament, book I, ch. 15), who assert that the Hebrew language is simpler than the Chaldaic, are mistaken about this. See § 125.

LVIII.

This renders Aramaic likely to have been fixed, that is to say, written, first, then Hebrew, and finally Arabic. And since these three languages are sisters, that is to say, not just modifications of a single language, with a mother common to all three, it follows from this that Hebrew, before being as it is now, i.e., in the time before it was written, was identical with Aramaic, from which it only gradually and little by little moved away, until becoming another idiom; likewise, Arabic was in older times similar to Hebrew, and in an even more distant era, similar to Aramaic.

This judgment, so far probable, will obtain, at least concerning the Chaldaic and Hebrew languages, a high degree of moral certainty from what will be explained in the continuation of these Prolegomena (from § 104 to § 141) regarding the fundamental rules of grammatical formation in these two languages (1).

(1) Priority is commonly assigned to the Hebrew Language, for reason that Genesis takes from this language the etymology of several names of the oldest antiquity. These etymologies are: 1. אִשָּׁה *woman*, from אִישׁ *man*; 2. חַוָּה *Eve*, from חַי *living*; 3. קַיִן *Cain*, from קָנִיתִי *I acquired*; 4. שֵׁת *Seth*, from שָׁת *he put*; 5. נֹחַ *Noah*, from יְנַחֲמֵנוּ *he will console us*; 6. פֶּלֶג *Peleg*, from נִפְלְגָה *it was divided*; 7. בָּבֶל *Babel*, from בָּלַל *he confused*. One must observe, however:

    a) that five of these names have an equal etymology in Aramaic, which has חַי *living*, קְנָא *to acquire*, נַחֵם *to console*, פְּלַג *to divide*, בַּלְבֵּל *to confuse*.

    b) that the verb פְּלַג *to divide* is in fact Aramaic rather than Hebrew, being found in the sacred Scripture only two other times,[11] and these only in a poetic

---

[11] In addition to Genesis 10:25, this verbal root appears in Job 38:25 and Psalm 55:10. Luzzatto does not count the occurrence in 1 Chron. 1:19, where the phrase is identical to that of Genesis.

style, akin to Chaldean (§ 67), and occurring very often in the Chaldaic Targums, where the Hebrew has בָּתַר, חָצָה, חָלַק:

c) that בָּבֶל is much more analogous to בַּלְבֵּל than to בָּלַל:

d) that although the Chaldean that has come down to us (which is not the most ancient, [since] we have nothing older than [the book of] Daniel) does not show the form אִית *man*, corresponding to the Hebrew אִישׁ, it does however have the forms אִית, אִיתַי, corresponding to Hebrew יֵשׁ *there is*; from this it is deduced that the sound IS (to which is related the Greek ἐστι, *is*; Latin *esse, est*; Germanic *ist*, and the Sanskrit AS *to be*) was in the primitive monosyllabic language used to vaguely express *being, existence, entity, the individual, man*; that this sound belonged equally to Aramaic and Hebrew, but, as per the customary pronunciations of the two peoples, Hebrew pronounced it אִישׁ, and Chaldean אִית; that the Hebrew language preserved its אִישׁ in the sense of *individual, man*, and formed from it the other word יֵשׁ, which it used to signify *being, existence*, i.e., *there is*; and that Aramaic instead preserved its אִית in this last sense of *there is*, and gave for *man* two new nouns, the one derived from the primitive אִית, אִישׁ, and is אֱנָשׁ, with the insertion of an epenthetic Nun (not unlike Hebrew did in the plural אֲנָשִׁים, and also in the feminine אִשָּׁה, in which the dagesh in the Shin supposes a Nun), and the other from a totally different root, and is גֶּבֶר, properly, *strong*:

e) that the verb שׁוּת *to put*, from which the sacred Scripture derives the name שֵׁת *Seth*, albeit monosyllabic, does not seem primitive, but probably shares a common origin with the Chaldean verb of equal value שַׁוִּי; that is to say, the primitive sound indicating *putting, placing something stably*, was probably SHA from which is derived שֵׁת, שַׁוִּי, שָׂם (with Sin, originally Shin, see § 102), and also שָׁם *there*, no less the [Aramaic] nouns שְׁתֵאסָא, שָׁתוֹת, אָשְׁיָה *foundation*,[12] [Hebrew] שֵׁת, שָׁתוֹת *buttocks*; and from this primitive SHA can be derived the name שֵׁת *Seth*, with added Tav, as were derived from it the words שֵׁת, שָׁתוֹת, etc. with added Tav.

And besides this it is notable that the form יַפְתְּ which is met in the blessing of Noah over Japhet (Gen. 9:27) is purely Chaldaic; and that the Talmudists say (Sanhedrin fol. 38) that Adam spoke in the Aramaic language: אדם הראשון בלשון ארמי סיפר.

LIX.

However, this does not preclude that the Aramean Language, at the time in which it was written, could have already moved away from the original language in some of its parts, in which Hebrew has preserved, and as a result also preserved the simplicity of the mother. Thus the Hebrew language preserved the primitive noun אִישׁ in the sense of *individual, man*, while the Aramaic does not use its אִית in except in the sense of *there is* (see above note). The Hebrew language preserved also the primitive form of the infinitive קְטֹל, which Aramaic has replaced with מִקְטַל.

LX.

The Hebrew Language is also in the middle of Aramaic and Arabic with regard to the greater or lesser use of the vowel sounds: so to express *he killed* Aramaic says קְטַל Kᵉtal, a word with one and a half syllables; Hebrew קָטַל Katal, bisyllabic; and Arabic קָטַלַ Katala, trisyllabic.

LXI.

This indicates the pronunciation to have been primitively harder (at least in the family of the triliteral languages); and to have become successively softened.

LXII.

This very tendency toward the softening of sounds was in many cases the cause of the opposite effect, namely, that the less ancient pronunciation was shorter than the older one; this is observed here and there in all languages, especially in French and English, in which their orthographies have preserved many letters formerly pronounced and which are no longer pronounced.

LXIII.

The language of Canaan became the language of the Hebrews after Abraham was transported from Mesopotamia to Canaan. This Patriarch spoke Aramaic, the language that continued to be spoken by his brother, who remained on the other side of the Euphrates, and by his descendents.

LXIV.

Abraham's family, in their adoption of the language of the Canaanites, were able to preserve, at least for some time, various Aramaic words, forms, and manners; and this even more so, since Jacob returned to Mesopotamia, where he had a long sojourn, where he got married, and where almost all of his children were born and raised.

LXV.

Such traces of Aramaic must have disappeared little by little from the language of the Israelites, after they established themselves in Canaan under Joshua, and were in constant contact with the indigenous people, who for several centuries remained among the new holders of the land.

LXVI.

Indeed even during their sojourn in Egypt, the Israelites—inhabiting the region of Goshen, a province which, in the opinion of the most eminent modern Orientalists (1), and supported by several Biblical passages (2), was very close to Canaan—were able to continue communication with the Canaanites, and from then their language must have continued losing its Aramaic tint, more and more approaching the Phoenician, with which it finally identified (3).

(1) Johann David Michaëlis, Rosenmüller, and Gesenius.

(2) Exodus 13:17, 1 Chron. 7:21.

(3) During their sojourn in Egypt there were introduced into their language, in small number however, several Egyptian terms. Such are the nouns אַחוּ and יְאֹר, and such is the pronoun אָנֹכִי I, in Coptic *Anok*. Already the Talmudist R. Nehemiah observed (see Yalkut [Shim'oni], Pentateuch, § 286) the form אָנֹכִי to be Egyptian.[13]

---

[13] The Coptic pronoun is, of course, a cognate of the Hebrew; see A. Rubin,

LXVII.

The Aramaisms or Chaldaisms, having become archaisms, in other words antiquated or at least lesser-used forms, were welcomed, even sought out, by the poets (1), who in all languages usually love terms and forms which are less popular [*volgare*] and less common in use. We will call these forms and words, frequent in the poetic elements of Scripture, and all imitating the Aramaic language, poetic Aramaisms or Chaldaisms. Examples of this are the forms תַּגְמוּלֹוהִי (Psalm 116:12) with an absolutely Aramaic suffix, instead of תַּגְמוּלָיו; מִטָּתוֹ שֶׁלִּשְׁלֹמֹה (Cant. 3:7), in the style of שְׁמֵהּ דִּי אֱלָהָא (Dan. 2:20), and, with the omission of the preposition, בְּנוֹ בְעֵר (2); שַׁלָּמָה (Cant. 1:7) *so that not*, in the style of the Chaldean דִּי־לְמָה (Ezra 7:23); אָתָא and אָתָה, instead of בּוֹא; אֱנֹושׁ for אָדָם; מִלָּה for דָּבָר; קָטַל for הָרַג; רָמָה for הִשְׁלִיךְ; גָּזַר in the sense of *to decree* (Job 22:28); אָחַז in the sense of *to close* (Psalm 77:5) from the Chaldean אֲחַד; מָלָא (or better מָלֵא) in the sense of *to draw* (Isaiah 2:6), as in Chaldaic מַלִּי; כָּלִיל in the sense of *crown* (ib. 2:18); מִיק in the sense of *to deride* (Psalm 73:8), from the Syriac and Palestinian Targumic מַיִּק; and many others.

(1) Gussetius [Jacques Gousset] had a glimmer of this (*De lingua ebraica*, Introductory remarks to his Lexicon),[14] but concluded from it that the Chaldeans enjoyed those forms which were more rarely used by the Hebrews.—But how is it that these forms became rare in the Hebrew language?

"An Outline of Comparative Egypto-Semitic Morphology," in *Egyptian and Semito-Hamitic (Afro-Asiatic) Studies in Memoriam Werner Vycichl*, ed. Gabor Takacs (Leiden, 2003), pp. 454–86. Luzzatto's suggestion (and that of his predecessors) are understandable, given that the other major Semitic languages which exhibit a *k* in the first person singular pronoun, namely Akkadian and Ugaritic, were unknown at the time. His footnote is especially interesting, in that this comment by R. Nehemiah—which deals with why God used *ānoki* in Exod. 20:2—probably contains, however unknowingly, the first common Afro-Asiatic word to be recognized.

[14] Jacques Gousset, *Commentarii linguae ebraicae* (Amsterdam and Utrecht, 1702). The second edition of this work bore the title *Lexicon linguae hebraicae* (Leipzig, 1743).

(2) Likewise, in my opinion, קְצִירוֹ רָעֵב (Job 5:5) meaning *the harvest of the hungry*; and מִימִינוֹ אֵשְׁדָּת (Deut. 33:2) *from the right of the slope*, that is to say, from the South of Mount Nebo, to which Sinai, Seir, and Paran are southerly.

LXVIII.

The Hebrew language was fixed by Moses in his divine Codex, and adapted to stable rules. So the word מָן, an Aramaic word, signifying *what?* was still used in the time of the Israelites, who upon seeing Manna, with which they were not familiar, exclaimed (Exod. 16:15) *Man hu*, that is to say, *what is it?* But this expression, not having been adopted in the Pentateuch by Moses, remained excluded from the Hebrew language.

LXIX.

The various dialogues reported by the sacred Scripture, since spoken in times prior to its recording, must not make us believe that they were uttered by their different interlocutors precisely as they are written; and that therefore the language of Moses was the very same one as that of Jacob, of Abraham, of Noah, of Lamech, and even of Adam. Such reasoning would also make us deem that the same was the language of the Pharaohs, and that of Laban, who, on the contrary, as we know, spoke Egyptian and Aramaic, respectively. It is necessary to recognize then that the divine Writer conveyed the other peoples' speech in his own language, and that therefore the Hebrew discussions of Jacob and of his forefathers and sons could have been uttered in a Hebrew somewhat different from that of Moses, and closer than it to Aramaic.

LXX.

The Hebrew language remained for nine centuries in the same state, in which Moses fixed it, without notable alteration (1), since the sacred Text of the law was in that time the most influential Text of the language, at least for Scholars and Writers, [and since] the nation did not have during this interval lasting relations, friendly or hostile, with peoples of a different speech.

(1) Two slight alterations that the language underwent after the time of Moses are met in the forms הוא and נער, that are usually used indiscriminately by Moses

for both genders, while the subsequent Writers always say היא and נערה for the feminine.—I suppose here, with the whole of antiquity, that Moses was the author of the Pentateuch, without ignoring that several modern [scholars], as reported and refuted by Rosenmüller in the Prolegomena to the Pentateuch,[15] profess this sacred Book to be far less ancient. Johann David Michaëlis, in the Preface to Lowth,[16] wondered how, the words of Ezra being less elegant, the Mosaic writings could be attributed to that same author; he concluded, however, there was no cause for astonishment, since a very similar enormity was ventured by Arduino,[17] who maintained that the works of Cicero and Virgil were written by some monks in the Middle Ages (!!). To perceive the frivolousness of the arguments of those people who deny the antiquity of the Pentateuch, I would be tempted to think that the true origin of their obstinacy was the fear of having to admit both divine Revelation and supernatural miracles. In fact, the Pentateuch contains predictions that were fulfilled, for example the dispersion of the Hebrews upon all the face of the earth (Deut. 28:64), an event without parallel, and which at the time of Moses could not have been humanly predictable. Thus the miracles become undeniable, if they were written by a contemporary historian, and under the eyes of the very people who it is said to have been witness to it.—On the other hand, it is by sheer mistake (inevitable in the works of such a vast periphery) that in the *Dizionario enciclopedico delle scienze, lettere, ed arti*, by the great Scholar Antonio Bazzarini (Tome IV, p. 1028), Maimonides is counted among those (Spinoza, Hobbes, Voltaire, etc.) who deny Moses as the author of the Pentateuch. Maimonides put as one of the fundamental articles of the Hebrew faith that of believing the entire book of the Law to have been written by Moses at the dictation of God. He regards Moses as God's copyist, and in this sense it can be said that he did not see him as the author of the Pentateuch, holding God alone as the true author: but is this opinion confusable with that of Spinoza and Voltaire?—This false accusation against Maimonides is found repeated in *Parnaso straniero* which is currently printed in Venice (Vol. I, p. 1321),[18] and gets extended to Ibn Ezra as well. The latter was certainly the first Critic who imagined some small amount of words to have been introduced into the Pentateuch by the Writers subsequent to Moses (a judgment refuted by me in

---

[15] Probably *Biblia Hebraica, ad optimas editiones inprimis Everardi van der Hooght ex recensione Aug Hahnii expressa. Praefatus est Ern. Fr. Car. Rosenmüller* (Leipzig, 1834).

[16] Robert Lowth, *De sacra poesi Hebraeorum* (Göttingen, 1758).

[17] It is unclear which Arduino SDL is referring to.

[18] *Parnaso straniero* was a series. The first volume, now extremely rare, was entitled *Poesie scritturale* (Venice, 1834).

Bikkurei ha-Ittim 5588 [= 1827–88], pp. 155–161);[19] but he did not leave in his numerous writings any sign that he was of the opinion that Moses was not the author of the Pentateuch.

LXXI.

Whether the sacred Text was less or more read and known by the population, is not of consequence, as would be thought by some. The Priests and the Levites, who did not have their own land, turned to the tribes in order to seek the subsidies for which only the Mosaic law gave them right; they, out of institution, interest, and necessity, would teach and inculcate that Law, which alone ensured their means of subsistence. In every era, they kept alive the law of Moses and his language. In times of greater disorder and anarchy, the Levites did not cease to be regarded as the most suitable for the religious ministry. The same Micah who had established in his own house a superstitious oracle, called himself blessed when he was able to find a Levite that he employed to be a priest for him (Judg. 17:14 [17:13]).

LXXII.

The popular language could vary somewhat in the various times and in the various provinces of the Israelite Republic; but that which was used by the Writers and Poets was always the language of Moses, the language of the Priests and of the Prophets; roughly comparable to the illustrious vernacular [*volgare illustre*] of Italy,[20] which is used in writing, in public speaking, and with every distinguished person, without it being precisely the municipal dialect of any city (1). However, I say roughly [*a un di presso*], since there is no evidence that Hebrew was ever divided into dialects so diverse from one another as are the dialects of Italy.

(1) See Dante, De Vulgari Eloquentia, Book I, Ch. 16, 17.

---

[19] On the journal *Bikkurei ha-Ittim*, see § 41, end.

[20] SDL's use of the word *illustre* 'illustrious, prestigious', is borrowed directly from the eloquent passages in Dante to which he refers. Dante explains his choice of the word in his ch. 17.

LXXIII.

Largely then, the language of Moses must have been preserved universally among the Israelites, at least on the level of an illustrious [prestige] language, after the time of David, when the Jews had a common center in Jerusalem, civil as well as religious, to which all the people rushed every year.

LXXIV.

And even though the popular dialects could differ somewhat in the different provinces, the illustrious language always remained universally understood. The Allocutions of the Prophets, proffered before the people for universal instruction, are proof of this. Nothing is more arbitrary and baseless than claiming, as someone did (1), that the Prophets used to interpret for the people and vulgarize their own speech.

(1) Encylopédie, art. Hebraïque (Langue) III.[21]

LXXV.

In the period in which the Judean kingdom had to submit in the face of Babylonian power, the Hebrew language itself must also have yielded to the Chaldean idiom; and this happened in two ways.

a) It declined in use among the population, which forgot it little by little, as the people became accustomed to the language of their masters.

b) The Scholars themselves, who continued to use it, more or less mixed with it Barbarisms, that is to say, Aramean and Persian forms, and Aramaizing locutions which were contrary to the rules of pure Hebrew. These can be called Aramaisms or Chaldaisms of later times. Many of these are met in the books written after the exile, namely, Ezra, Nehemiah, etc.

Examples of Aramaic words are the names of the months אֲדָר, נִיסָן etc., as well as the nouns אִגֶּרֶת, גִּזְבָּר, גִּיל (כְּגִילְכֶם Dan. 1:10), גְּנָזִים (גִּנְזֵי Esther 3:9), כְּנָת (כְּנָוָתוֹ Ezra 4:7), תַּכְרִיךְ, פִּתְגָּם, צֹרֶךְ, רִשְׁיוֹן, שַׁרְבִיט; the

---

[21] *Encyclopédie, ou, Dictionnaire raisonné des sciences, des arts, et des métiers*, ed. D. Diderot and J. Alembert (17 vols; Paris, 1751–72), s.v. "Hébraique (Langue)," section III.

verbs אָחַז in the sense of *close* (Nehemiah 7:3), גָּזַר in the sense of *decree* (Esther 2:1), תִּרְגֵּם ,חִיֵּב. Examples of Aramaizing locutions are וּשְׁנֵיהֶם הַמְּלָכִים (Dan. 11:27) with redundant Suffix; בְּיוֹמָם *by day* (Neh. 9:19), from בִּימָמָא, whereas in Hebrew the final Mem changes the noun יוֹם into an adverb [יוֹמָם], as happens in חִנָּם, רֵיקָם, in which manner it is not possible to say בְּיוֹמָם, just as one does not say בְּחִנָּם, בְּרֵיקָם; פָּקַד עַל in the sense of *command* (Ezra 1:2, 2 Chron. 36:23), a locution which in pure Hebrew means *to call for inspection, to take account of others' actions, to punish*; צִוָּה עַל in the sense of *command* (Esther 4:8, a translation of the Chaldean פְּקַד עַל), a locution which in older Hebrew means *to prohibit* (see Ibn Ezra, Genesis 2:16).

LXXVI.

It is not true, however, that as soon as the Jews returned to the ancient homeland under Cyrus, they lost knowledge of their own language; and even less [true] that they had forgotten it already some centuries earlier, as someone has asserted (1). Nehemiah (13:24) says only that the children of Hebrew fathers and non-Hebrew mothers did not know how to speak Hebrew well, but half of them spoke the language of their mothers. This does not mean that these people did not understand Hebrew, and even less that the better part of the nation had lost the ancient language; and so much the less, since these foreign women were repudiated by the same Nehemiah. The Prophets Haggai, Zechariah, and Malachi continued to speak to the people in Hebrew, and in the time of Nehemiah a long oration was recited before the people (Neh. 9:5–37), meant to encourage the people to undertake an oath of loyalty to the Law of God; it is not said that it was interpreted and expounded otherwise, since it was generally understood. The sacred Text of the Law was not translated for the people by the Levites, but rather commented on and illustrated (2).

(1)   Encyclopédie, ubi supra [§ 74, note 1].

(2)   The Levites are here called מְבִינִים אֶת־הָעָם (Nehemiah 8:7, 9) *causing the people to understand*, never מְלִיצִים or מְתַרְגְּמִים *translators*. The form מְפֹרָשׁ from Nehemiah (8:8) does not mean *interpreted, translated*, as is believed by many, after the Talmud (Megillah fol. 3, Nedarim fol. 37), nor *faithfully, verbatim*, as Gesenius wants (Geschichte [der hebräische Sprache und Schrift], p. 45 and Lexicon manuale [hebraicum et chaldaicum], p. 843); but rather it means (and

likewise the corresponding מְפָרַשׁ of Ezra 4:18) *clear, distinct*, that is, *clearly, distinctly*, like the כְּתָב מְפָרַשׁ of Onkelos (Exodus 28:11), which signifies *clear and distinct writing.*

LXXVII.

However, the Hebrews who did not return with Ezra to Palestine (who were the greater number), remaining in Babylon, became accustomed little by little to the language of the country, losing the use of Hebrew. These, later on, being transported in droves to settle in the Holy Land, contributed more and more to the expansion of the use of Aramaic there, at the expense of the Hebrew Language. To this was added at the outset the dependence of the Hebrew population on the Persian king, in whose court (according to what appears in the books of Daniel and Ezra) the Aramaic language was in use; and after some centuries, the matters of war with and dependence on the king of Syria, a country whose language was pure Aramaic.

LXXVIII.

Nevertheless, the Hebrew language could not be called entirely dead, as long as the Second Temple lasted. Losing its universality century by century, it was preserved alive until after the fall of Jerusalem, among a large part of the nation, more or less. R. Meir, living in the second century of the vulgar era, comforted with the promise of the rewards of the next life all those who maintained stable residence in Palestine, and who spoke the Holy Language (Jerus. Talmud, Shabbat, ch. 1 [fol. 3]); this proves that the Hebrew Language at that time was becoming less common every day, but that it had not yet lost all use among the people. Nothing more can be deduced with certainty from the passages of Josephus Flavius and from the books of the New Testament, cited by R. Azariah [dei Rossi] and by [Giovanni] De Rossi (1), except that the Hebrew Language was at the time of Titus less common in Palestine than was the Chaldean language.

(1)   Me'or Enayim, chaps. 9 and 57—From Christ's own language.[22]

---

[22] Azariah dei Rossi cites the Aramaic expressions used by Jesus (e.g., *talitha kumi*, Mark 5:41) as evidence for the common language of the time.

LXXIX.

The Hebrew of the Second Temple abounded in non-Biblical forms, of which, however, a great many are not barbaric or exotic words, but are Hebrew words, albeit not met in the books of the sacred Scripture. This happened in three ways:

a) vocabulary belonging to the language of Moses and the Prophets, which they did not have occasion to make use of, and which were preserved traditionally among the people: such is, for example, the word זֶרֶת *little finger* (from זְעֵרֶת *small*), not used in the Scripture except in the sense of *span*, certainly a secondary meaning, derived because the span is the length of the open hand from the end of the thumb to the tip of the little finger; and such is the substantive חָלָל *void, empty space*, a non-Biblical noun, from which, however, have been derived חַלּוֹן *window*, חָלִיל *drum* [more often: *flute, pipe*], מְחִלָּה *cavern*, and חָלָל *pierced, run through*:

b) vocabulary belonging not to the illustrious vernacular of the Prophets, but to the popular dialect, no less ancient than the illustrious language:

c) vocabulary adopted by the Hebrew people after Biblical times (§ 84).

LXXX.

This Hebrew is quite Aramaized, containing:

a) Aramaic terms, for example, אֲבָר *lead*, in place of Hebrew עֹפֶרֶת; אִילָן *tree*, in place of עֵץ; אַרְכּוּבָה *knee*, for בֶּרֶךְ; גֵּף *to embrace*, for חִבֵּק; חִגֵּר *lame*, for פִּסֵּחַ; טַס *slab, sheet*, for פַּח or לוּחַ; כְּרַךְ *walled city*, for קִרְיָה; סוֹמֵא *no*, for לֹא; לָקָה *to be struck*, for הֻכָּה; הִלְקָה *to strike*, for הִכָּה; סוֹמֵא *blind*, for עִוֵּר; סַיִף *sword*, for חֶרֶב; סְפָר *boundary*, for גְּבוּל; סַפָּר *barber*, for גַּלָּב; סָתַר *demolish*, for הָרַס or נָתַץ; נִתְקַל, תָּקַל *to stumble*, for כָּשַׁל:

b) Aramaic mannerisms, for example, the union of the Participle and the personal pronoun, as מֵפְרָשׁ אֲנִי for אֲנִי מֵפָרֵשׁ; so מוּפְרָשְׁנִי, גָּזַר אֲנִי for גּוֹזַרְנִי; מֶרְחֲצָאוֹת is similar, with added Alef, or rather, with the addition of the קמץ which in Aramaic is characteristic of the feminine plural:

c) new forms, combinations of Hebrew and Aramaic; for example הֲרֵי *here is*, from הִנֵּה and אֲרֵי; כְּמוֹת *like*, from כְּמוֹ and כְּוָת; שֶׁמָּא *so that not*, probably שְׁמָא, for שֶׁלָמָה (§ 67), from דִּילְמָא.

It contains, in addition, many Greek and Latin words (1).

(1) See the work *Thesauri linguae hebraicae e Mischna augendi* (Rostock 1825, 1826) by Anton Theodor Hartmann, which in several folios contains a Grammar and a Vocabulary of the Mishnaic language. The author counts in the Mishnah 760 terms from Biblical roots, but with different form or meaning than they have in the sacred Scripture; 273 Greek or Latin words; and 1720 non-Biblical words, not exotic, but proper to the language of the Mishnah. What a pity that this work is so unsatisfactory in terms of accuracy!—However, the Dictionary of the Mishnaic language could be enriched by examination of the Tosefta and other writings containing statements of the ancient Scholars (§ 81). Another collection of Mishnaic terms was already mentioned in § 42.

LXXXI.

Such a later Hebrew Language—that is to say, of later times—is that in which the Mishnah, Baraitot (scattered within the two Talmuds), the Tosefta (printed in the Talmudic Compendium by [Isaac ben Jacob] Alfasi),[23] and the so-called קְטַנּוֹת הֲלָכוֹת were written down; as well as a great number of statements and narratives of the Talmudic Scholars (אמוראים) of Palestine, scattered in the two Talmuds, and in the Midrashim. These voluminous Texts would provide an abundant crop for a Dictionary of later Hebrew, in which, in addition to the many non-Biblical roots, the Biblical roots would be enriched by the many fine and beautiful forms, mannerisms, and locutions of every sort.

LXXXII.

R. Joḥanan, living in the third century of the vulgar era, speaking about the slight differences that in an identical word are met now and then in the use of this later Hebrew as compared with the Biblical (e.g., מָזַג to *temper the wine*, which in the Scripture is expressed by מָסַךְ, and רְחֵלוֹת *sheep*, which in the Bible is רְחֵלִים), gives later Hebrew the name חֲכָמִים לְשׁוֹן *Rabbinic Language*, distinguishing the Biblical by the name תּוֹרָה לְשׁוֹן (Avodah Zarah fol. 58, Ḥullin fol. 137). This denomination may certainly make one think that in those times the use of the Hebrew Language was mainly restricted to the Rabbis, but never that Rabbinic Hebrew was instituted by

---

[23] The Tosefta was first printed in an edition of Alfasi's *Sefer ha-Halachot* (Venice, 1521).

the Rabbis themselves, without ever having been popular in Judea (1). It bore all the characteristics of a living language spoken by an agricultural people, practicing all the mechanical arts, who were the Hebrew nation. The Mishnah treats in detail all rural matters, all the instruments of the arts and trade, and all that which concerns contracts, lawsuits and Courts, without ever making use of those circumlocutions, to which Scholars who want to write a dead language are often forced to resort.

(1) As [Solomon] Löwisohn held in a Dissertation on the Rabbinic language, inserted in his בֵּית הָאֹסֶף, and reprinted in the text of the Mishnah (Vienna, 1815), against Maimonides, for whom see his Commentary on the Mishnah, Terumot ch. I § 1 and Kilaim ch. II § 3.

LXXXIII.

If the Rabbinic language had not been spoken, but was all the doing of the Rabbis, and it was desired to revive the Hebrew language in their academies, they would not have had in their instituting it a model other than the sacred Scripture. They certainly would have been able, and would have had to, compensate for its scarcity, adopting exotic terms; but their zeal (be it religious, political, or literary) would have impeded them from altering the purity of the ancient Hebrew by introducing into it, without any necessity, foreign or new terms (§ 80), where the scriptural language afforded the equivalent. In addition to this, they would not have used so many Biblical terms with meanings different from what they have in the Scripture; nor would they have excluded from their language so much vocabulary of such very frequent use in the holy books, for example הִנֵּה, הֲלֹא, אֲשֶׁר, אֲנַחְנוּ, מַדּוּעַ, לְמַעַן, כִּי, יַעַן.

LXXXIV.

Much less understandable would be the origin of the numerous non-Biblical, non-exotic words that are proper to the Rabbinic language; that is to say, drawn from Hebrew roots with a freedom that is natural for a people speaking a language, and is inconceivable for Scholars who want to speak a dead language. Such are the words בִּשְׁבִיל *on account of* (properly *by way of*, as in German *wegen*, from *Weg*), כְּלַפֵּי *near* (from לְאַפֵּי), כֵּיצַד *in what way?* (from כְּאֵי צַד), אֲפִילוּ *even if* (from אַף אִלּוּ), אַחֲרַאי *guarantor* (from אַחַר *after*, i.e., the one who replaces another in an obligation), אָמַד *to estimate, calculate approximately* (from מָדַד), תָּפַח *to swell* (from נָפַח), עִמֵּץ *to close* (from עָצַם), הִתְעַכֵּל *to be consumed* (from אָכַל), הִתְחִיל *to begin* (from תְּחִלָּה), תָּרַם *to separate the sacerdotal rights from the provisions* (from תְּרוּמָה), מָסַק *to harvest olives* (from שָׂק, properly *to bag*).

LXXXV.

In addition to this living language in vulgar use, the Scholars of the Mishnah knew how to use a more pure language, not living, but imitated, not of the people, but of the Scholars; and it is in this language that the Compilation of the Prayers is written down. This language, quite different from the preceding, generally imitates the Biblical Hebrew, except for a very small number of terms which it retains from the later Hebrew. This could only be called Rabbinic Language, since it was never of the people, but belonged exclusively to the Rabbis and Scholars. This did not admit, except exceedingly sparingly, barbarous forms and foreign terms, nor Biblical terms with meanings different from the scriptural ones; it uses frequently all those Biblical words which were unknown to later Hebrew (§ 83); and it sometimes successfully imitates the poetic style of the Holy Books.

(1)   In 1821 there came out in Vienna the first volume of the Prayers [*Orazione*] of the German Israelites, with my Italian translation; in 1829 the second volume came out, of which, however, the final pages (124–165) are not mine. In the same year 1829, the Prayers of the Italian Israelites were published in Vienna, with only my translation.[24]

LXXXVI.

Since, however, this [Hebrew of the Prayers] is not without neologisms proper to later Hebrew, which quite naturally must have been introduced into it: thus, as [Ḥayyim ben Naphtali] Köslin already observed in his בְּאֵר רְחֹבוֹת (1), the advice of some modern German Israelite Grammarians (2) was not sound, that they undertook to amend, according

---

[24] *Seder Tefillah ke-fi Minhag ha-Ashkenazim, Formulario delle orazioni degl'Israeliti* (Vienna, 1821–29); *Formulario delle orazioni degl'Israeliti secondo il rito italiano* (Vienna, 1829).

to the rules of Biblical Hebrew, what they met in the Compilation of the Prayers, which more or less moved away from these rules; however, they should be commended for the correction of many errors independent of these neologisms, and attributable only to the carelessness and ignorance of the copyists.

(1) Booklet inserted into the Hebrew Journal מאסף year 546 [1785], month Tevet [December], and reproduced in בִּכּוּרֵי הָעִתִּים year 585 [1824–25], pp. 116–124.

(2) [Solomon ben Judah] Hanau (שערי תפלה), [Isaac ha-Levi] Satanow (וַיֶּעְתַּר יִצְחָק), and [Judah Löwe] Ben-Zeev (תְּפִלָּה זַכָּה).

LXXXVII.

Such Rabbinic language, which, besides the Compilation of the Prayers, includes several passages met in the Talmud, was successfully used until the sixth century of the vulgar Era, the age of the last Talmudists (1). There also exists an elegant Hymn which is believed to postdate the Talmudists by several centuries (2).

(1) See Berachot 16, 17, Moed Katan 25, Avodah Zarah 24, and Jerus. Talmud Moed Katan Ch. 3.

(2) אֲשֶׁר הֵנִיא עֲצַת גּוֹיִם which is believed to have been composed at the time of the Geonim [ca. 589–1038].[25]

LXXXVIII.

Up to this point, the Hebrew Language was a living language, that is to say, spoken more or less universally by the Hebrew nation. Biblical Hebrew was alive and popular, at least in the capacity as an illustrious vernacular [see § 72]; the later Hebrew of the Mishnah was also living, at least in the first three centuries of the vulgar Era, i.e., until the time of Rabbi Joḥanan and his disciples, whose great many sayings are Hebrew.

---

[25] Morais notes, "A poem in alphabetical order, each sentence of which begins with a letter of the twenty-two letters of the Hebrew alphabet. It is inserted into the Ashkenazic ritual for the eve of Purim."

LXXXIX.

We can therefore distinguish three periods of the Hebrew language:

a) the golden age which embraces all the sacred books before the Babylonian emigration, in other words, the age of pure Biblical Hebrew;

b) the silver age, which contains the scriptural books subsequent to the emigration, in other words, the age of later Biblical hebrew;

c) the copper age, namely, that of non-Biblical later Hebrew, commonly called the Rabbinic Language.

XC.

These various types of Hebrew all belong to the science of the Hebrew language; that is, all should be contemplated in the Grammars and Lexicons of the Hebrew Language; if it is true that a Language does not lose its name due to the adoption of new terms, and due to small and minor alterations which, with the passing of the centuries, it receives in its inflections, as long as such new inflections and new terms are ratified by the use of the same people (1).

(1) One of my annotated Lexical Specimens of Mishnaic Hebrew can be seen in [the journal] *Bikkurei ha-Ittim*, 589 [1828–29], pp. 123–32.

XCI.

In later times (from 1000 of the vulgar Era on), with the number of Hebrew writers multiplying, almost as many types of Hebrew were created as there were authors. Such varieties of Hebrew [*Ebraismi*], because they were never in vulgar use, but were the exclusive propriety of the Scholars, do not belong to the science of the Hebrew Language, but to the critical study of the Rabbinic writings.

XCII.

These Hebrew types, which we will call *recenziori*, that is, more recent, can be arranged into six classes:

A) Rabbinic *recenziore* Hebrew, used by the Rabbis and all of the writers of Talmudic material, Rashi, the authors of the Tosafot, and generally the

Ritualists (פִּסְקִים). The basis of this language is Mishnaic Hebrew, peppered, however, with Talmudic Aramaic expressions. It makes almost no use of terms or phrases found in the Bible that are not in the Mishnah.

B) Philological *recenziore* Hebrew, used by the Philologists, Ibn Ezra, Kimḥi, Abravanel, and the other Writers of varied erudition. This, in contrary to the preceding, is amicable to Biblical expressions and phrases, and makes very scarce use of Chaldean locutions from the Talmud.

C) Philosophical *recenziore* Hebrew, introduced by those who translated philosophical works from Arabic, namely, the Tibbonides (Judah, Samuel, and Moses), translators of the אֱמוּנוֹת of Saadiah, the חוֹבַת הַלְּבָבוֹת of Bahya [ben Joseph], the כּוּזָרִי of Judah ha-Levi, the מוֹרֶה נְבֻכִים of Maimonides, etc., and imitated poetry of some philosophers who wrote in Hebrew, for example Gersonides (רלב"ג). This language is distinguished by its usages taken not from Hebrew or Aramaic, but rather from Arabic.

D) Oratory *recenziore* Hebrew, in which is written prose of an elevated and elegant style; these are divided into 1) non-rhymed, 2) fixed to rhyme, 3) with rhyme thrown in at will. This language likes classical phrases, paronomasia, and plays on words; things which it does not refuse, even if they consist of non-Biblical, or even non-Hebrew vocabulary. In the most recent times, some Germans have used an elevated prose without rhyme, without paronomasia, and without barbarisms.

E) Poetic *recenziore* Hebrew, in which are written compositions in verse, which are divided into rhymed and blank verse, and into measured and non-measured; these last are subdivided into:

a) following the rules of meter (מִשְׁקָל), that is, with the vowels and semi-vowels (תְּנוּעָה and יָתֵד) in fixed positions:

b) with the semi-vowels regarded as if they were not there (*Philoxenus*, pp. 92–94):

c) with the semi-vowels counted as vowels, and used promiscuously:[26]

This [style], among the most ancient Italian and German Poets, loved rare and anomalous words; among the Spaniards and Africans it is more regular and pure. In the seventeenth century it became excessively amicable to plays on words and amphibologia, which rendered it obscure: it was brought back to life by the famous Paduan, Moses Ḥayyim Luzzatto.

---

[26] Morais notes: "In his *Oheb Ger* [*Philoxenus*], Luzzatto illustrates these different styles minutely."

F) Imitative *recenziore* Hebrew, which embraces the following three types:

a) Recenziore Hebrew imitating the language of Biblical prose. Example of this are the סֵפֶר הַיָּשָׁר,[27] the בֶּן־גּוּרְיוֹן,[28] and the French and Ottoman History of Joseph [ha-]Cohen:[29]

b) Recenziore Hebrew imitating the language of Biblical poetry, examples of which are the Psalms of modern authors, and [Isaac] Satanow's מִשְׁלֵי אָסָף.

c) Recenziore Hebrew imitating Mishnaic language. Maimonides makes use of this in his grand ritual work, entitled מִשְׁנֶה תּוֹרָה.

---

[27] This is a medieval work which some claimed was the book of the same name mentioned in the Bible (cf. Joshua 10:13, 2 Sam. 1:18). It was first published in Naples (1552).

[28] Morais notes: "A spurious translation of Josephus' works." This is the *Sefer Yosippon*, thought throughout the middle ages to be a Hebrew version of Josephus, and valued as an important historical source. Its many printed editions, and its early translation into so many languages—including Arabic, Latin, Yiddish, Ladino, Ge'ez, Russian, and Czech—testify to its importance. It is now known to have been written in southern Italy in the mid-tenth century. Printed editions referred to the author as Joseph ben Gurion, but this attribution was a creation of later editors. Joseph ben Gurion is just the Hebrew name that the author gives to the historical Josephus; its true author is unknown. A critical edition of the work was published by David Flusser (Jerusalem, 1978).

[29] *Divrei ha-Yamim le-Malchei Tsarfat ve-Malchei Beit Otoman ha-Togar*, by Joseph ben Joshua ben Meir ha-Cohen, first published in Venice (1534).

FUNDAMENTAL LAWS OF THE GRAMMATICAL FORMATION OF WORDS.

XCIII.

Concerning the following fundamental laws it is fitting to note that these are not to be regarded as if physical or mathematical laws, the effects of which are necessary and inevitable; but rather they are moral laws: that is to say, that they express the tendencies and, as it were, the inclinations, or the preferences, of languages in general, or of a given language in particular. Every language is the sum of the customs of a people as to the means of expressing their own ideas; every language is therefore a system of voluntary acts, not of one man, but of a great many people. Every voluntary act has its own motive, which, however, can be slight and imperceptible, and the imperceptibility of the motives often makes human volition appear capricious and inconsistent. The voluntary acts related to the formation of languages have, like all the others, their own slight and imperceptible motives. And in the same way that man has various tendencies and natural inclinations, and from their continuous conflict it happens, according to the most minute circumstances and internal and external conditions, that sometimes one wins out, sometimes another; so equally every language has various laws, or let us say tendencies, which produce an infinite variety of phenomena, and an inconstancy that may seem arbitrary and unbound from any law. However, the laws or the tendencies do not cease to exist; though the discovery of these, and the exact determination of their number, proves exceedingly difficult. This I wanted to attempt; and my attempts will be successful, if they will be carried through to final perfection by others.

XCIV.

And owing it to the fundamental laws particular to the Hebrew Language to state first those that are proper to the Aramaic, I should mention here that under the name of the Aramaic language, I mean the most ancient and pure Aramaic. Such is not the Biblical Chaldean of Daniel and Ezra, which, as was already observed by Ludwig de Dieu (in his comparative grammar),[1] is not without a mixture of Hebraisms. Such is also not the language of the Targums, nor the Syriac language; since these belong to a later time (being posterior to the vulgar Era), and they abound in Hebraisms, Grecisms, Latinisms, and Neologisms. The ancient and pure Aramaic is a language already lost: the source of all Aramaic dialects, it can only be reassembled through the accurate collation of all these dialects. The Biblical Chaldean, as the most ancient, gives evidence to the antiquity and purity of that which is met in the less ancient Chaldaic and Syriac writings; and conversely, the purity of that which is found in Daniel and Ezra is confirmed by the agreement with the books of the Syrians. The things then which are particular to the Biblical Chaldean, or to Syriac, must be judged of suspect and uncertain antiquity and purity.

XCV.

It should also be recognized that that Biblical-Chaldaic pointing is by no means fixed and uniform, for example, the verbs הֲוָת, מְטָת, are read sometimes with קָמֵץ, sometimes with פַּתַח (see also § 137); a fact which must undoubtedly be attributed to the copyists, ignorant of Chaldaic Grammar, who easily confused the vowels קמץ and פתח which to them both sounded like *A*. Highly reliable regarding such things are the Syrians, who have cultivated the Grammar of their language from the time in which it was their vernacular (1), and who (the Westerns at least) give to the pronunciation of קמץ (Zekofo) and פתח (Pethoho) two completely different and unconfusable sounds.—The pointing of the Targumic Chaldaic is generally rather incorrect and variable.

(1) See Hoffmann, Gram. syr., p. 27.

---

[1] *Grammatica linguarum Orientalium Hebraeorum, Chaldaeorum et Syrorum inter se collatarum* (Leiden, 1628; Frankfurt am Main, 1688).

XCVI.

Also the orthography of the Biblical Chaldaic is by no means fixed, as can be seen in the verbal form אֶתְפְּעֵל, which is met sometimes with א, sometimes with ה; in the feminine nouns, which terminate either in ה or in א; in the letters Vav and Yod, which in the same word are found written or omitted (see, e.g., § 128). These should be attributed in part to the copyists, and in part to the writers themselves.

ARTICLE I.

Fundamental Laws Common to All Languages.

XCVII.

The goal of all speech being that of making known the thoughts or sentiments of our minds, it is evident that the primary law of every language must be that of Perspicuity. That is to say, every people in forming its own language principally tends to see to it that each of its ideas have a particular sign or expression; in such a way that it might be distinguished from any other idea.

XCVIII.

It is the law, or rather the need, of Perspicuity, that in all languages has prompted the manifold inflections of verbs, intended to distinguish one tense from another, one mood from another, one person from another, and so on; and to distinguish number and gender among the nouns. Such inflections, very few in the beginnings of languages, are multiplied as the need for them is felt, and then the seal is placed on their development only when the speech is almost inalterably fixed, becoming a written language, and used in writings of some celebrity.

XCIX.

In addition, every language tends toward brevity, and this tendency gives rise to a second law of every language, to the law of Brevity, which, contrary to that of Perspicuity, tempers and moderates the latter's impulses, which, in the interest of greater clarity would render words and sentences overwhelmingly long.

C.

The Law of Brevity acts:

a) in the primitive formation of words (1), not allowing the law of Perspicuity to express with more syllables what can be expressed with only one, nor with two vocables what just one would sufficiently express.

b) after the primitive formation of words, shortening them in various ways. Such shortenings are sometimes adopted as law, as in Latin *movi*, *motum*, instead of *movui*, *movitum*; and sometimes they are left to the arbitrary decision of the speaker or writer, as in [Latin] *audii*, *amasti*, in place of *audivi*, *amavisti*.

However, the tendency for brevity acts on single words according to the frequency of their use in daily speech; for this reason, it happens that the words in most frequent use are in all languages usually the shortest and most anomalous.

(1) It should be noted that these fundamental laws deal with everything concerning the *grammatical* formation of words, and not their *lexical* formation. *Amavisti*, for example, is certainly a not primitive lexeme [*parola*], as it has only the syllable AM for its root; but *amavisti* can be a primitive word [*voce*], relative to its grammatical formation, or let us say inflection; on the other hand, *amasti*, which is a shortening of it, is of a secondary and derived formation and inflection.

CI.

A third law is that of Facility of pronunciation, or Euphony, by which every language tends to avoid sounds that are harsh and difficult to pronounce, as well as sounds grating to the ear of the listener. Regarding this statement, languages differ widely from each other, according to the varied climates and different characters of the nations (1).

Someone could deem that this law should be divided into two, to distinguish the law of facility of pronunciation, intended for the comfort of the speaker, from that of Euphony, intended for the pleasure of the listener. It seems to me, however, that the sounds that grate upon the ear of the listener are at the same time the most harsh and difficult to pronounce, and vice-versa. This will not be denied when one understands that the harshness of sounds does not lie only in the piling up of consonants, but in all those things that somewhat impede or retard pronunciation. Now hiatuses, and the concurrence of identical or similar syllables, retard the speaker, to the extent that if he does not pay attention to them, it will happen that he leaves out one or the other of those vowels or syllables, or even pronounces them confusedly and out of order. The heaping up of monosyllables also retards pronunciation, multiplying the intervals necessary between words. The verse:

Nè si fa ben per uom quel che il Ciel nega

could, without retarding the pronunciation, be uttered:

Nessì fabèn peruòm quelchèl cielnega;

but then who would understand it? The reader is almost forced to put in various pauses that render the sounds of it slow and hard. Now, a retarded and forced pronunciation naturally proves hard and disagreeable to the listener.—The following verse from the Dittamondo:[2]

Fa quel che déi, e poi ciò che vuol sia,

does not prove equally cacophonous, because it can be read, without such pauses, as:

Fa quelchedèi epòi ciocchevuòl sia,

and still be intelligible and gentle to the listeners.

(1) Nulla enim est lingua, says [Francis] Bacon of Verulam, quin vocalium concurrentium hiatus, aut consonantium concurrentium asperitates aliquatenus refugiat. Sunt et aliae respectivae, quae scilicet diversorum populorum auribus gratae aut ingratae accedunt. Graeca lingua diphthongis scatet: latina longe parcius. Lingua hispanica literas tenues odit, easque statim vertit in medias. Linguae quae ex Gothis fluxere aspiratis gaudent. *De dignitate et augmentis scientiarum.* Book VI, Chap. I.[3]

CII.

This law of the facility of pronunciation is usually the cause of various changes in words. It is through this that the ancient name *Clothowechus* was transformed first into *Chlodevicus* and *Clovis*, then into *Ludovicus* and *Lovis*, and finally into *Luis, Luigi, Luì (Louis)*. Similarly the Portuguese gave to the Greek aspirate letter X, and the French to the Latin aspirate CH, the softer

---

[2] An allegorical poem by Fazio degli Uberti, written circa 1346–67, and first printed in 1447.

[3] "For there is no language that does not to some extent avoid the hiatus of concurring vowels or the roughness of concurring consonants. There are respective others which are pleasing or displeasing to the ears of different peoples. The Greek language abounds in diphthongs; Latin uses them more sparingly. The Spanish language dislikes *tenues* letters [voiceless stops], and changes them into *mediae* [voiced stops]. The Germanic languages delight in aspirates."

sound SH, a pronunciation that the Germans gave to SCH, altering its primitive value, which was certainly a compound sound, as seen in the words *schreiben* and *Schule*, derived from [Latin] *scribere* and *schola*.

Likewise in Hebrew, the ה, originally always aspirate, almost always lost its sound at the end of a word, and remained as a quiescent letter; and the ש, primitively always *Shin*, was in many roots pronounced simply *Sin*, on account of the difficulty that many among the Hebrews found with it (see Judges 12:6).

Hence it happens sometimes that a word with *Shin* derives from another with *Sin*, or with ס, and vice versa. Thus מִשְׁאֶרֶת *kneading trough*, derives, as observed already by [Isaac] Abravanel, from שְׂאֹר *leaven*. Thus שַׂעֲרוּרִיָה *a horrible thing*, is from שָׂעַר *to horrify*, originally from שֵׂעָר *hair*, so properly *to make hair stand on end*. Thus מִשְׁפָּחָה *family*, and שִׁפְחָה *servant-girl*, derived from סָפַח *to join* (1).

(1) [Giambattista] Vico has observed in *Scienza nuova* (Book I [Section II], Axiom 78) the affinity of the Latin words *familia* ['family'] and *famulus* ['servant'], but the Latin language could not, nor could the Greek, supply a root that would offer a plausible derivation of these two nouns; so he was forced to imagine (Book II [Section IV], Chap. [II] on the families of servants) that since the ancient Heroes were men of fame [Latin *fama*] (Gen. 6:4), those unfortunate ones who sought their protection were called *famuli*. How likely this etymology is, everyone will see for themselves.

In Hebrew, מִשְׁפָּחָה *family* means properly an *aggregation* of people, and שִׁפְחָה *servant-girl* means an *aggregated* person, received into the fold of the family. We observe that this latter noun is not used in the masculine gender, the full reason for which is given by the customs of the ancient Orientals. One was able to aggregate into the family the servant-girl, who not unusually was taken with the agreement of the lady of the house in order to make children for the man; but this could not be said of the servant-boy, whose master was too jealous to create a potential rival.

CIII.

A fourth law common to all languages can be called Inconstancy. Since languages depend on the use of people, even the commoners, use is:

Arbiter, judge, and standard of speech (1).

Now in the use [of language] by people scattered in various provinces, it is impossible that any rule be constantly followed, even more so over the course of a long time. Hence arise the exceptions to which the grammatical laws of all languages are subjected.

All grammatical phenomena, as many as there are, are born from the conflict of the three laws, of Perspicuity, of Brevity, and of Euphony. Sometimes one, sometimes another prevails, certainly not without cause, but through slight and imperceptible circumstances, the effects of which, constituting the inconstancy of languages, are usually attributed to popular whim (see § 93).

(1)   ... usus quem penes arbitrium est, et jus et norma loquendi.[4] Horace, *in arte poet.* [72].

---

[4] More literally: "Usage, in whose power is judgement, and right, and the standard of speech."

ARTICLE II.

*Fundamental Laws Particular to the Aramaic Language
and Primitively Common Also to Hebrew.*

CIV.

A fundamental law in Aramaic Grammar is the conservation of the nature of some syllables, so that long, mixed, and strong syllables, as far as is possible, must remain such.

CV.

I call:

a) long [*lunghe*] syllables those that have quiescent letters, be they simple or mixed [i.e., open or closed]; for example בִּי, בּוּ, בִּין, בּוּן; as well as those that have קָמֶץ, for example בָּ, בָּל (see §§ 158, 159);

b) short [*brevi*] syllables those, simple or mixed, that have neither a quiescent letter, nor קָמֶץ; for example בַ, בְ, בַּר, בֶּר;

c) tenuous [*tenui*] syllables those that are both short and simple, for example בַ, בְ;

d) strong [*forti*] syllables those that consist of three consonants, with a vowel on the middle letter, for example גְּבַר;

e) hard [*dure*] syllables those that consist of three consonants, with the vowel on the first, for example קִשְׁט.

This is in addition to the usual denomination of simple [*semplici*] syllables given to those that end in a vowel, for example, *ba, be, sta, sto*; and of mixed [*miste*] syllables to those that terminate in consonants, for example, *er, per, sper.*

CVI.

From the law of conservation of long, mixed, and strong syllables, proceed the following phenomena:

a) the immutability of long syllables, for example פְּתְגָם, יְקוּם ;יְקוּמוּן פִּתְגָמַיָּא;

b) the דגש, or the epenthetic Nun, which is added after the Preformative to verbs deficient in the second radical, for example in Syriac נֶבּוּז, for נְבְזּוּז, and in Hebrew יִתֵּם, יַתֵּם, for יְתְמֵם, יִתְמֹם; since its only purpose is to preserve the first syllable as mixed [closed].

c) the דגש of the Chaldaic form אֶתְפֵּל, and the epenthetic ת of the Syriac form אֶתְתְפֵל; which are equivalent forms for אִתְפְּעֵל in those verbs where we should say אִתְפֵּל [i.e., middle weak verbs], for example יִתְּשֵׂם, אֶתְתְּרִים, יִתְּזִין; since its purpose is to preserve the second syllable as strong (1).

(1)   The very learned Hoffmann observed this (*Gram. Syr.*, p. 216), but without ceasing to regard as unusual the form אֶתְתַּפְעַל imagined by Ludwig de Dieu, which is really only the אֶתְּפְעַל of verbs ע"ו; it is not reasonable to place in the group of Syriac verbal forms a form for which no example with a sound root is provided by the Peshitta, the most ancient and pure work extant in the Syriac language. Some examples that are met in Writings of lesser antiquity and purity are not enough to legitimize it.

CVII.

A second fundamental law in Aramaic is the conservation of vowels, from which it proceeds that if a vocalized letter is lost (which does not occur except when the preceding letter or letter before the preceding has a Schwa), or its vowel is lost, the vowel shifts to the preceding consonant. Hence it is that the following words are changed:

a) סְבַב into סַב, סָבַב into סֹב (1), לְבַב into לֵב, בְּנַת into בַּת, etc.;

b) יְנְתַּן into יִתַּן, יְכַתַּת into יַכַּת, etc. (2);

and that from גְּבַר is made גּבְרָא; from קְטַל קָטַל, קָטְלֵה; from קְשֹׁט קֶשְׁטָא.

(1)   The fundamental Rule of the conjugation of geminate verbs in Hebrew is this: *Omit the second radical every time that in the conjugation of regular verbs it would be (in actual Hebrew, or at least in the primitive) preceded by Schwa: then the first radical changes its Schwa to the vowel proper to the omitted letter.* The form סַבּוּ does not derive from the attested Hebrew סָבְבוּ, but rather from the Aramaic, that is, from the primitive Hebrew, סְבָבוּ (from which also derives the form found with suffixes פְּקָדוּנִי, etc.); and it was precisely this obvious derivation of סַבּוּ from סְבָבוּ that made me (along with the already considered Aramaic origin of the segholate forms) suspect the existence of a primitive Hebrew, different from the attested, and closer to Aramaic. Likewise the feminine סַבָּה does not

originate from the attested Hebrew קְטָלָה ,סָבְבָה, but from the primitive קְטָלַת ,סָבְבַת; however, not directly, but indirectly, namely from קָטַלַת (§ 153), from which are the suffixed פְּקַדְתַּנִי, etc. From קָטַלַת Hebrew, truncating the final letter (§ 121 *h*), made קְטָלָה (סָבְבָה, from which סָבָּה), then קְטָלָה, and finally קָטְלָה.

(2) Grammarians take these and similar forms from the הָפְעַל (יֵתַץ = יִנְתַץ), which the meanings of such words do not permit. This is because יֵתַץ does not signify *will be made demolished by others*, nor is יֻכַּת *will be made crushed by others*, nor is יֻקַּח *will be made taken*, nor is יֻקַּם *will be made avenged*, nor is יֻתַּן *will be made given*, nor is תֻּתַּשׁ *will be made broken*, nor is יוּשַׁד *will be made plundered*, nor is יֻחַק *will be made inscribed*; but rather *will be demolished*, *will be crushed*, *will be taken*, etc. Similarly, a number of words whose meaning demands a נִפְעַל, are usually taken by Grammarians as קַל: such are the forms יִדַּח (2 Sam. 14:14), just like the following Participle נִדָּח; תִּתַּךְ (Jer. 42:18), just like the preceding Preterite נִתַּךְ; יִסְחוּ (Prov 2:22), similar to וְנִסַּחְתֶּם (Deut. 28:63); and so יִשַּׁק in the text of Proverbs (24:26), where it means not *will kiss*, but *will be kissed*; and יִקֹּם in Joshua (10:13), where the sense is *until the nation had avenged itself of its enemies*, not *they had avenged their enemies*. The form יִשַּׁק (and likewise can be said of all the others) stands in place of יִנָּשֵׁק, as the primitive form of this word was יִנְשֵׁק (as in Aramaic יִתְפְּעַל, § 125 Note 2), from which was made (omitting the דגש in the letter pointed with Schwa) יִנְשֵׁק, then (assimilating the Nun) יִשֵּׁק, and finally (on account of the great resemblance with the קַל, with which the ancient population, and in later times, the Grammarians, confused this נִפְעַל) יִשַּׁק.

CVIII.

A third law seeks the elimination of unaccented tenuous syllables (§ 105 *c*), which must therefore, as much as possible, lose their vowel, and be joined (by assuming a Schwa) to the following syllable.

CIX.

It is natural for every consonant to draw to itself the following vowel, so it proves difficult to separate a vowel from the consonant that precedes it, as can be seen when trying to pronounce *bar-a*, where the organs [of speech] lead us involuntarily to pronounce instead *ba-ra*. It happens therefore, on account of the law of facility of pronunciation, that augments consisting of a vowel, e.g., אָ֑, or beginning with a vowel, e.g., ־ְךָ, ־ֶה, ־ִין, ־וּן, are necessarily joined to the final consonant of the word, so that instead of forming from בַּר, בַּר־אָ, from שֵׁם, שְׁמַ־א, from תִּפְקַד, תִּפְקַד־וּן, from סְפַר־ין, סְפַר, from בְּשַׂר, בְּשַׂר־ֵה, or from קְטַל, קְטַל־ֵה, one involuntarily says קְטָלֵה, בְּשָׂרֵה, סְפָרִין, תִּפְקְדוּן, שְׁמָא, בָּרָא (1). Now since Aramaic rejects unaccented tenuous syllables, the forms תִּפְקְדוּן, שְׁמָא, בָּרָא change to תִּפְקְדוּן, שְׁמָא, בְּרָא. On the three other forms קְטָלֵה, בְּשָׂרֵה, סְפָרִין, see § 117.

(1)   Hence the Syrians write אַטְאָב instead of אַטָאָב; אֶשְׁאַל for אֶשְׁאָל; אֶתִידַע for אֶתְידַע; נַבֵשׁ or נַבֵשׁ for נִבְאֵשׁ; אֶתְּבַאֵשׁ, אֶתְאַבֵשׁ, or אֶתְּאַבֵשׁ in place of אֶתְבְּאֵשׁ or אֶתְּבְּאֵשׁ. The Olaf added before the first radical is to avoid the tenuous syllable, changing it into a long syllable; it does not originate, as Hoffmann believes (*Gram. syr.*, p. 213), from the great resemblance that verbs with a second radical א have with verbs פ"א.

CX.

But where—thanks to perspicuity (1), facility of pronunciation, or whatever reason—the language wishes that an unaccented tenuous syllable not be lost, the following consonant becomes doubled, so that the syllable ceases to be tenuous. Examples of this are the substantives עֵדֶן, לֵשָׁן, the adjectives שַׁפִּיר, חַכִּים, קַדִּישׁ, חַסִּיר, and the intensive forms קַטֵּל, גַּנֵּב, אִתְקַטַּל.

(1)   That is, the objective of distinguishing different ideas, or various shades of a the same idea.

CXI.

In place of geminiation of the second radical,

   a) sometimes a new letter is added, usually a liquid (ל, מ, נ, ר), or quiescible (Vav and Yod, and in Syriac also Olaf);

   b) sometimes the third radical is doubled.

CXII.

A letter is added

a) after the first radical, as in גּוֹלֵל, formerly גּוֹלֵל, instead of גָּלַל; in שַׁרְבִיט, דַּרְמֶשֶׂק, שַׁלְאֲנָן, זַלְעָפָה, סַרְעֵף; and in the Syriac verbal forms קַרְטֵל, קַמְטֵל, קַיְטֵל, קַוְטֵל (1):

b) after the second radical, as in פַּרְנֵס, מָעֶזְיָה for מָעֶזְיָה, פֶּרֶס for פֶּרֶס:

c) after the third radical, for example שַׁלְמוֹנִים for שִׁלּוּמִים.

(1) See the examples of these in Hoffmann (*Gram. Syr.*, p. 186) and Gesenius (*Lehrgebäude*, pp. 863–864).

CXIII.

The third radical is doubled in צְמִתֻתוּנִי, אֻמְלַל, שַׁאֲנָן, רַעֲנָן, פִּרְחָח (read הָעֶרְכְּךָ), הָעֶרְכְּךָ (read הָעֶרְכָּךְ), and in the Syriac verbs עֲבֵד, פְּרֵד, אֶתְבַּעֲרַר, פַּרְכֵּךְ (1).

In all these ways the loss of a syllable is avoided, by it not becoming tenuous.

(1) See Hoffmann *ib.*, p. 185.

CXIV.

The tenuous syllable is not eliminated where the vowel is improper and a substitute for Schwa, added only for the facility of pronunciation. Improper vowels of such type are:

a) in Biblical Chaldean, the initial וּ, e.g., וּפִשְׁרָא, which is for וְפִשְׁרָה, and the עֲ in the noun עֲטָה, for עֲטָה.

b) in Syriac, every initial אַ, אֶ, יְ, e.g., אֱלָהָא, אֱמַר, יֱלֵד, for אֱלָהָא, יֱלֵד, אֱמַר (1).

Belonging here are the two Syriac nouns יַלוּדָא *child*, and יַלוּפָא *Scholar*, in which the initial Schwa was changed to *A* due to the difficulty of pronunciation. Other examples are חֲמוּצָא *sour*, עֲמוּטָא *dark*, עֲנוּדָא *foreigner*. This improper *A* deceived the very learned Hoffmann, who (*Gram. syr.*, p. 242) imagined a nominal form קַטוּל. The same thing can be said about the noun חֲסִי ,חַסְיָא *pious*, which does not at all support the form קְטֵל introduced by the same Hoffmann (ib., p. 241).

(1) In fact, the Eastern Syrians pronounce the word אַלָהָא with a double *l* (see [George] Amira, *Gram. chald.*, *Praeludia*, third page; [Giuseppe] Assemani, *Bibliot. Orient.* Vol. III, Part II, p. 379; Hoffmann, *Gram. syr.*, p. 105); however, it is not the case that they use such doubling in all the numerous cases of an improper vowel forming a tenuous syllable.

CXV.

Biblical Chaldean has another category of improper vowels, and these are the rapid vowels (חטפים), substituting not for mobile [Schwa], but silent Schwa; e.g., רַחֲמִין, which is for רַחְמִין. Here also a tenuous syllable comes about, namely the one that precedes the Ḥatef. It is, however, quite probable that such a diastole, completely unknown to the Syrians, was in Biblical Chaldean a Hebraism introduced by the Hebrew Pointers; and that the ancient Arameans pronounced רַחְמִין, with a muted ח, just as the Syrians pronounce it.

CXVI.

The fourth and final law of Aramaic, born from the third common to all the languages (§ 101), does not permit any syllable to begin with three consonants, that is to say, with two Schwas, as would be the syllables *scri* (סְקְרִי), *stra* (סְטְרָא).

CXVII.

Therefore, in the words קְטַלָה, בְּשָׂרֵה, סְפָרִין, where, eliminating the tenuous syllable, one would say קְטָלָה, בְּשָׂרֵה, סְפְרִין, a new vowel is added between the first two consonants, and one says קַטְלָה, בְּשָׂרֵה, סִפְרִין.

CXVIII.

This new vowel is
    a) the same vowel that is proper to the second consonant, e.g., קַטְלָה from קְטָלָה, גַּבְרָא from גְּבַר:

b) another, but analogous to the primitive [vowel], e.g., קְשָׁטָא from קְשׁשָׁא, from קְשַׁט:

c) the vowel *I*, as in בִּשְׂרֵה, סִפְרִין (1):

d) the vowel *A*, which occurs very frequently in Syriac, e.g., וַלְכוּן, דַלְכוּן, and sometimes in Hebrew, e.g., מַלְכִּי from מֶלֶךְ, primitively מְלֶךְ.

(1) Thus צַד, which is for צָדַד (§ 107 *a*), makes צִדוֹ, for צָדדוֹ, for [earlier] צָדְדוֹ; the vowel *a* does not change irregularly into *i*, as Gesenius thought (Lehrgeb., p. 166),[5] and the צ did not primitively have *e* (צֵד), as claim Schultens (p. 153)[6] and Ewald (p. 468).[7] In the same manner, from מַס one says מִסִּים, for מְסְסִים, as in Chaldaic (like סִפְרִין), without the addition of the Hebrew Kamets (מְסָסִים).

---

[5] Gesenius (*Lehrgebäude*, § 45.4 Anm. 1) claims that the *a* changes to *i* because of the following dagesh. In the latest English edition of Gesenius' grammar (*Gesenius-Kautzsch-Cowley*, § 27s), this rule has been made more vague: "The attenuation of *ă* to *ĭ* is very common in a toneless closed syllable."

[6] Albert Schultens, *Institutiones ad fundamenta linguae hebraeae* (Leiden, 1737; 2nd ed., 1756). It is unimportant which edition SDL was using, since the second edition is essentially a corrected reprint of the first. The page numbers cited by SDL apply to either edition. There was apparently another second edition (*editio secunda*) from 1743, which I have not had occasion to examine; presumably, it was also nearly identical to that of 1737 and 1756 (the *editio altera*).

[7] Heinrich Ewald, *Kritische Grammatik der hebräischen Sprache* (Leipzig, 1827).

ARTICLE III.

Fundamental Laws Particular to the Hebrew Language.

CXIX.

The Hebrew Language, since, in its attested state, is posterior to the Aramaic, possesses over the latter a certain degree of perfection and polish.

It surpasses it in

a) Softness [*Soavità*],

b) Harmony [*Armonia*],

c) Richness [*Ricchezza*].

CXX.

The first fundamental law of Hebrew is Softness, that is to say, the universal law of facility of pronunciation is carried through in Hebrew to a degree of delicateness much greater than it is in Aramaic. It is because of this that Hebrew likes to avoid strong syllables (at least where the first letter is a radical), hard syllables, and often also final mixed syllables; and in general, compared with Aramaic, it abounds in vowel sounds. It is also fond of variety.

CXXI.

Thus it happens that

a) a Kamets is commonly added to the first part of strong syllables beginning with a radical letter, and so one says פָּקַד instead of Aramaic פְּקַד, בָּשָׂר for בְּשַׂר, שָׁלוֹם for שְׁלָם. Such a קָמֵץ is to be called "Hebrew"; this is to accurately distinguish it from the primitive, or Aramaic קָמֵץ, as is that of שְׁלָם:

b) nominal forms consisting of a strong syllable, e.g., קְשֹׁט, חְלֵב, גְּבַר, are commonly made bisyllabic segholates, e.g., גֶּבֶר, חֶלֶב, קֶשֶׁט; also, bisyllabic [words] ending in a strong syllable are made trisyllabic segholates, e.g., מִשְׁמֶרֶת instead of מִשְׁמְרַת, from מִשְׁמָרָה; מַצֶּבֶת for מַצְבַת, from מַצֵּבָה. This was practiced by the Hebrews even in the pronunciation of Aramaic words, saying e.g., אֲמֶרֶת (Dan. 5:10) for אֲמְרַת; הִתְגְּזֶרֶת (id. 2:34,

45) for הִתְגַּזְרַת ;הִשְׁתְּכַחַת (id. 6:23) for הִשְׁתַּכְּחַת ;הַדֶּקֶת (id. 2:34, 45) for הַשְׁכַּחַת ;הַדְּקַת (id. 2:25) for הַשְׁכַּחַת (1):

c) the vowel פתח (*A*) is replaced many times by the compound or diphthong קמץ (*OA*) at the end of nouns; e.g., בָּשָׂר from the Aramaic בְּשַׂר:

d) tenuous syllables are not eliminated, but the vowel is preserved as is, as in זְקֵנִים; or (more frequently) it changes into a compound vowel, so that instead of (בְּשָׂרוֹ, בְּשָׂרֵהּ, קְטַלֵהּ, בְּשָׂרֵהּ, סָפְרִין, one says סָפְרִין סָפְרִים (סְפָרִים), קְטָלֵהּ (קְטָלוֹ:

e) strong syllables are broken into two, via the addition of a final קמץ; e.g., פָּקַדְתָּ from the Aramaic פִּקַדְתְּ:

f) the קמץ is moved from the penultimate to the ultimate letter, e.g., תִּפְקְדוּן from תִּפְקְדָנָה, גָּלָת from גְּלָתָה (2), סוּסָךְ from Aramaic סוּסֵךְ:

g) a quiescent Yod is added in the verbal form הַפְעִיל, primitively הַפְעֵל or הַפְעַל, so one says הַקְטִיל instead of הַקְטֵל (Aramaic הַקְטֵל or מַקְטְלִין), מַקְטְלִים instead of מַקְטְלִים (Aramaic מַקְטְלִין):

h) sometimes the final non-radical consonant is omitted, e.g., פְּקָדָה instead of Aramaic פְּקָדַת, תִּפְקְדוּ instead of תִּפְקְדוּן:

i) sometimes a final vowel is added, e.g., פָּקַדְתִּי, from the Aramaic פְּקַדֵת:

l)[8] after the accent, that is to say, the stress, it does not tolerate three consonants, as there would be if one said בַּרְזֶל *bàrzel*, פָּקֶד *pikked*, סַבְּתָ, תְּסָבְנָה, סַבְּנוּ (3), nor two consonants preceded or separated by a quiescent Vav or Yod, which we find for example in תְּקִימְנָה, וַיִּיצֶר, וַיּוֹסֶף, anomalous forms, in place of which are regularly written וַיִּצֶר, וַיֹּסֶף, תְּקֻמְנָה (4); or which would be found in תָּקִים, תָּקוּם, if these words had the accent on the penult:

m) the succession of two or more long syllables is avoided many times, on account of variety, writing for example קָרְבִּים, גָּדְלִים, תָּמְמִים, צַדְּיקִים, גָּדְלוֹת, קָרְבּוֹת, instead of צַדִּיקִים, תְּמִימִים, גְּדוֹלִים, קְרוֹבִים, גְּדוֹלוֹת, קְרוֹבוֹת; also avoided is the succession of the same sounds, e.g., תֶּחֱרַשׁ and תַּחֲרַשׁ, instead of תַּחֲרֹשׁ; תֶּחְפַּץ and תַּחֲפֹץ, instead of תַּחְפֹּץ.

---

[8] The letters *j* and *k* are not native to Italian, so SDL does not use them in his outlining. I have avoided them also, only to help keep references consistent between the English and Italian editions.

(1)   This hypothesis accounts for

a) some irregularities of declension, by which segholate forms seem to follow the laws of the forms פָּעַל, פָּעֵל; e.g., הֶבֶל, הֲבַל חֲדַר, חֶדֶר:

b) some nouns used indiscriminately in segholate form and in the form פָּעֵל, פָּעַל, פְּעַל; e.g., גָּדֹל and גְּדָל; שְׁכֶם and שֶׁכֶם; זֶרַע and זְרַע; גְּבַר and גֶּבֶר (Exod. 15:16); גֹּבַהּ and גָּבַהּ (1 Samuel 16:7):

c) some nouns of the form פָּעֵל (primitively פִּעֵל), that are declined in part like the segholates; e.g., כֶּתֶף, כָּתֵף; גֶּדֶר, גָּדֵר:

d) the two forms that the infinitive פְּקֹד takes when joining with certain suffixes: פָּקְדְךָ from פְּקֹד, and פְּקָדְךָ as if from פְּקַד:

e) נִשְׁבַּחַת, נִבְכַּחַת, Chaldaizing Preterites, primitively נִבְחַת, נִשְׁבַּחַת:

f) יָחְנְךָ, לְהַפְרְכֶם, where the verbal forms הָפֵר, יָחֹן, losing the Hebrew קמץ upon joining with the suffixes, and becoming הָפֵר, יָחֹן, were changed into הֵפֵר, יֵחֹן, and then from them were made הַפְרְכֶם like מַלְכְּכֶם, and יָחְנְךָ like קָדְשְׁךָ:

g) the double form of מִשְׁמָרָה and מִשְׁמֶרֶת, and the like. The construct form of מִשְׁמָרָה was מִשְׁמֶרֶת. The strong syllable מְרַת was, as usual, changed to מֶרֶת. Then, since the segholate forms serve indifferently for the absolute state and for the governed [construct], the new form מִשְׁמֶרֶת became used in both these states; more often, however, in the governed state, to which it fundamentally belongs.

Schultens instead supposes the segholate forms to have primitively had, as they still have in Arabic, the vowel on the first consonant; e.g., פֶּ, פַּקְ, פְּקֹד, פָּקַד.[9]

To this judgment, I counter

a) that it leads to vocables with nearly impossible pronunciations; e.g., חְקַק, לְבְב, גַּנְן, חֶלְי, פֶּרְי, גָּדְל, נְבְל, סְפְר, נְדְר, tolerable only by the Arabic language, which normally adds to these the [case] ending ON (*nidron, sifron,* etc.):

b) that יָדַעְתָּ and the like, where the primitive form terminated really with two Schwas (יָדְעְתָּ), have dagesh in the ת; whereas דַּעַת and the like, the primitive form of which is claimed to have been דַּעְתְּ, have ת without a dagesh:

c) that אַתְּ and נָתַתָּ, which are for אַנְתְּ and נָתַנְתָּ, have the ת with dagesh, while בַּת and מַתַּת have rafe; so it appears that the primitive form of these latter two words was not בַּנְתְּ and מַתַנְתְּ, but בְּנַת and מַתְנַת:

d) with the analogy of the geminate verbs, where, as an example, the Imperative סֹב is undoubtedly contracted from סָבַב, not from סְבֹב.

---

[9] Schultens was quite correct on this point.

It would do no good to counter with the analogy of quiescent final-He verbs, e.g., יִפֶן, which is for יִפֶן, from יִפְנֶה. This is because here it is not necessary that the harsh pronunciation יִפֶן was ever in use, being from יִפְנֶה and having passed immediately in speech into יִפֶן, with regression of the Seghol (§ 153); whereas in the Schultensian doctrine, the very harsh sounds נְבָל, לְבָב, etc., were in actual use, which is extremely unlikely.

(2) To tell the truth, I judge סוּסָךְ to be more ancient than סוּסְךָ, on account of the following etymological conjectures. It seems to me that some of the very first sounds, with which man expressed to his fellow man the pleasant sensation that his sight caused to rise in his chest, were TA and KA, which in the mind of our new speaker confusingly had the values of *you* (from which the afformative תָּ, the pronoun אַתָּה *you*, and the suffix ךָ *you, your*), of *you come* (from which אָתָא *to come*, in the imperative אֱתָא), and of *here* (from which the Chaldaic particle כָּה *here*, and the Hebrew כֹּה *here* and *there*); it seems to me also that the first sounds, with which the speaker indicated his own self, were I, NI, TI, from which the suffixes ־ִי, ־ִנִי, and the afformative תִּי. Now joining the primitive כָּה to a noun, one first said סוּסָךְ; but the Arameans, due to that harshness that was proper to their pronunciation, moved the קָמֵץ from the simple final syllable (where it is most often mutable, § 133) to the preceding letter, saying סוּסָךְ; then the Hebrews, dedicated as they were to greater gentleness [*dolcezza*], restored the final vowel, saying סוּסְךָ. The same thing has happened to the personal pronoun אַתָּה, which having originally had the sound אַנְתָּה, אַתָּה, תָּה, was shortened by the Arameans to אַנְתְּ, אַתְּ, then was restored by the Hebrews to the older form אַתָּה.—However, my hypothesis that Hebrew ךָ is not primitive, but derives from ־ָךְ, accounts for why, although beginning with a consonant, [the suffix] is often (in the manner of the weak suffixes beginning in a vowel) preceded by קָמֵץ; for example, דְּבָרֶךָ, חֶכְמָתְךָ, rather than by פַתַח, as [is] the suffix כֶם [e.g., דְּבַרְכֶם], which also primitively began with a consonant, being sounded in Chaldaic as כוֹן.

(3) Therefore the vowel added in תֵּשֶׁב בִּינָה, סַבֹּנוּ, סַבֹּתָ, is not, as Schultens claims ([*Institutiones*,] p. 324), to avoid the concurrence of two quiescent Schwas, nor, as Gesenius (*Lehrg.*, p. 358) and Ewald ([*Kritische Grammatik*,] p. 470) write, because the דָּגֵשׁ would be otherwise less perceptible; but because the gentleness of Hebrew pronunciation does not tolerate three consonants after the accent. Since the second person plural is derived from the second singular, from סַבֹּתָ is made סַבֹּתֶם with the added vowel, even though it would be possible to pronounce סַבְתֶּם without harshness.—So also appears the erroneousness of the imagined reading by Schultens וָאֶבְרְכֶם [Gen. 48:9],

with the accent on the בָ. He was led to support this reading by the Seghol that several editions have on the כ; without a doubt a false Seghol, in place of which the Spanish Codices, as was noted by [Menaḥem] Lonzano and [Jedidiah] Norzi, have צְרִי.[10]

(4) So instead of קוּמְנָה , one regularly says קָמְנָה. In מְשִׁיבַת נָפֶשׁ [Psa. 19:8], מַחְכִּימַת פֶּתִי [ib.], and probably also in בִּתְשֹׂוּמֶת יָד [Lev. 5:21] (from תְּשֹׂוּמָה), the accent is retrograde, and the two words are to be regarded as forming a single word, מְשִׁיבַתְנָפֶשׁ, etc. But מְשִׁיבַת and the like, pronounced isolated, would be intolerable sounds in the Hebrew Language.

CXXII.

The second law of Hebrew is Harmony, by which the Hebrew language loves to drop the accent, the tone, or the pause [i.e., stress], onto the second syllable; so that syllables deprived of a pause and the accented ones possibly come to alternate.

CXXIII.

From this it happens that

a) no Hebrew קמץ is added when the accent would come to fall on the third syllable; e.g., בְּשָׂרוֹ, פְּקַדְתֶּם (1):

b) the succession of two accents is avoided, which is done

    I. via the regression of the first of the two, which is called נָסוֹג אָחוֹר;

    II. by joining the two words as one, so that the first loses its accent; this is called מַקֵּף *united, connected* (2):

c) a semi-pause [secondary stress marker] (מֶתֶג) is added, if possible, when the stress necessarily falls after the second syllable; e.g., מֶחְכְמָה .

(1) The same is the reason for the construct forms בְּשַׂר־קֹדֶשׁ, בְּשַׂר־אִישׁ, and the like. The first being subordinate to the following noun, it forms with it a compound noun, and both are treated as if a single word; so where בָּשָׂר had

---

[10] The Leningrad Codex (Codex Leningradensis), considered the most authoritative complete Masoretic text, has a *tsere* as well. The reference to Lonzano and Norzi is certainly to Norzi's *Minḥat Shai*, for which Norzi sought help from his friend Lonzano.

to be pronounced, and the accent falls on the third syllable, or even later, the primitive form בְּשַׂר is retained. The construct form is never an unusual form, but rather it is the primitive form. So מַלְכֵי, the construct form of the Hebrew plural, is the primitive plural of Syriac (מַלְכֵא) and Talmudic (מלכי), to which was added a Nun (מַלְכִין), which Hebrew changed to a Mem (מְלָכִים). Poetic Hebrew, amenable as is it to Chaldaisms, often uses the primitive form instead of the lengthened one, especially with nouns that are found in some way subordinated to the following word, e.g., אֹהֲבֵי לָנוּם, יֹשְׁבֵי עַל־מִדִּין, אֱלֹהֵי מִקָּרוֹב, מַשְׁכִּימֵי בַבֹּקֶר. The construct form of the feminine plurals reassumes the vowels of the Aramaic singular. So instead of צְדָקוֹת one says as a rule צִדְקוֹת, analogous to the Chaldaic singular צִדְקָה. The construct form of the feminine singular is then the same among the Hebrews and the Arameans.

(2) Grammarians mean by this name the line itself that joins the two words; and, taken in this sense, several moderns (after [Johann] Dantz) have rightly observed that it should better be pronounced מַקֵּף. But the Masoretes, the first to use this denomination, applied it to the word joining to the following, and wrote מקף, not מקיף, as they would have written if they had pronounced it מַקִּיף.—However, the retreat of the accent signifies (no differently than the joining line) that the two words are pronounced as if they were only one, and the receded accent acts in place of the semi-accent that the two words would have if they were joined; e.g., עָמַדְשָׁם = עָמַד־שָׁם = עָמַד שָׁם. The joining line is not usually used except in cases in which the regression of the accent could not take place, either because the first of the two vocables is monosyllabic, e.g., כָּל־אָדָם; or because the penultimate syllable of the first word is mixed [closed], and therefore equally incapable of [having] a semi-accent, and of [having] a receded accent taking the place of a semi-accent; e.g., וַיִּקְרָא־לוֹ, דִּבֶּר־לוֹ. The joining line has also another purpose, which is to avoid the concurrence of two or more non-disjunctive [non distinguenti] accents; and it appears if the preceding word does not have the right to a disjunctive accent, as happens in וַיִּפֹּל עַל־צַוָּארֵי (Gen. 35:20), הוּא מַצֶּבֶת קְבֻרַת־רָחֵל, בִּנְיָמִן־אָחִיו (ibid, 45:14), וְיִכָּתֵב בְּדָתֵי פָרַס־וּמָדַי (Esther 1:19), where without the joining line the words קְבֻרַת, בִּנְיָמִן, and פָּרַס would have a non-disjunctive accent, preceded by another non-disjunctive; such a concurrence of two servile [ministri] accents is never tolerated before טִפְחָא (except in the case of מֵרְכָא כְּפוּלָה), and could not be avoided except by marking with תְּבִיר the words עַל־צַוָּארֵי, מַצֶּבֶת, and בְּדָתֵי, which, being in a governing state, i.e., strictly subordinate to the following [word(s)], do not have the right to a disjunctive accent, as תְּבִיר is.

CXXIV.

Aramaic, free as it is from the laws of Softness and Harmony, proves more uniform and constant than Hebrew. Hebrew is more luxuriant; and the greater number of laws that it must follow produces greater conflict, which is a necessary reason for greater variety and inconstancy. Thus it is that long syllables are not always preserved in the Hebrew Language, as can be seen in תָּקֹמְנָה, וַיָּקָם, יָקוּם; הִפְקַדְתָּ, הִפְקִיד.

CXXV.

The Hebrew Language is, from a grammatical point of view, richer than the Aramaic, inasmuch as

a) it possesses a greater number of nominal forms (1);

b) it possesses two verbal forms unknown to Aramaic, namely, the two passives פֻּעַל and הָפְעַל (2).

(1) The Hebrew nominal forms occurring with perfect roots are, according to [David] Kimḥi, circa 150, and are distributed by Gesenius into thirty-seven classes. Hoffmann, carefully following the method of Gesenius, distributes the Syriac nominal forms into 27 classes, which, adding to them the quadriliteral form, are 28, and they embrace just 80 different forms, many of which Syriac would have probably added to those [inherited] from the ancient Aramaic.

(2) Of the verbal forms in common use, Aramaic has just three active, פַּעֵל, קַל, אַפְעֵל, corresponding to Hebrew קַל, פִּעֵל, הִפְעִיל; and the two reciprocals אִתְפְּעֵל and אִתְפַּעַל, corresponding to Hebrew נִפְעַל and הִתְפַּעֵל. The אִתְפְּעֵל was changed in Hebrew to הִנְפְעַל, then to נִפְעַל, conserving, however, the ה in the infinitive and in the imperative.

The active Aramaic forms each have two Participles, an active and a passive: קָטֵל, קָטִיל; מְקַטֵּל, מְקַטַּל; מַקְטֵל, מֻקְטַל. Hebrew has created from the two passive Participles מְקֻטָּל, מֻקְטַל, the two complete conjugations פֻּעַל and הָפְעַל. It did not do the same with the passive Participle of the קַל, since the law of softness prevented קְטִילְתָּ or קָטוּלְתָּ from being pronounced (§ 121 *l*).

The Hebrews that learned the Chaldaic language during the Babylonian exile used sometimes in their Chaldean (the Biblical Chaldean) the form הָפְעַל, e.g., הֵסַק, הָחֳרַבַת, הָתְקְנַת, etc. This is not all [that they did]; drawn from the analogy of the Hebrew forms פֻּעַל and הָפְעַל, daughters of the Chaldean passive Participles מְקַטַּל and מֻקְטַל, they began to create a new passive conjugation, a daughter of the passive Participle of the קַל, that is, taken from פְּעִיל, from which they made the past קְטִיל, קְטִילוּ, קְטִילַת, תְּקִלְתָּ;[11] a conjugation unknown to the Syrians, as well as to the Targumists and Talmudists.

CXXVI.

As for the correspondence of the Hebrew vowels to the Aramaic, it is to be noted that

a) the Aramaic קָמֶץ is preserved in Hebrew words, and in fact remains immutable, e.g., כְּתָב, שְׁאָר, גְּנַב; otherwise (and this is more frequent) it changes to וֹ, e.g., קָל, קוֹל; דָּר, דּוֹר; גְּבַר, גִּבּוֹר; שָׁלָם, שָׁלוֹם:

b) the חִירֶק with Yod is changed often times into שׁוּרֶק, and vice versa; e.g., זוּ, דִּי, זוּ (1); אָחִיהוּ, אֲחוּהִי, אֲבִיהִי, אֲבוּהִי; קָטוּל, קְטִיל.

(1) אֲבוּ, not אָב, is the primitive form of the word used by the triliteral languages to express the noun *Father*. Likewise אֲחוּ, not אָח, is the primitive noun for *Brother*. *Abù* and *Achù*[12] are among the first sounds that children tend to utter. From this comes the plural אָבוֹת with a feminine form, since אבו has a desinence proper in Aramaic to feminine nouns, e.g., זָכוּ, גָלוּ. From אֲחוּ is made the masculine plural אַחִים, due to the necessity of distinguishing brothers from sisters.

The primitive form of אֵם *Mother* is אֲמַם or אֲמֶם = *Mamma*, also a primitive sound among babies.

---

[11] This last word refers to the form תְּקִילְתָּה found in Dan. 5:27.

[12] Properly this should be *Abù*, but SDL did not know this. I have kept his transcription since he is maintaining that the primitive sound uttered by children is [x] and not [h].

APPENDICES

APPENDIX I.

Objections that could be made to the law of § 108, and their solutions.

CXXVII.

OBJECTION I.

In Biblical Chaldean, unaccented tenuous syllables are met before a guttural or semi-guttural letter that should have a dagesh; e.g., פֶּחָר for פַּחָר [Dan 2:41], וְתֶרֹעַ for וְתֵרֹעַ [Dan. 2:40].

RESPONSE.

Syriac does not know any sign for the doubling of consonants, a doubling that the Western Syrians do not use even in pronunciation. The Eastern Syrians, however, pronounce some consonants doubled; for example, שְׁמַיָּא *Shemayyà*, קַדִּישָׁא *Kaddishà* (1).

That the gemination of consonants was in use among the most ancient Arameans, as it is among the Hebrew, the Arabs, and the Eastern Syrians, seems probable. The guttural letters then, either were doubled by the ancient Chaldeans, as the Arabs still do, in which case the pointing of the word פֶּחָר and the like would be a Hebraism; or, because of the great difficulty of pronunciation, were not doubled, without such an exception at all invalidating the law that demands *as much as possible* the elimination of unaccented tenuous syllables.

(1) See the authors cited in § 114, Note 1.

CXXVIII.

OBJECTION II.

Biblical Chaldean has many other unaccented tenuous syllables.

RESPONSE.

In the greater part of these words, the orthography (as a Hebraism, or due to copyist error) is defective; that is to say, that the Hebrew Writers have omitted the quiescent letter which the Syrians consistently wrote; or else the pointing itself is Hebraizing, rather than truly Chaldean. Thus:

אַרְכֻבָתֵהּ (Dan. 5:6) is for אַרְכוּבָתֵהּ; if it is not instead to be read אַרְכָּבָתֵהּ, with קמץ; the Syrians in fact say רְכָבָא.

הַרְהֹרִין (id. 4:2) is for הַרְהוֹרִין; or else to be read, as the Syrians do, הַרְהָרִין.

יְדֻרוּן (id. 4:9) is for יְדוּרוּן.

יְקֻמוּן (id. 7:24) is for יְקוּמוּן, just as is read in Dan. 7:10, 17.

יְשֵׁיזִב (id. 3:17), וְשֵׁיזִב (id. 3:28) are for יְשֵׁיזִב, וְשֵׁיזִב, as we have elsewhere יְשֵׁיזְבִנְכוֹן (id. 3:15), יְשֵׁיזְבִנָּךְ (id. 6:17), מְשֵׁיזִב (id. 6:28). The editions, however, vary in this. The Syrians have שַׁוְזֵב.

לְהוֹדָעֻתַנִי (id. 2:26, 5:15) is for לְהוֹדָעוּתַנִי (id. 4:15, 5:16).

לְמֵזֵא (id. 3:19) is for לְמֵאזֵא. In the same manner,

לְמֵמַר (Ezra 5:11) is for לְמֵאמַר, which is read in Dan. 2:9, and

לְמֵתֵא (Dan. 3:2) is for לְמֵאתֵא. The Syrians do not omit the radical Olaf. The Targumists and the Talmudists change the א into Yod. In any case, the syllable is not tenuous, but long.

מְדֹרָךְ (id. 4:22, 29) is for מְדוֹרָךְ, as is read elsewhere מְדוֹרֵהּ (id. 5:21); or else we should read מְדָרָךְ, like מְדָרְהוֹן (id. 2:11).

רַעְיֹנָהִי (id. 5:6) is for רַעְיוֹנָהִי, as it is in Dan. 4:16, and like רַעְיוֹנַי (id. 2:30), רַעְיוֹנָךְ (id. 7:28), רַעְיוֹנָךְ (id. 2:29, 5:10); or perhaps instead it is to be read רַעְיָנָהִי, as the Syrians have. The editions also vary here.

שִׁלְטֹנַי (id. 3:2, 3) is for שִׁלְטוֹנַי, as some editions have in verse 3, or is to be read שִׁלְטָנַי, as the Syrians say שׁוּלְטָנָא.

שֻׂמַת (id. 6:18) is for שׂוּמַת.

תְּחוֹתוֹהִי (id. 4:9, 18) is for תְּחוֹתוֹהִי, from תְּחוֹת (id. 7:27, Jeremiah 10:11); or it is to be read תַּחְתּוֹהִי, like in Dan. 4:11. The Syrians have both תַּחְתִּי and תְּחוֹתִי (Amira, p. 444).[1]

תִּלָתֵהוֹן (id. 3:23) is for תִּלָתֵיהוֹן with the Yod of the plural, like the Syrians have (Amira, p. 235).

In Biblical Chaldean, there remain eight unaccented tenuous syllables, all pointed with צְרִי.

בְּטֵלַת (Ezra 4:24). This is without a doubt a Hebraism. In the Syriac manner, it would be בְּטֵנַת, on the model of בְּטֵנַת (1); and in the Targumic, בְּטֵילַת, with quiescent Yod, like נְסִיבַת (Gen. 3:6).

גְּזֵרַת (Dan. 4:14). This is a Hebraism. The Syrians say גְּזָרָא.

יְקֵדַת (id. 7:11). A Hebraism. The Syrians have יְקֵדָא.

לֵוָיֵא (Ezra 6:16, 7:13). The Syrians also say לֵוָיֵא Levite. In foreign names, the original orthography is often preserved.

רֵוֵה (Dan. 2:31),

שֵׁגְלָתֵה וּלְחֵנָתֵה (id. 5:2, 3, 23). These three nouns are unknown to the Syrians. The Targumists write רֵינָא and לְחֵינָתָא with Yod. שֵׁגַל is unknown to the Targumists also.

לִשְׁלֵוְתָךְ (id. 4:24). The Targumists have שְׁלֵיוְתָא, שְׁלֵיוָא, with quiescent Yod. The Syrians say שָׁלֵיוּתָא.

(1) See Amira, p. 304; Ch. B. Michaëlis, *Syriasmus*, p. 40; Hoffmann, p. 168.

CXXIX.

OBJECTION III.

Unaccented tenuous syllables are frequently met in Syriac, in the middle of a word, when the א gives up its vowel to the preceding letter which lacks a vowel; e.g., סֵנָאא, which is for סֵנְאָא, וָמָאא, which is for וָמְאָא, מַלאָכָא, which is for מַלְאָכָא (which should be for מַלְאָכָא, see § 114 b); likewise the Yod gives up its אַ (חִירֶק) חְבָצָא to the preceding letter, e.g., אֶתִידַע, which is for אֶתְידַע, which would be for אֶתְיְדַע.

---

[1] George Amira, *Grammatica syriaca, sive chaldaica* (Rome, 1596).

RESPONSE.

This softened pronunciation is not primitive, and it is likely that the most ancient Arameans said סְנָאָא ,וְמָאָא, or וּמָאָא, etc., just as we find in Biblical Chaldean, and as the Hebrews say יְגָאַל ,יִשְׁאַל, and the like.

CXXX.

OBJECTION IV.

There are in Syriac many tenuous syllables in the third person plural of the Preterite with paragogic Nun, e.g., קַרֵבוּן, אֶתְקְטִלוּן, קְטַלֵין, קְטַלוּן, אַשְׁלֵמוּן.

RESPONSE.

The Syrians, who, in such words vocalized the second radical, pronounced these words with penultimate stress, so that the tenuous syllable was accented. Otherwise, they would have said אֶתְקַטְלוּן, קַטְלֵין, קַטְלוּן, etc., as they say with suffixes קַטְלוּנִי, קַטְלוּךְ, קַטְלוּהִי, etc., and as they say in the Future נֶתְקַטְלוּן, תֶּתְקַטְלוּן, not נֶתְקְטְלוּן, תֶּתְקְטְלוּן.

CXXXI.

OBJECTION V.

Syriac has unaccented tenuous syllables every time that the first of two successive Schwas changes to a vowel, e.g., מְשַׁמְלְיָא, which is for מְשַׁמְלְיָא, נְבִנְיָן for נֶבְנְיָן, נְפַרְשָׁן, חֶכְמְתָא for חֶכְמְתָא, מַדְנְחָא, which is for מַדְנְחָא, נְפַרְשָׁן.

RESPONSE.

Already [George] Amira showed (pp. 43, 46) that such a diastole, whose sign is the line known as *Mehagyono*,[2] was not used except in verse, by

---

[2] The Syriac sign *mehagyono* 'vocalizer' is a horizontal line placed below the letter to indicate the presence of a short epenthetic vowel *e*, or, before gutturals or *r*, the

necessity of the meter; or in prose, to avoid an overwhelmingly harsh or difficult pronunciation. Now this is not in opposition to the law that requires, *if it is possible*, the elimination of unaccented tenuous syllables.

Since, however, the first of two successive Schwas is rather frequently found in the Polyglott of London changed into Reboṣo [= ē] (see the *Syriasmus restitutus* of [Heinrich] Opitz,[3] 1678, pp. 11, 12, and Hoffmann, p. 148), it is useful, so that this pointing will be recognized as illegitimate and false, to repeat here the words of Amira (p. 46). He says: "Unde colligas licet, non tantam, quantam variae indicant opiniones, esse difficultatem, quoties enim, ut dictum est, vel propter metri necessitatem, vel pronunciationis difficultatem, Mehagyono litteram afficere quis cogitur, afficiat: si verum nullum horum accidat, illi Marhetono apponat."[4]

However, it is extremely likely that the most ancient Arameans did not count the syllables of their verses, nor did they make such a division of one syllable into two.

CXXXII.

OBJECTION VI.

Syriac has unaccented tenuous syllables in some masculine nouns, whose plural ends in וָתָא, e.g., אַרְיָוָתָא, כְּנָוָתָא, לִילְוָתָא, כַּרְסָוָתָא, etc. (1).

---

vowel *a*. See L. Costaz, *Grammaire Syriaque* (5th ed., Beirut, 2003), § 23; C. Brockelmann, *Syrische Grammatik* (8th ed., Leipzig, 1960), § 12.

[3] *Syriasmus facilitati et integritati suae restitutus* (Leipzig, 1678).

[4] "As far as it is fitting for one to gather, there is not so much difficulty as various opinions indicate, for as it has often been asserted, either on account of the necessity of the meter or the difficulty of pronunciation, if one is forced to affix a letter for *Mehagyono*, one should do it: but if none of these things should occur, let him place on it *Marhetono*." (translation Daniel Berman and Philip Baldi.) The Syriac sign *marhetono* 'accelerating' is a horizontal line placed above the consonant, to indicate the complete absence of a vowel (Costaz, § 24; Brockelmann § 12). This sign is also used as a *linea occultans*, to indicate that a consonant is not to be pronounced at all. It is noteworthy that Amira's nearly seven-page discussion of *mehagyono* and *marhetono* (pp. 40–46), complete with copious examples, is far more comprehensive than the meager treatments (one paragraph or less) found in twentieth-century grammars.

REPONSE.

The Biblical pointing has קָמֵץ in כְּנָתֵהּ, אַרְיָוָתָא, כָּרְסָוָן; and these pointings are preferable to those of the modern Syrians. This is because in כְּנָתָא, מְנָתָא, עְלָתָא, the קָמֵץ is, in the language of Michaëlis and Gesenius, impure and immutable קָמֵץ, since it underlies an א (2); or, according to my principles, an Aramaic קָמֵץ, primitive and immutable. It is therefore evident that in these three words, כְּנָתָא, מְנָתָא, עְלָתָא, the Syrians have altered the ancient pronunciation, substituting פתח for קָמֵץ. Now it is believable that the same thing happened also in the other plurals with the same termination, so that the ancient Arameans pronounced with קָמֵץ the words כָּרְסָוָתָא, אַרְיָוָתָא, as they are read in Biblical Chaldean, and so likewise אַתְרָוָתָא, אָסָוָתָא, and all the others; and that the modern Syrians have in all these plurals changed the קָמֵץ into פתח (3).

Some other objections might by chance be drawn from the Targumic Chaldean, and from Syriac. But the Targumic Chaldean is too inaccurate and variable in its pointing to be able to use alone as evidence; and Syriac, not having דָּגֵשׁ forte, offers far too many apparently tenuous syllables which were probably not so in primitive Aramaic; for example, קַטֵל, הִתְקַטַל, and the like, where the second radical was primitively doubled.

(1) See Amira, p. 90, Joseph Acurense,[5] pp. 27–42, Opitz, p. 68, Ch. B. Michaëlis, pp. 83, 84, Hoffmann, p. 255.

(2) See Gesenius, Lehrg., p. 607, and Lexicon Manuale [p. 493] under the Art. כְּנָת.

(3) Without a doubt mistaken is Amira, who (pp. 26 and 91) reads in the singular כַּנְתָּא instead of כְּנָתָא, which [Edmund] Castell and [Johann David] Michaëlis have in their Syriac Lexicon (p. 422),[6] as do Gesenius in his Lexicon manuale (p. 493) and, the most authoritative of all, Joseph Acurense, Patriarch of Antioch (p. 19). Hoffmann (p. 255) has כַּנְתָּא; but in the Errata (p. 417) he correctly substitutes כְּנָתָא.

---

[5] *Grammatica linguae syriacae* (Rome, 1647).

[6] *Lexicon syriacum* (2 vols.; Göttingen, 1788).

APPENDIX II.

Clarifications regarding the Aramaic קָמֵץ.

CXXXIII.

The קָמֵץ appearing in Aramaic words in simple [open] final syllables is mutable; for example, מַלְכָּא, מַלְכִין, מַלְכֵיהוֹן: excluding this one case, the קָמֵץ is immutable and indestructible in Chaldean, as well as in Syriac. Buxtorf has already observed (*Gram. chald. et syr.*, Book III) concerning the word שָׁעֲתָא (Dan. 5:5), that the קָמֵץ of the penultimate syllable does not change in the emphatic form, and therefore that from שָׁעָה one says שָׁעֲתָא, with קָמֵץ rather than פתח under the שׁ. Ch. B. Michaëlis (*Syriasm.*, p. 15) showed that the vowel O (the Zekofo, corresponding to the קָמֵץ) in final mixed [closed] syllables is regularly invariable. He was followed by Hoffmann (p. 143), who elsewhere (p. 262) showed further, always talking about the Noun, however, that the Zekofo ordinarily rejects any mutation. Up until now, no one that I know of has observed this property of the Zekofo in its universality, much less presented the reason for it (§§ 104, 105, 158, 159).

CXXXIV.

The following examples of the immutability of the Zekofo, that is, of the Aramaic קָמֵץ, are taken from the Syriac Grammars of George Amira (Rome, 1596), and of Joseph Acurense (Rome, 1647), both [Maronite] Patriarchs of Antioch.

I.

In the final Syllable.

A. In the Noun:

The emphatic form

1) of the masculines עֲבַד, עַבְדָא, חֲבָל, חֲבָלָא; בּוּסָם, בּוּסָמָא; פּוּרְקָן, פּוּרְקָנָא, etc. (Amira, p. 147); שְׁרִי, שַׁרְיָא; רוּמִי, רוּמָיָא, etc. (idem, p. 148, see also p. 159):

2) of the feminines עֶלְתָא, עֲלָת; בְּעֶתָא, בְּעֶת; מִנְתָא, מְנָת (Acurense, p. 55).

B. In the Verb:

1) the conjugation of middle weak verbs, in the Preterite of the Qal: דָּשׁ, דָּשֶׁת, דָּשְׁנַן, דָּשְׁתּוּן, etc. (Amira, p. 289); דָּן, דָּנְתּוּן, etc. (Acurense, page 303):

2) the second and third person feminine plurals with suffixes: תֶּפְרְשָׁן, תֶּפְרְשָׁנַה, תֶּפְרְשָׁנָךְ, etc.; נֶפְרְשָׁנָכוֹן, נֶפְרְשָׁנָךְ, נֶפְרְשָׁן, etc. (Amira, p. 387; Acur., pp. 239, 240. See also Amira, pp. 375, 376, 382, 399):

3) the third person feminine singular of final weak verbs with suffixes: בְּנַת, בְּנָתֵהּ, בְּנָתָךְ, בְּנָתְכוֹן (Amira, p. 373; Acur., p. 284); on the contrary, בְּזַת (from בַּז) is with suffixes בַּזְתֵהּ, בַּזְתָךְ, etc. (Amira, page 379).

C. In the Particles with suffixes: חִלָּפַי, חִלָּף; קְדָמַי, קְדָמַיכוֹן, קֳדָם; לְוָתָךְ, לְוָתְכוֹן, לְוָת; חִלָּפַיכוֹן (Amira, p. 442; Acur., pp. 546–548).

II.

In the penultimate Syllable.

A. In the Noun:

1) the emphatic form
   a) of the masculines: מָרְיָא, מָרֵא, כָּהֲנָא, כָּהֵן; יַלְדָא, יֶלֶד, etc. (Amira, p. 154, Acur., p. 53); פָּרוּק, פָּרוּקָא; פָּתוּר, פָּתוּרָא (Amira, p. 147):
   b) of the feminines: סָבְתָא, טָבְתָא, etc. (Amira, p. 110), עֶקְתָא, דַּרְתָּא, רָחֲמְתָא, שָׁעְתָא, etc. (Amira, pp. 155, 156):

2) the construct form: קָרְיַת, קָרֵי; עֲקַת, עֲקָא; שָׁעַת, שָׁעָא (Amira, p. 65).

3) the plural form
   a) of the masculines: שַׁלִּיטָנֵי, שַׁלִּיטָנָא; חֶטְהֵי, חֶטְהָא; טָבֵא, טָבָא; אִילָנָא, אִילָנָא (Amira, pp. 76, 77); דַּיָּנָא, דַּיָּנֵי (Acur., p. 307); מָרְיָא, מָרְיָא; בָּעֲיָא, בָּעֲיָא; שָׁטְיָא, שָׁטְיָא, etc. (Amira, p. 79):
   b) of the feminines: סָבְתָא, טָבְתָא; סָבְתָא, מָרְתָא: מָרְתָא, דִּינָתָא (Amira, p. 84); עֲלָיָתָא, עֲלָיָתָא, etc. (Am., p. 82); דִּינָתָא (Acur., p. 307):

4) the movement of a noun, or the passage of an adjective from masculine to feminine gender: סָבָא, סָבְתָא; טָבָא, טָבְתָא (Amira, p. 110); דָּוְיָא, דָּוְיתָא; שָׁטְיָא, שָׁטִיתָא (not so דַּכְיָא, with פתח, from

which דְּכִיתָא, Amira, p. 112); מְשַׁבְּחָנִיתָא, מְשַׁבְּחָנָא, etc. (Amira, p. 113); עֲלָיָא, עֲלָיתָא, etc. (Amira, p. 114); דִּינָא, דִּינָתָא, דְּיָנָא (Acur., p. 307).

5) nouns joined to suffixes:

   a) the masculine nouns: רָחְמָא, רָחְמִי, רָחְמָךְ, etc. (Amira, p. 184; Acur., p. 95) See also Amira pp. 204–213):

   b) the feminine nouns: חֶכְמָתָא, חֶכְמָתָךְ, חֶכְמָתְכוּן, etc. (Ami., p. 182).

B. In the Verb:

  1) Participles coupled with personal pronouns: פָּרֵשׁ, פָּרְשַׁתְּ (Amira, p. 297; Acur., p. 207); פָּרְשִׁיתוּן, פָּרְשָׁן, פָּרְשִׁין, פָּרְשִׁינַן, פָּרְשָׁתִין (Amira, p. 298; Acur., p. 208); בָּנֵין, בָּנֵינַן, בָּנֵיתוּן, בָּנְיָן (Amira, p. 260; Acur., p. 267); בָּזֵין, בָּזֵינַן, בָּזֵיתוּן; בָּזָן, בָּזְיָן, בָּזְתִין (Amira, p. 283):

  2) The Infinitive with suffixes: לַמְשַׁבָּחוּתֵה, לְמַשְׁבָּחוּתֵה, etc. (Acur., p. 422):

C. In the numerals: תְּמָנַעְסַר, תְּמָנְיָא, תְּמָנֵא, תְּמָנֵעֶסְרֵא (Amira, p. 224), (idem, p. 226), תְּמָנִין (idem, p. 227), תְּמָנֵמָאא (idem, p. 228); תְּלָתִין, תְּלָתִינָיָא; תְּמָנִין, תְּמָנִינָיָא (idem, p. 233), תְּלָתֵיכוּן, etc. (id., p. 235).

III.

In the antipenultimate Syllable.

In the Noun:

  1. The emphatic form: פְּרוּקֵי, פְּרוּקָיָא (Amira, p. 148):

  2. The plural form

    a) of the masculines: שְׁמַיָּנָיָא, שְׁמַיָּנָיָא; עָרוּמֵא, עָרוּמָא (Amira, p. 76); גְּבוּלָא, גְּבוּלֵא (Acur., pp. 210, 250):

    b) of the feminines: כִּנְיָיתָא, כִּנְיָיתָא, etc. (Amira, p. 82); קָיֵמְתָא, קָיֵמְתָא, etc. (Amira, p. 88); גְּבוּלְתָא, גְּבוּלָתָא (Acur., pp. 210, 250); דִּיָנָתָא, דִּיָנוּתָא (Acur., p. 308):

  3. The movement of a noun [masculine to feminine]: רָחוּמְתָא, רָחוּמָא, etc. (Amira, p. 111); גְּבוּלְתָא, גְּבוּלָא (Acur., pp. 210, 250):

  4. The abstract form: גְּבוּלוּתָא from גְּבוּלָא (Acur., p. 210), שָׁלוּחוּתָא from שָׁלוּחָא (id., p. 250).

CXXXV.

To all of these are to be added the compound nouns סְיָמִידָא from סָיָם אִידָא (1 Tim. 4:14), לְעָלַמְעָלָמִין from לְעָלַם עָלְמִין (Rom. 16:27 [26]), and the construct noun לְשָׁוֹחַבְרֵה [sic] (Gen 11:7); as well as the prepositions חְלָף and קָדָם, which are properly nouns, and every time that they precede another noun are construct nouns, and so still retain the קמץ.

CXXXVI.

Following are all of the anomalies that I have been able to collect from the above-mentioned Grammars, that is to say, the Syriac forms in which the Zekofo proves mutable.

a) מְנָתָא, מְנַתָא, etc., regarding which see § 132.

b) חָתָא *sister*, plural אַחְוָתָא (Amira, p. 97). This is a true anomaly. The Hebrew אָחוֹת also loses its וֹ in the plural, becoming אֲחָיוֹת.

c) תְּלִיתָיָא from תְּלָתָא, תְּמִינָיָא from תְּמָנְיָא. These are anomalous. Likewise in Hebrew, one says from שְׁלֹשָׁה, שְׁלִישִׁי; from שְׁמֹנָה, שְׁמִינִי. However, it should be observed that while the Zekofo is lost, the primitive length of the syllable is preserved, with the addition of the Yod.

d) אֶשָׁתָא *fever*, plural אֶשְׁתְּוָתָא (Amira, p. 98). An anomaly. Perhaps the Zekofo was added to the שׁ because the word means *fever* and is not to be confused with אֶשְׁתָּא, which means *bottom, lowest part.*

e) אִיסְרָאִיל *Israel*, אִיסְרָלָיָא *Israelite* (Amira, p. 109). A simple anomaly in a foreign word.

f) From אָרָם *Syria*, אָרָמָיָא *Syrian*; but from אָרָם, the name of an ancient Gentile city, is made אַרְמָיָא: so Amira (p. 110), who I suspect is mistaken. The examples given by [Edmund] Castell, namely Gal. 2:3, 14, Acts 19:10, 17, demonstrate that the words אַרְמָיָא, אַרְמָאִית do not derive from the name of any city, but rather from the use of later [*seriore*] Hebrew, which usually called any gentile, by synecdoche, אֲרָמָאי *Aramean*. The Christian Syrians, wanting to distinguish the Arameans, or Syrians, from the Gentiles, or Idolaters, retained the ancient pronunciation where the word was used in its proper sense, meaning *Aramean, Syrian;* and where it was used in an improper sense, and meant *Gentile, Idolater*, they slightly altered the vowels, saying אַרְמָיָא, and hence the adverb אַרְמָאִית.

g) עַדְמָשׁ *hitherto,*[7] a form contracted from עַד הָשָׁא (Acur., p. 57), or perhaps rather from עַדְמָא לְהָשָׁא. One should note that הָשָׁא also is a compound word from הָא שָׁעָא, like Talmudic השתא, from הָא שָׁעְתָּא. Therefore in עַדְמָשׁ two Zekofos are lost, both primitively in simple [open] syllables, and thus mutable (§ 133), namely that of the Mem of מָא, and that of the He of הָא.

h) Amira (p. 154) attributes to some of the Syrians an irregular pronunciation, saying from עָלְמָא (1) not עָלַם, according to the rule, but rather עַלַם; a pronunciation, as he says, now in use, especially among the Maronites. Nevertheless, we have already seen (§ 135) that the form לְעָלְמָעָלְמִין was pointed by these same Maronites with Zekofo under the first ע.

(1) To understand this expression it is necessary to know that the Syrian Grammarians, as Hoffmann correctly observed (p. 258, Note 1), call simple, common, and genuine, that which we call the emphatic Form; calling then the contracted form that which we call absolute; that is to say, instead of regarding גְּבַר, for example, as a primitive form, and גַּבְרָא as an extended one, they hold this latter form to be primitive, and consider the former as if shortened from the latter. This manner of looking at things stems from the fact that the emphatic form is, among the Syrians, in greater use than the absolute; and it is generally a very common error to believe as primitive those things to which we are most accustomed.

CXXXVII.

The Biblical Chaldean offers several other anomalies, which certainly should be blamed on the incompetence of the Copyists. So in Daniel (2:32) we read דְּהַב with קמץ, a vowel which vanishes דַּהֲבָא. But we read דְּהַב with פתח in Dan. 3:1 and Ezra 7:15, 16; and so it is found pointed by the Syrians. Vice versa, in Daniel 4:33 we meet the noun יְקָר erroneously pointed with a פתח, but correctly pointed with a קמץ in verse 27 of the same chapter. In Ezra 7:18, שְׁאָר has פתח; but in nine other passages in

---

[7] This form is given as עֲדְמָשׁ in J. Payne Smith, ed., *A Compendious Syriac Dictionary* (Oxford, 1903) and C. Brockelmann, *Lexicon Syriacum* (2nd ed., Halle, 1928).

Daniel and Ezra it has קָמָץ.[8] Finding the emphatic forms יְקָרָא (Dan. 2:37, 5:18, 20), שְׁאָרָא (ib. 7:7, 19) with קָמָץ, a pointing confirmed by the use of the Syrians, we must regard as incorrect the construct forms שְׁאַר, יְקַר, with פַּתַח. Likewise the פַּתַח of שַׁעְתָּא (ibid 3:6, 15, 4:30, 5:5) must be considered incorrect, since we find שָׁעָה (ibid 4:16) with קָמָץ confirmed by the Syrians. In כַּהֲנָא, כַּהֲנַיָּא, כַּהֲנוֹהִי (many times in Ezra 6 and 7), קָמָץ should be substituted for פַּתַח, after some editions (e.g., that of [Jacob] Lombroso), also after the use of the Syrians, corroborated by the analogy of the Participles, which have in Hebrew חֹלֵם and in Aramaic קָמָץ (Heb. פֹּקֵד, Chald. פָּקֵד), and by the fact that in Hebrew the noun כֹּהֵן has the participial form. Likewise in בַּבְלָיֵא (Ezra 4:9), the first בּ is erroneously pointed with פַּתַח, the noun בָּבֶל having קָמָץ (Dan. 4:26, 27; Ezra 5:13).

Similar errors abound in the Targums, in which, for example, the noun סָהֲדוּתָא is consistently found with פַּתַח. In the Biblical [Hebrew] text, שָׂהֲדוּתָא (Gen. 31:47) and וְשָׂהֲדִי (Job 16:19) have קָמָץ. Of the great many anomalies met in the Targumic Chaldean, it is not worth making mention, given the very well-known inaccuracy and inconstancy of its pointing.

CXXXVIII.

In the passage of Aramaic words into Hebrew, the Aramaic קָמָץ, where it does not change to וֹ (§ 126 a), normally preserves its immutability, though not with the same constancy as in Aramaic.

CXXXIX.

Examples of the immutability of the Aramaic קָמָץ in Hebrew words are:

a) The nouns פִּתְגָם, שְׁאָר, כְּתָב, יְקָר, which preserve the קָמָץ in the construct state (1):

b) The nouns גָּלוּת, גָּלוּתִי (in Aramaic גָּלוּתָא, גְּלוֹ); שָׁבוּעַ, שָׁבוּעוֹת (in Syriac שְׁבוּעָא); בָּגוֹדָה (from the Chaldean form כָּרוֹזָא):

c) The words מַלָּחֵיהֶם, אִכָּרֵיכֶם, חָרָשֵׁי, from the Aramaic form דַּיָּנָא; and מַעֲבָדֵיהֶם from the Chaldean מַעֲבָדָא מַעֲבָּדוֹהִי) Dan. 4:34).[9] The noun

---

[8] In the Leningrad Codex, this word is found with קָמָץ in 7:18 as well.

[9] The Leningrad Codex has in Dan. 4:34 מַעֲבָדוֹהִי.

תּוֹשָׁב has in the construct תּוֹשַׁב with פתח, but in the plural תּוֹשָׁבֵי. Syriac has (in the Lexicon of [Edmund] Castell) both the forms תַּוְתָּבָא and תַּוְתָּבָא:

d) The nouns הַכָּרָה, אַזְכָּרָה, נֶחָמָה, נֶאָצָה, בַּקָּשָׁה (derived from the Aramaic Infinitives אִקְטָלָה, קַטָלָה), preserving the קמץ in בַּקָּשָׁתִי, הַכָּרַת, אַזְכָּרָתָה, נֶחָמָתִי, נַאֲצוֹתֶיךָ.

(1) Thus it is evident that we should say כְּתָבֵי, כְּתָבֵיכֶם, כְּתָבֵיכֶם, and not כְּתָבֵי, כְּתָבֵיכֶם. Likewise, from Rabbinic שְׁטָר (taken from Syriac שְׁטָרָא) one says שְׁטָרֵי, not שְׁטָרֵי. This renders less probable the opinion of J. D. Michaëlis (Lex. Syr., p. 55), who derives the name *Estrangelo* from שְׁטָר אַנְגִיל *writing of the Gospel;* since the ט, having Zekofo, cannot be left without a vowel, as happens in אֶסְטְרַנְגְּלָא. In addition, שְׁטָר signifies rather *a writ, a book* (as Amira, p. 28, interprets it), and never *a manner of writing, an alphabet.* If the interpretation of Michaëlis regarding the second part of the word Estrangelo is to be accepted (which is doubtful), I would prefer to regard to first part rather as a metathesis of סְרְטָא *line, letter.*

CXL.

Since, however, the Hebrews usually changed Aramaic קמץ into וֹ, so that the primitive קמץ became rare, and the Hebrew קמץ, unlike the Aramaic, was very frequently mutable: it happened that the Hebrews, confusing the diverse nature of the two קמץ, sometimes robbed the Aramaic קמץ of its immutability and indestructibility. Examples of this are:

a) the nouns חָרָשׁ and דָּיָן changing the קמץ into פתח in the construct state; and קָרְבָּן which has the construct form קָרְבַּן, and in the plural with suffixes קָרְבְּנֵיהֶם:

b) אָרָם instead of the Syriac אָרָם, and אֲרָמִי instead of אָרָמִי. It is notable that in the feminine one says אֲרָמִית, with kamets under the ר. So also פַּדַּן אֲרָם, instead of פַּדַּן, from Syriac פַּדְנָא:

c) the noun חֲנָיוֹת, instead of חָנָיוֹת, from Syriac חָנוּתָא:

d) the noun הִתְחַבְּרוּת, derived from the Chaldean Infinitive construct הִתְנַדְּבוּת, הִתְקַטְּלוּת:

e) the noun יְרִיעָה, in Syriac יְרִיעָא:

f) the verbs with a quiescent second radical, changing the קמץ into פתח in קָמְנוּ, קַמְתֶּם, קַמְתִּי, קַמְתָּ, and the like, instead of קָמְתָּ, etc., as in

Biblical Chaldean שָׂמְתָ (Dan. 3:10), and as the Syrian Grammarians have (§ 134 I.B.1).

CXLI.

Johann David Michaëlis, in § 22 of the Appendix added to his Hebrew Grammar, believed to be able to explain the immutability of the kamets of § 139, making recourse to the Arabic language, asserting that such kametses supposed a following quiescent Alef, which in the corresponding Arabic words is actually written, and that those kametses owed their immutability to such an Alef. Since the Arab Grammarians called *impure* those vowels that are followed by a quiescent letter, he gave the denomination *impure Kamets* to such kametses. This doctrine was followed by Gesenius and other notable Orientalists.

Regarding this doctrine, I counter:

a) that the addition of an Alef after the kamets to indicate length, though maybe very common in Arabic, is almost unknown in Hebrew, the only example of it being צַוָּאר, and the words of irregular orthography רֹאשׁ, וְקָאם, הַשָּׁאטִים (1):

b) that in the one word in which Alef appears constantly in Hebrew, namely the noun צַוָּאר, the kamets is not immutable, the form of the construct singular being צַוַּאר, and in the plural צַוְּארֵי (2):

c) that also in Arabic the impure Fatḥa is far from immutable, since in the Verbs we find כֻּנְתְּ, כֻּנְתָּ, etc., from כַּאן, where the Elif is lost throughout the conjugation, as happens in all those with a quiescent second radical; and in the Nouns, the forms פֶּעָאל and פַעָאל make a plural פֻּעֻל; the form פַאעֶל makes פַעֲלָת, פֻּעוּל, and פֻּעְלָאן; and the form פֻּעָאל, and sometimes also the פַעָאל, make a plural פֶּעְלָאן.[10]

---

[10] It seems worthwhile to rewrite this section on nouns using Roman transcription: "the forms *fiʿāl* and *faʿāl* make a plural *fuʿul*; the form *fāʿil* makes *faʿalat*, *fuʿūl*, and *fuʿlān*; and the form *fuʿāl*, and sometimes also *faʿāl*, make a plural *fiʿlān*." Examples are *kitāb-kutub* 'book', *sayāl-suyul* 'mimosa tree', *kāfir-kafarat* 'unbeliever', *šāhid-šuhūd* 'witness', *rākib-rukbān* 'rider', *ǧulām-ǧilmān* 'boy', *ǧazāl-ǧizlān* 'gazelle'.

(1) Regarding such an orthography, Roorda (Vol. 1, p. 11) said: Verum haec scribendi quaedam negligentia potius, quam consuetudo, appellanda est.[11]

(2) The Kamets of צַוָּאר is mutable, since it is not Aramaic, there being in Daniel (5:7, 16, 29) צַוְּארָךְ, צַוְּארֵה, and in Syriac צַוְרָא. Probably the א was added to this noun, if only with the object of making it distinguishable from צוּר.[12]

    I do not speak of the noun מְלָאכָה, since the Alef is not originally quiescent here, the primitive form of it being מְלָאכָה. In every form, the Kamets, despite the Alef, is mutable (מְלַאכְתּוֹ, מְלֶאכֶת). Likewise, the Kamets disappears in מַלְכֵי, דָּגִי, although, by an irregularity of orthography, we meet דָּאג (Nehem. 13:16), הַמְּלָאכִים (2 Sam. 40:1),[13] with quiescent Alef.

---

[11] "In truth, this should rather be called a certain negligence of writing, as is the custom." (translation Philip Baldi.) SDL is quoting from Roorda's *Grammatica hebraea* (Leiden, 1831–33).

[12] The second paragraph of this note did not appear here in the Italian edition, but rather at the end of the book (p. 204), as an addendum, with the heading "Addition to Note 2, page 151". It was presumably added just prior to publication.

[13] The Leningrad Codex reads הַמַּלְאָכִים here, but notes that very many manuscripts have the reading given by SDL.

APPENDIX III.

Origins of some inconstancies particular to the Grammar of Hebrew.

CXLII.

Hebrew Grammar is not, strictly speaking, the theory of the Hebrew Language which was spoken by the ancient Hebrews, and which was written by the Biblical Authors; but it is the Grammar of the scriptural books, as they were read and chanted by the ancient Hebrew Scholars living during the time of the second Temple.

CXLIII.

These Scholars, whose names and dates are uncertain, and who were, after the return from the Babylonian emigration, the founders of Judaism, fixed the Canon of the sacred Books, and, together with it (by means of verbal instruction), the reading and chanting thereof, for use especially in public recitations in the Houses of Prayer (1).

(1)   These Scholars are known under the title of Soferim (סֹפְרִים) *Scholars, Literate Men*. Their ritual institutions bear the name *Divrè Soferìm* (דִּבְרֵי סֹפְרִים), and the reading taught by them is called *Mikrà Soferìm* (מִקְרָא סֹפְרִים).

CXLIV.

The reading of the Hebrew Text, as it was fixed by these Scholars, was undoubtedly in substantial conformity with the ancient manner of pronouncing Hebrew in the times of the Biblical Authors (1); it contains, however, several things which were instituted by these Scholars. Such are:

a) the pronunciation of the tetragrammaton, changed to אֲדֹנָי (2):

b) the pronunciation of the verb שָׁגַל, and of the words עפלים, שיניהם, חראיהם, changed via euphemism to שָׁכַב, טְהֹרִים, צוֹאָתָם, מֵימֵי רַגְלֵיהֶם:

c) the pronunciation of many other words slightly modified, so that

1) the antiquated pronunciation no longer in use was substituted by the one in use; e.g., the forms הוּא and נַעַר changed in the feminine to הִיא and נַעֲרָה (§ 70, Note); יְרוּשָׁלֵם changed to יְרוּשָׁלַיִם; אַתִּי, נָתַתִּי, and other

second person feminine singulars (as the Syrians write), changed to אַתְּ, נָתַתְּ (as the Syrians also pronounce):

2) several anomalies in use by the sacred Writers conformed to the laws of the language; e.g., בַּאַוַּת נַפְשׁוֹ שָׁאֲפָה רוּחַ (Jer. 2:24) changed to נַפְשָׁהּ:

3) various apparent or real errors of the copyists were emended; e.g., several לֹא changed into לוֹ. All these modifications in the reading of the sacred Text were made by means of verbal teaching, without ever touching (as the Samaritans did) the Text itself. The lection of the Text is called כְּתִיב *the written*, and the lection instituted by the Scholars is called קְרִי *that which is read* (3).

d) the pronunciation of many syllables, modified

1. due to the chanting, e.g., מִקְּדָשׁ [Exod. 15:17], הַצְּפִינוֹ [Exod. 2:3],[14] where the euphonic דגשׁ increases by a half syllable these two words carrying accents of long chanting, and renders them all the more chantable:

2. to prevent the elision of certain letters, as happens with the advanced accent of סוּרָה אֲדֹנִי סוּרָה אֵלַי [Judg. 4:18], and the like; the recession of the accent, rendered incomplete by a half accent added at the end, e.g., וַיֹּצֵא צִיץ [Num. 17:23], הֲשָׁמַע עָם [Deut. 4:33], שָׁלַח חֹשֶׁךְ [Psa. 105:28]; and finally, the irregular changing of vowels, e.g., בְּכָתֵף פְּלִשְׁתִּים [Isa. 11:14] instead of בְּכְתֵף (see [David Kimḥi's] Michlol, fol. 203), חָצֵב בּוֹ [Isa. 5:2] instead of חָצַב בּוֹ:

3. for strength and emphasis, e.g., the דגשׁ of וַיֹּאמְרוּ לֹא, קוּמוּ צְאוּ (§ 197); as well as the שׁורק of תְּהֹמֹת יְכַסְיֻמוּ, which forms an Onomatopoeia, representing the falling into a deep, dark abyss:

4. to remove any cacophony, e.g., the דגשׁ of גָּאֹה גָּאָה (4), כַּדְכֹד, כַּלְכֵל, aiming to avoid the repetition of the same sounds; as well as that of מִי כָמֹכָה, to avoid the succession of the sounds מִיכָה מִכָּה (5):

5. to remove any sound capable of producing any indecency or scandal. Thus the כ of יִדְמוּ כָּאָבֶן received a dagesh, so that these two words would not produce, as [Jedidiah] Norzi notes [in *Minḥat Shai*], the sound יִדְמוּךָ אָבֶן, *stones are similar to you*. Perhaps belonging here is the form הַצְלִיחָה, normally stressed on the penult, but stressed on the ultima in הַצְלִיחָה נָא (Psalm 118:25); since הַצְלִיחָה נָא would have produced a

---

[14] The Leningrad Codex reads here הַצְּפִינוֹ.

sound confusable with the woman's name חַנָּה. In more modern times, some think that the פ of פִּי יְ [Deut. 8:3] should have a dagesh, on the grounds that *Fi* is, in French, an Interjection indicating contempt and abhorrence. See Norzi at Deut. 8:3.

It is on the same principle that the pronunciation of the Tetragrammaton was changed to אֱלֹהִים instead of אֲדֹנָי, whenever it appeared next to the latter Name, since there would have been an immediate repetition of the same Epithet, a repetition that, not being a vocative, would have seemed indecent to the audience.

(1) See Gesenius, *Geschichte*, pp. 211–218. The Talmudist Rabbi Isaac (Nedarim, fol. 37) takes the Mikra Soferim as far back as Moses.

(2) Ibn Ezra (Exodus 3:15) says: "Moses pronounced the name of God as it is written, since he was holy; so the ancients have had to substitute an epithet," i.e., they had to substitute *the Lord* for the name of God; so that the sacred name was not profaned, by being irreverently spoken by the most unworthy people, specifically, those who very often, swearing and blaspheming, call on the supreme Being.

(3) The Grammarians and the Critics wrote *Keri*, which is an erroneous pronunciation. קְרִי or קֱרִ, from Ezra (4:18, 23) is a third person Preterite passive קְטִיל (§ 125, Note 2). However, the passive Participle of verbs with a quiescent third radical have not חירק, but צרי; for example, בְּנֵה (Ezra 5:11) *built*, שְׁרָא (Daniel 2:23 [2:22]) *settled* (שָׁרוּי of the Rabbis), חֲזֵה (Dan. 3:19) *fitting* (= רָאוּי). The plural then of קְרִי is in the masculine קְרָיִן, like שָׁרָיִן (Daniel 3:25), and in the feminine קָרְיָן, not קְרְיָן as [Johann] Simonis writes in the title of his opuscule *Analysis et explicatio lectionum Masorethicarum Kethibhan et Krijan vulgo dictarum* (3rd ed., Halle, 1824).

(4) So [Solomon ibn] Parḥon (in Heidenheim, משפטי הטעמים, fol. 41),

ושינו עוד ואמרו כי גאה גאה. משפטו גאה גאה, אבל לא רצו
להשים שניהם ממין אחד, שמא תתגנה המלה, לפיכך דגשו השניה

that is: They have changed גָּאֹה גָּאָה, where the [second] Gimel should have rafe; but not wanting to make them both of the same type, lest the words produce an indecent sound, they have added dagesh to the second.

(5) The first מִי כָמֹכָה of this text (Exodus 15:11) does not have dagesh: these two words being repeated rather soon after, it would cause cacophony if the כ had dagesh or rafe in both instances.

CXLV.

It is difficult, perhaps impossible, to determine which things [originally] belonged to the language, and which were institutions by the Scholars. There can be doubt, for example, with regard to the change of vowels in pause, a change unknown to kindred languages, and to the ancient interpreters. The double pronunciation of the letters בגד כפת is surely not an invention of the Scholars, being common also to Syriac; but it may have been unknown to the ancient Israelites, and introduced after the Hebrews (and the Syrians) had developed relations with the Greeks and learned their language. The letters בגד כפת produce the mediae [voiced stops] (B, Γ, Δ), the tenues [voiceless stops] (Π, K, T), and the aspirates [fricatives] (Φ, X, Θ) of the Greeks. However, the claim of Ewald, that this double pronunciation was unknown even to the Pointers, is an absurd hypothesis; it is equally absurd to agree with this author ([*Kritische Grammatik*,] page 84) that the Syrian Grammarians introduced this double pronunciation after taking it from Hebrew Grammar.

CXLVI.

The reading fixed several centuries before the vulgar Era by the ancient Scholars called Soferim, and handed down traditionally from century to century, that is, via oral teaching, until the time of the Pointers [*Puntatori*] (בעלי הנקוד) living in the sixth century of the vulgar Era, was by these latter men newly and more stably fixed, by putting it in writing via the invention of the vowel Points and Accents. The Pointers followed the Soferim faithfully, even adopting all of the modifications that they had introduced into the reading of the sacred Text. The reading adopted by the Pointers necessarily formed the basis of Hebrew Grammar, which, if it wanted to free itself [from the reading tradition], would become a completely arbitrary and uncertain discipline.

CXLVII.

The Punctuators [*Punteggiatori*], namely, the Nakdanim (נַקְדָּנִים), men educated in Hebrew Grammar, whose profession was the punctuating of Bible manuscripts that were written by the calligraphers (the modern Soferim) without vowel points or accents; as well as the correction of

Bibles already pointed; introduced in the Pointing some minor novelties, aiming to facilitate correct pronunciation for less learned readers. They increased the [number of] compound Schwas and semi-accents [*methegs*]; they added some unusual דגש (§§ 163, 194–200); they duplicated, in words with penultimate stress, the accents of fixed position (§ 190); and they introduced into the reading other slight modifications of a similar type; all of these things are to be distinguished by the name *Secondary Pointing*, as opposed to the *Primary Pointing*, which was the work of the Pointers. The Punctuators, or Nakdanim, lived from about one thousand to the year fourteen hundred of the vulgar Era. The first and the most famous of these were Ben-Asher and Ben-Naphtali. The things belonging to the Punctuators are recognizable by the discrepancies present among them in the codices and editions.

CXLVIII.

The discrepant opinions of the Punctuators are the true reason for many anomalies that are encountered in the sacred Text, insofar as the more modern Punctuators, and the editors of printed Bibles, have carelessly followed sometimes one, sometimes another of the different systems of the Nakdanim; as a result, their punctuation proves in many places unstable and inconsistent. The words בִּיקְרוֹתָיִךְ [Psalm 45:10],[15] כִּיתְרוֹן [Ecc. 2:13] can serve as examples of this (§ 199).

---

[15] In the Leningrad Codex, this word is pointed as בִּיקְרוֹתָיִךְ.

APPENDIX IV.

On Hebrew and Aramaic vowels.

I.

HEBREW VOWELS.

CXLIX.

The Hebrew Pointers instituted seven vowel signs, which the ancient Grammarians called שִׁבְעָה מְלָכִים, and which are contained in the two mnemonic words וַיֹּאמֶר אֵלְיָהוּ. The Kibbuts is not to be regarded as an eighth vowel, since it is only a substitute for the Shurek, where the Vav is missing; the same word can have שׁוּרק or קבוּץ, depending on whether or not it has the Vav; e.g., יְשׁוּבוּן, יְשֻׁבוּן (see § 166).

CL.

As for the sounds of these seven vowels, five of these are known well enough: there is no doubt that פתח is sounded *A*; צֵרי *E*; חירק *I*; חלם *O*, שׁוּרק and קבוּץ *U*. Less certain are the sounds of סגול and קמץ.

CLI.

I attribute to סגול the sound of open *E*, and to צרי that of closed *E*; and this observing that

a) the צרי often times stems from חירק, e.g., פְּלֵטִים, פָּלִיט; נֵפֶן, תֵּפֶן, from נִפְנֶה, תִּפְנֶה; and the סגול from פתח, e.g., הֶחָכָם for הַחָכָם; יֶגֶל for יָגֶלה; יֶחֱזֵאל for יְחֶזְקֵאל; אֶכֶלְךָ for אַכֶלְךָ; יֶדְכֶם for יָדְכֶם;

b) the צרי often changes into חירק, e.g., נֵדֶר, נִדְרִי; and the סגול into פתח, e.g., מֶלֶךְ, מַלְכִּי; and into קמץ, as happens in pause, e.g., גֶּפֶן, גָּפֶן.

c) the guttural letters, which attract broad [*larghi*] sounds, often assume a seghol in the declension of nouns; e.g., עֶזְרָה, חֶדְוָה, חֶלְקִי.

To this it can be added that the ancient Grammarians called the Seghol little Patah; and that [Abraham de] Balmes says that Seghol is pronounced by dilating the extremity of the lips, and the Tsere by pressing them together.

CLII.

This judgment will be contested by the Schultensian Grammarians, saying that it is not probable that we should assign an open sound for the vowel which so very often is furtive, that is, which is added to primitively unvocalized letters, as happens in all of the segholate forms; e.g., in גֶּבֶר, originally גִּבְרְ. However, we have already seen (§ 121 *b*) that I give to the segholate forms an altogether different origin than that which Schultens attributes to them. This objection is therefore of no force against my opinion.

CLIII.

To the Seghol that Schultens calls furtive, I give a three-fold origin. These are:

a) a Seghol that regresses (by the law of § 107), with the loss of final He, from the second radical to the first; e.g., יִפֶן from יִפְנֶה:

b) a transformation of primitive פתח; e.g., גֶּבֶר from גָּבַר, מִשְׁמֶרֶת from מִשְׁמָרַת. Specifically, by moving the accent from the ultima to the penult, גָּבַר became גָּבַר, and מִשְׁמָרַת מִשְׁמֶרַת; then both of the פתח were changed into the kindred vowel סגול. Relics of these forms גֶּבַר and מִשְׁמֶרַת are preserved in the Targumic Chaldean, where the form קְטַלַת instead of קְטִלַת is very common (see Buxtorf, *Gram. chald. et syr.*, Book I, chap. 7), a form which is still familiar to the Hebrews in the reading of the Talmud, and from which is also derived the form קְטֶלַת of the Biblical Chaldean (§ 121 *b*):

c) a transformation of the non-primitive פתח, in the form קֹדֶשׁ, which was primitively pronounced קָדְשׁ, passing first into קֹדְשׁ, then into קֹדֶשׁ. Vestiges of this פתח are also found in the Targumic Chaldean, which has קָדַשׁ, כּוֹתַל, קְטוֹרֶת, and the like, with the accent on the penultimate syllable and פתח in the ultima, as we read in the very accurate Targum of the Pentateuch of Sabbionetta from 1557.[16]

---

[16] This edition of Targum Onkelos was until the mid-twentieth century

CLIV.

The genuine sound of קָמֵץ has long been lost. The [Syriac] Zekofo (זְקָפָא), the vowel corresponding to קָמֵץ, is pronounced *A* by the eastern Syrians, *O* by the western. The northern [*settentrionali*] Hebrews (German and Polish) pronounce it *O*; the southern ones [*meridionali*], when it is accented or in a simple [open] syllable, pronounce it *A*; in unaccented mixed [closed] syllables, they give it the sound *O*.

CLV.

Being extremely unlikely that the Hebrew Pointers, who took such care to avoid all ambiguities in the reading of the sacred Codices, to the point of greatly abounding in signs for vowels and semi-vowels, would institute a sign that had to represent in some cases *A*, and in other cases *O*; several philologists have judged the קָמֵץ to have been intended by the Pointers to represent exclusively the vowel *O*; an opinion strengthened by the name of קָמֵץ itself, which in Chaldaic means *closing*, *pressing*, as opposed to פתח, which means *opening*. So Jean Morin (*Exercitationes biblicae*, p. 543)[17] and Gesenius (*Hebr. Gram.* 1834 [11th ed.], p. 26).

CLVI.

This opinion is demonstrated to be false by the following argument. The final guttural letters, which are preceded by one of the four vowels E, I, O, U, consistently assume a furtive פתח, which is omitted where the gutturals are preceded by the vowel A. But the gutturals preceded by קָמֵץ never have furtive פתח; e.g., מִזְרָח, מַדָּע. Therefore such a קָמֵץ (namely, that of an

---

considered to be the most accurate in print. It was reprinted with annotations by A. Berliner (Berlin, 1884; itself reprinted in Jerusalem, 1974). The best printed edition of Targum Onkelos is now that of A. Sperber, *The Bible in Aramaic*, vol. 1 (Leiden, 1959; reprints 1992, 2004).

[17] *Exercitationes biblicae de hebraici graecique textus sinceritate* (Paris, 1633). A second edition (1669) went under the title *Exercitationes ecclesiasticae et biblicae*, as did a reprint (1686), which included an earlier work.

accented syllable) must be sounded A, not O: otherwise it would be followed by a furtive פתח (1).

(1)   This reasoning is from Mr. Samuel Vita Lo-ly [Lolli] (see § 42).

CLVII.

Others consider the קמץ to have the sound of A mixed with O (so [Sebastian] Münster, *Opus gram. cons.*, p. 2, and [David] Kyber,[18] p. 21), or to be something in between A and O (so [Johannes] Reuchlin, p. 9,[19] and [Francesco Mario di] Calasio,[20] p. 19). This hypothesis, however, does not explain why the קמץ forms a long syllable (§ 105 *a*) and is immutable (§§ 133–135).

CLVIII.

Finally, still others regard the קמץ as a compound vowel, or diphthong, the components of which are A and O. Ibn Ezra (at the beginning of צחות) says that the sound of קמץ is a compound of those of חלם and פתח, and therefore its shape (ָ, in some manuscripts and ancient editions ָ) is taken from the forms of these two vowels.

[Abraham de] Balmes says simply that the קמץ is pronounced OA;[21] and more clearly, the author of שיח יצחק (fol. 9) says:[22] ומה שאמרנו למעלה שהקמץ מורכבת מחולם ומפתח. היינו שהקמץ נקראת תחלה חולם ואחר כך פתח. i.e., "That which we have said above, that the Kamets is compounded from Ḥolem and Pataḥ, should be understood to mean that the Kamets is pronounced first Ḥolem, then Pataḥ." This same

---

[18] *Yesod Ha-Dikduk, De re grammatica hebraeae linguae* (Basel, 1552).

[19] *De Rudimentis Hebraicis* (Pforzheim, 1506).

[20] *Canones generales linguae sanctae* (Rome, 1616).

[21] *Mikne Avram* (Venice, 1523).

[22] Isaac ben Samuel ha-Levi, *Siaḥ Yitsḥak* (Prague, 1627/8).

double sound OA is attributed to the Kamets by [Alhardt] de Raadt.[23] Gennaro Sisti, on the other hand (pp. 69–72), reads the Kamets AO.[24]

CLIX.

This opinion, that the sound of Kamets contains both the vowels A and O, will be perceived as probable, considering that it

a) explains why the קמץ forms a long syllable (§ 105 *a*):

b) explains why the קמץ of Aramaic words changes to וֹ in the corresponding Hebrew words (§ 126 *a*):

c) explains the origin of the variant pronunciations of קמץ among the eastern and western Syrians, and among the northern and southern Hebrews; since the Kamets originally contained in itself the two sounds A and O, and this compound vowel produced (in its very frequent appearance in Hebrew and Syriac words) a tiresome and unrewarding pronunciation, it came to be separated into its elements, so that some pronounced it *A*, and others *O*.

Between the two diphthongs *AO* and *OA*, I am inclined to attribute to קמץ [the sound of] the latter, but accented on the second vowel: OÀ. This hypothesis explains why the קמץ is not followed by furtive פתח (§ 156), and accounts for the origin of קמץ חטוף (§ 161).

CLX.

The קמץ is divided into Aramaic, or primitive, and Hebrew, or supplementary, which was in origin שוא or פתח (§ 121 *a*, *c*). Both of these types of קמץ are included under the denomination of wide קמץ (רָחָב), since in both cases the קמץ is pronounced *A* by the southern Hebrews.

CLXI.

Hebrew, which likes to abound in vowel sounds (§ 120), instead of O and U, often times pronounced OÀ; that is to say, that where there was חלם,

---

[23] *Sugiat ha-Nikud, hoc est De Punctationis hebraicae natura Commentarius* (Leiden, 1671).

[24] *Lingua santa da apprendersi anche in quattro lezioni* (Venice, 1747).

שורק or קבוץ, they sometimes substituted קמץ; e.g., from *gòdel* (גֹּדֶל), instead of saying *gudlò* (גֻּדְלֹו), they sometimes said *guadlò, goadlò*, that is, גֻּדְלֹו.

CLXII.

Such an expansion of the sounds *O, U*, did not occur in simple [open] syllables, nor in accented mixed [closed] syllables; since the vowel in such syllables, being naturally somewhat long, does not easily permit an alteration such as the addition of an *A*. Hence it is that this קמץ does not occur except in mixed [closed] unaccented syllables.

CLXIII.

Such a קמץ as the one that was originally *O* or *U*, was also pronounced *O* by the southern Hebrews. With the purpose of distinguishing it from wide קמץ (§ 160), the Punctuators usually added a שוא to the right of it (חֶכְמָה), giving to it the form of a rapid קמץ, or a semi-vowel, called קמץ חטוף. So a single name, חטוף קמץ or קמץ חטוף, was applied indiscriminately to the semi-vowel קמץ, deriving from שוא, and to the vowel קמץ, deriving from *O* or *U*, to which the denomination חטוף *stolen* or *rapid* was not at all fitting. Later the ambiguity was removed, the name קמץ חטוף remaining for the semi-vowel קמץ, and giving the name קמץ חטוף (1) to the vowel קמץ, an improper denomination, which was preserved even after they stopped writing חָכְמָה and the like with [both] שוא and קמץ.

(1)   This distinct nomenclature, used indiscriminately by the earlier Grammarians, was used consistently by Elijah Levita, followed by all subsequent Grammarians.

CLXIV.

The קמץ חטוף is peculiar to Hebrew; the Syrians preserve the primitive *U*, e.g., תּוּקְפָא, קוּדְשָׁא; or make use of another vowel, e.g., חֶכְמְתָא. The קמץ חטוף of Biblical Chaldean are all Hebraisms. They are in fact rare in the Targumic Chaldean, which have instead, e.g., against חָכְמָה and שָׂכְלְתָנוּ in Daniel [1:4, 5:11], (in the manuscripts and ancient editions) חוּכְמָה and סוּכְלְתָנוּ (see, e.g., Deut. 4:6).

CLXV.

Neither Aramaic, nor Hebrew recognizes a division between long and short vowels; but rather a distinction between long and short syllables. No single vowel constitutes a long or short syllable; but rather the presence or absence of quiescent letters. The קמץ is excepted, which in Aramaic forms a long syllable, since the קמץ is not a vowel, but a diphthong.

CLXVI.

Vowels occur without distinction in both long and short syllables. The פתח is to be excepted, which does not tolerate a following quiescent letter, since every time A is in a long syllable, it becomes $O\hat{A}$, and the פתח is changed to קמץ; e.g., בָּנָה, which is the same form as פָּקַד (1). The שורק and the קבוץ, the first of which does not appear in short syllables, and the second of which does not appear in long syllables, are not two [different] vowels, but rather two signs for the same vowel (§ 149). The Pointers would have been able to always mark the vowel U under the consonant, a quiescent Vav following it or not; precisely as they always marked the I in a single manner, a Yod following or not. Except that possibly wanting to reduce the confusion produced by the already too numerous interlinear signs, they took advantage of the small space that the body of the Vav offered them, and inserted into it the שורק; decreasing in this way the multitude of points under the letters. They did not do the same thing with the Yod, given the extreme smallness of this letter, in which for necessity alone did they insert the דגש.

(1) The He that follows the פתח in מַה־טֹּבוּ [Num. 24:5] and the like is not quiescent, but otiose.

CLXVII.

Some Grammarians, attempting to assign fixed rules regarding the קמץ רחב and חטוף, and the mobile or mute שוא, observed that

a) קמץ is read רחב in all simple [open] syllables, and in all accented syllables; and vice versa, the חטוף in all mixed [closed] unaccented syllables:

b) שוא is mobile after חלם, צרי, קמץ רחב, unaccented, שורק, and חירק followed by Yod; and, vice versa, it is mute after סגול, פתח, קמץ חטוף, and usually also after קבוץ, and חירק not followed by Yod.

These two assertions are then followed by a third, which is

The שורק, חלם, צרי, קמץ רחב, and חירק followed by Yod are not met in mixed [closed] unaccented syllables; and vice versa

The קבוץ, קמץ חטוף, סגול, פתח, and חירק not followed by Yod, when they are not accented, are usually found in mixed syllables.

And so the vowels are divided into two classes, which are distinguished by the names of greater (גְּדֹלוֹת) and lesser (קְטַנּוֹת), or long and short.

CLXVIII.

There is nothing to oppose the property of long vowels. As for that of the short vowels, one can counter with the many cases in which חירק not followed by Yod, and קבוץ, have the property of long vowels.

On the other hand, if the Pointers had thought of such a division of the vowels,

a) they would never have put צרי in the Chaldaic forms שְׁאֶלְתָּא, שֵׁשְׁבַּצַּר, בֵּלְטְשַׁאצַּר, and סֶגוֹל in the first radical of the Hebrew names יְבֶרֶכְיָהוּ, מְשֶׁלֶמְיָה, שֶׁלֶמְיָהוּ:

b) they would not have put קבוץ in וְיַעְזְרֶכֶם and the like, where the syllable is simple [open]; but they would have adopted another sign for defective שורק (that is, without quiescent Vav), and not have had a single sign common to the long and short vowels:

c) they would have instituted two different signs for long and short חירק:

d) they would have distinguished with the two different signs the חטוף קמץ רחב and.

CLXIX.

Even though the division of the vowels into long and short is certainly not in accordance with the mentality of the Pointers, nor with the ancient manner of Hebrew pronunciation, and even though it allows some exceptions; it can not be denied that

a) it facilitates the teaching of the rules of reading, according to our current pronunciation:

b) it abbreviates the expression of several rules concerning the changing of vowels.

The customary division can therefore be retained, provided that it is regarded as a convenient method of expression, and not as a principle or fundamental of the science.

CLXX.

[Jacob] Alting maintained that every syllable had to contain, in addition to the consonant with which it begins, an entire *mora*, that is, two measures. A long vowel is of two measures, a short, of one measure only. Hence the measure, or half mora, that a short vowel lacks, is compensated for in various ways, the vowel being followed

a) by an expressed consonant, e.g., מִן:

b) an implicit consonant, compensated by דגשׁ, e.g., וַתִּקַּח:

c) by an implicit consonant, not compensated by דגשׁ, e.g., אָחָד:

d) by a quiescent letter, e.g., עָשָׂה:

e) by an accent, e.g., דְּשָׁא :

f) by a semi-accent [*metheg*], e.g., נַעֲשָׂה:

[Johann] Dantz accorded a measure to every consonant as well, and therefore gave three measures to every syllable. The syllable פָּ, for example, has three measures, one of the consonant and two of the long vowel. The syllable קַד in the same manner has three, two of the two consonants, and one of the short vowel. However, two consonants before the vowel, e.g., פְּקֹד, only have a single measure.

This system offers false hope to students, teaching in letter *c* that the measure that is lacking for short vowels can be compensated by a non-existent consonant, which is not even indicated by דגשׁ; this is like saying that the measure that is never supposed to be lacking, is lacking completely in אָחָד, מַהֵר, שָׁחֵת, יְרְחַם, and so on.

It would have been better to allow an exception. But this allowed, the system falls apart. If it was important to the Language or to the Pointers that the two (or three) measures were not lacking, why did they not point יְרְחַם, שָׁחֵת, מָהֵר, אֶחָד, with a long vowel?

Still more peculiar is the opinion of Dantz, who attributes equal measure to קַד and פְּקֹד, that is to say, to a single consonant, and to two consonants separated by Schwa mobile.

If any truth still looms in the Altingian system, it comes from the law, not of Hebrew, but of Aramaic (§ 108), which desires, as much as possible, the elimination of unaccented tenuous syllables; a law, however, which does not suppose any division between long and short vowels, but only that distinction which is between the simple vowels and the קמץ, which is a compound vowel or diphthong.

CLXXI.

Dividing the vowels (as is done by several modern [scholars]) into three classes, according to the three elements of Ibn Ezra and the three vowels of the Arabs (§ 7, Note 1), is completely useless; such a division is certainly not provided in the system of Hebrew Pointing, on which all of Hebrew Grammar must necessarily be based (§§ 142, 146) (1).

(1)   The doctrine of the three classes of vowels is adduced by Gesenius (*Hebr. Gramm.*, 1834, p. 32) to account for the three חטפים. However, it is not sufficient to give special attention to the vowels that were chosen to form the Ḥatefim. This is because if חטף פתח corresponds to the *Fatḥa* of the Arabs and חטף קמץ to the *Damma*, then the *Kasra* should correspond to a חטף צרי, not to חטף סגול; since צרי is the vowel fundamentally analogous to *Kasra*, while סגול most often corresponds to *Fatḥa*. This same ambiguous nature that can be attributed to *Seghol* (making it correspond usually to *Fatḥa*, and sometimes to *Kasra*) is also proof that the three-way division of the vowels was never contemplated by the Institutors of the Hebrew Pointing: and it proves at the same time that the Hebrew Pointing was not instituted in imitation of the Arabic.—On the other hand, the reason why the חטפים were formed only from פתח, קמץ, and סגול, seems to me very simple. The חטפים being essentially intended to ease [*dilatare*] the pronunciation of the guttural letters, it was natural that they were taken from the most open vowels, which are פתח (*A*), סגול (open *E*), and קמץ (*OÀ*), rather than from the vowels *I* and *U*, naturally closed, צרי (closed *E*), or חלם, which is a less open sound than that of קמץ.[25]

---

[25] This entire note did not appear in the main body of text in the Italian edition, but rather after it (p. 204), as an addendum, with the heading "Note to § 171". It was presumably added just prior to publication.

II.

ARAMAIC VOWELS.

CLXXII.

It is probable that the ancient Arameans had the same number [of vowels], and the same vowels that the Hebrews have, excepting the קָמֵץ חַטוּף (§ 164), which, however, did not have a particular sound, distinct from that of the קָמֵץ רחב. The ancient Arameans most probably did not have vowel signs, just as the ancient Hebrews did not.

CLXXIII.

The western Syrians, when they instituted their vowel signs, altered the ancient pronunciation, giving to the קמץ the sound *O*, as well as changing into *U* the חלם of Biblical Chaldean, saying, for example, לְהוּן, לְכוּן, שְׁלָמְכוּן, תִּקְרוּן, in place of תִּקְרוֹן, שְׁלָמְכוֹן, לְהוֹן, לְכוֹן. Not caring to distinguish the closed *E* from the open (§ 151), they instituted only five vowel signs:

A, פְּתָחָא, *opening* (of the lips), corresponding to the פתח of Biblical Chaldean:

E, רְבָצָא, *lying down*, corresponding to צרי, and to חירק not followed by Yod:

I, חְבָצָא, *tightening*, corresponding to חירק with Yod, and sometimes to צרי:

O, זְקָפָא, *elevating*, corresponding to קמץ, and sometimes to חלם:

U, עְצָצָא, *compression*, corresponding to the שורק, קבוץ, and חלם of Biblical Chaldean.

CLXXIV.

The Syrians, although they altered to *U* the *O* of the Chaldeans, preserved some distinction between the primitive *U*, e.g., that of נוּרָא, and the *U* derived from *O*, e.g., that of לְכוּן; specifically, they distinguished these two *U*'s in the script, in the name, and probably also in pronunciation. Those עְצָצָא that were primitively pronounced *O*, they marked with a point over the Vav (not unlike the Hebrew חלם), and called it אַסְקָא *elevating* (just like they called the O זְקָפָא), or with another name, דִּקְדָּם רְוִיחְתָּא *formerly dilated* (1), that is to say that in the past it did not have the closed sound of U, but rather the wide and open sound of O; or finally עֶצָּא כַרְיָא *short compression*, since, although the sounds of this vowel had already approached U, they still did not compress the lips so much in pronouncing it, as much as with the true, genuine, and primitive U. The other עֶצָּא, that is, the primitive U, they marked with a point under the Vav, and called it עֻמְקָא *depth*; or with another name, עֶצָּא אֲרִיכָא *long compression*, or else עֶצָּא אֲלִיצְתָא, *formerly squeezed, compressed*, that is to say, vowels that in the past and originally already had the closed and compressed sound U.

(1)   The particle קְדָם is a noun, which in the same form can be used in the absolute and construct states. This particle is commonly used subordinated to the following word, in the manner of a construct noun, and means *before* = לִפְנֵי. But it can be used in an absolute sense, with the meaning of לְפָנִים *in the past, formerly.*

CLXXV.

So Joseph Acurense (p. 10) counts six vowels, namely: חְבָצָא, רְבָצָא פְּתָחָא, עֶצָּא, זְקָפָא, and עֻמְקָא.

He says that the vowel עֶצָּא is marked with a point above the Vav, and gives as an example the word אֲרְכוּנָא, that is, Ἀρχων *Arcon*; and for the vowel עֻמְקָא he gives as an example the noun נוּרָא *fire*. This is how, with very convenient examples, he distinguishes primitive U, as is that of נוּרָא, from U derived from O, as is that of אֲרְכוּנָא.

CLXXVI.

[George] Amira also distinguishes long U, עֶצָּא אֲרִיכָא, from short, עֶצָּא כַרְיָא; and he adds that the former is marked with a point under the Vav, the latter with a point above it. He then gives many examples of both U's (pp. 54, 468, 469). He designates as long the U of the words פּוּמָא, תַּכְתּוּשָׁא, עֲמוּדָא, דְּמוּתָא, חוּבָּא, סְגוּלָא, שׁוּפְרָא, נוּנָא, בְּתוּלָא, כּוּבָּא, בּוּרְכְּתָא, קוּם, נְקוּם, of which all that occur in the Biblical Chaldean or Targumic, have שׁוּרק or קבוץ (1). On the other hand, he calls short the U *a*) of עֲבוּרָא פְּסוּקָא, nouns of the same form as Biblical Chaldean כָּרוֹזָא (Dan. 3:4) and Targumic קָטוֹלָא, as well as Hebrew בְּגוֹדָה:

b) of נְסִינָא, in Hebrew נִסָּיוֹן:

c) of יוּחָנָן, in Hebrew יוֹחָנָן:

d) of תּוֹמָא *Thomas*, from the Hebrew תְּאוֹמִים:

e) of כֵּל, in Hebrew and Chaldean כֹּל, ־כָּל:

f) of the suffixes הוֹן and כוֹ, which in Chaldean are pronounced הוֹן and כוֹ:

g) of the Diminutives, e.g., אֲנָשׁוּנָא, analogous to Hebrew אִישׁוֹן:

h) of the Futures of final weak verbs, for example, נֵבְנוֹן נֶתְבְּנוֹן, תַּאסוֹן, where the Biblical Chaldean has חלם; e.g., יִשְׁתּוֹן, יִקְרוֹן, יִבְנוֹן, יִשְׁנוֹן; noting (pp. 469, 470) that the Futures of other types of verbs, e.g., נֶתְבְּזוֹן תֶּבְזוֹן, נַאלְפוּן, נֶשְׁרְרוּן, נֶתְתְּדִישׁוּן (where the Biblical Chaldean has שׁורק) have long *U*:

i) of the Futures of geminate verbs, e.g., נְבּוּז from בַּז, which is for בְּזַז, where the Targumists have חלם (See Buxtorf, *Gramm. chald. et syr.*, Book I, Chap. 15).

All of these examples of long and short *U* used by Amira confirm my opinion excellently. Some other examples of short *U*, offered by that same author, are contrary to it, since they correspond to where Biblical Chaldean, Targumic, and even Hebrew [where applicable], have ו. These are:

a) the personal pronoun אַנְתּוּן, and the derived verbal ending תּוּן, e.g., עֲנֵיתוּן:

b) the Future of verbs with first radical א, e.g., נֵאכוּל:

c) the two nouns שׁוּעִיתָא and יֵשׁוּע.

However these anomalies are to be regarded, they are too few to be able, in the natural inconstancy of such things, to invalidate my opinion.

(1) Unique among these, the word סְגוּלָא *cluster* is met among the Targumists sometimes with שׁורק and sometimes with חלם. The derived grammatical name סְגוֹל has חלם, as does the Hebrew אֶשְׁכּוֹל.

CLXXVII.

David, son of Paul, an ancient Grammarian cited by Amira (p. 35), also lists six vowels. These are 1. זְקָפָא; 2. פְּתָחָא; 3. זְלָמָא *bending*, *curving*, corresponding, according to Amira, to רְבָצָא; 4. חִבָצָא; 5. אַסְקָא, which, in my judgment, is the *U* that was primitively *O*; 6. עְמָקָא, the primitive *U*.

CLXXVIII.

Elia, another ancient Grammarian, counts, according to the same Amira, seven vowels. They are:

1. זְקיפָתָא, the same thing as זְקפָא;
2. רְביצָתָא, the same as רְבָצָא;
3. פְתיחתָא, the same as פְתָחָא;
4. דִקְדָם מַסְקָתָא, according to Amira, the same as חִבָצָא כַרְיָא, short *I*;
5. דִקְדָם רְויחָתָא, according to Amira, the same as אַסְקָא or עְצָצָא כַרְיָא;
6. דִקְדָם אַליצָתָא, according to Amira, the same as עְמָקָא, that is, עְצָצָא אַריכָא;
7. דִקְדָם חְביצָתָא, of which Amira gives no explanation, nor any examples.

Of these, the first three are rather well known; the fifth and the sixth have been illustrated by me in the preceding §§; regarding the fourth and the seventh, of which Amira offers no examples, it is impossible to pronounce a judgment that is certain or close to certain. However, the examples that Amira (pp. 467, 468) provides for the short *I* suggest to me a probable conjecture concerning the fourth, and perhaps not improbable concerning the seventh of these vowels.

The *I* of many Syriac words was primitively *E*; e.g., ריחָא, in Hebrew רֵיחַ and in Targumic Chaldean רֵיחָא; דָאבָא, in Hebrew זְאֵב; נְאלַף נָאמַר, in Biblical Chaldean נֵאמַר; לְליָא, in Chaldean לֵיליָא; תְּתָא, in Hebrew תְּאֵנָה, in Targumic תֵּינְתָא; מֶסְכְּנָא, in Hebrew and Targumic מִסְכֵּן. Likewise in the originally Greek word פְּרַקְלְטָא, παράκλητος, in Latin *paracletus*; אֶסְכְּמָא, σχῆμα, in Latin *schema*. Sometimes Syriac *I* was primitively *A*; e.g., לַמְפּידָא, λαμπάς. Now to all of these words Amira attributes a short *I*. On the contrary he calls long the *I* of דִינָא, אַעְליני, אַסוּרני, which is primitive. I suppose that in the same way that the primitive *U* was regarded as longer than the one stemming from *O*, the primitive *I* was regarded and pronounced longer than the non-primitive, which was originally *E*, or even *A*. Hence Elia's fourth vowel, called short *I* by Amira, indicates the non-primitive *I*, called therefore זְדָקִים מַסְסָקְתָא, vowels *formerly raising* the lips, that is to say, having in origin a more open sound, for which it is necessary to raise and separate the lips more than the vowel *I* requires. On the contrary, the vowels of the seventh type are called זְדָקִים חְבִיצָתָא, *formerly narrowed*, which is to say, they were primitively the same as חְבָצָא, i.e., *I*.

CLXXIX.

Hoffmann (*Gram. syr.*, p. 91) gives to the word קָדֶם of Elia's last four vowels the meaning of *greatly* ([Latin] *magis*); this [definition] is without any other example in the Hebrew or Aramaic languages. This gratuitous interpretation is also inadequate for explaining the fifth vowel called זְדָקִים רְוִיחָתָא—that is, according to Hoffmann, *greatly dilated*—which according to Amira, is short *U*. Hoffmann was obliged to claim that this denomination (against the analogy of all the other six) was not taken from the opening of the lips in producing the vowel, but rather from the [graphic] form of the vowel itself. This being still to no avail, since the form of short *U* is only a point above the Vav, Hoffmann was compelled to imagine that this vowel was also marked with two points, one above, and one under the Vav; a form completely unknown to Amira and Acurense, and which is as unlikely to have been used to indicate the vowel *U*, as it is certain to be proper to the vowel *A*.

CLXXX.

The eastern Syrians, according to what [Bonifazio] Finetti relates in his *Trattato della lingua ebraica e sue affini* (pp. 57, 58), have seven vowel signs. Two diagonal [*perpendicolari*] points above the letter indicate long *A*, and are called זְקָפָא [see § 5 *a*]. One point above and one point below the letter indicate short *A*, and are named פְּתָחָא. Two diagonal [*perpendicolari*] points below the letter make long *E*, and are called זְלָמָא קַשְׁיָא. Two horizontal points under the letter signify short *E*, and are named זְלָמָא פְּסִיקָא. A point above the Vav makes *O*, and is called רְוָחָא; under the Vav makes *U*, and is named רְבָצָא; and under the Yod makes *I*, and is called חְבָצָא.

This system of pointing, compared with that of the western Syrians, appears much more analogous to the Hebrew pointing, in that—in addition to the two points of contact, already observed in § 5 (letters *a*, *c*), in which both systems of Syriac pointing coincide with the Hebrew—that of the eastern Syrians exhibits these other analogies with it:

a) the number of vowels is seven among the eastern Syrians, as well as among the Hebrews (§ 149), while the vowel signs used by the western Syrians are only five;

b) a point above the letter indicates the vowel *O* among the Hebrews and the eastern Syrians, but not among the western Syrians;

c) a point below the letter indicates the vowel *I* among the first and second equally, but not among the third;

If this account by Finetti, for which I have not attempted to recover the source, is genuine and accurate, it renders it very probable that the idea for the Pointing was suggested to the Hebrews by the example of the eastern Syrians; this further strengthens my opinion that the Hebrew Pointing is Babylonian in origin, rather than Palestinian.

Appendix V.

On the Accents.[26]

CLXXXI.

The Hebrew accents have three different functions, or values. They are musical Notes, or signs, intended to regulate the type of chanting that has been used since very ancient times in the public reading of the scriptural books.

This chanting being subordinate to the sense of the words, the Accents have at the same time the function of Punctuation [*Interpunzioni*].

They have mostly a third function, which is to indicate in every word the place of stress [*posa*].

These three functions of the Accents are distinguished with the names musical, syntactic, and grammatical.

CLXXXII.

Of the three functions explained so far, Wasmuth, Gesenius, and others have claimed that the two final, and especially the second—that is, the syntactic—were the primitive purpose of the Accents. However, the multiplicity of the servile [*ministri*] Accents (of which there is not any need for the syntactic value, and [of which] one alone would suffice for the grammatical function) proves, as Elijah Levita already observed (טוב טעם, Chap. II), that the Accents are originally musical signs; and all the more if one considers the quantity and fastidiousness of the laws that these same servile Accents obey, which, after all, if they were not intended to regulate the chanting, would be totally useless. The same thing is proven by the changes to which the disjunctive [*distinguenti*] accents are subject (§ 190), and the different systems of accentuation used in the prose and poetic books.

---

[26] SDL also dealt with the accents in the first fascicle of his *Grammatica della lingua ebrea* (Padua, 1853) and in an article in *Kerem Ḥemed* 9.

CLXXXIII.

The disjunctive accents of the prose [books] are the ten following, listed in descending order of their disjunctive value:

מְלָכִים Kings	1. סוֹף פָּסוּק, or סִלּוּק, e.g.,	סֵפֶר
	2. אַתְנָח, or אַתְנַחְתָּא,	סֵפֶר
שָׂרִים Princes	3. סְגוֹלְתָּא, סְגוֹל, or, שְׁרֵי,	סֵפֶֿר
	4. זָקֵף,	סֵפֶר
	5. טִפְחָא, or טַרְחָא,	סֵפֶר
	6. רְבִיעַ,	סֵפֶר
פְּקִידִים Prefects	7. זַרְקָא,	סֵפֶֿר
	8. פְּשְׁטָא,	סֵפֶֿר
	9. תְּבִיר,	סֵפֶר
	10. גֶּרֶשׁ,	סֵפֶר

In addition to these Accents, there is the line called לְגַרְמֵהּ (|) which occurs between two words both marked with a non-disjunctive accent, in which case the first of the two non-disjunctive accents acquires a minimal disjunctive value.

CLXXXIV.

The Accents essentially not being logical punctuation, but musical signs; these ten disjunctives cannot be compared to the full stop, colon, semi-colon, and comma of European languages. The סוֹף פסוק corresponds many times to the full stop; but since a verse does not always contain a complete sentence, but can contain just a part, a clause, or a phrase—as can be seen in Gen. 7:8, 23:17, Lev. 17:8, Num. 14:21–22, 31:22, 2 Sam. 17:27–28, Isaiah 7:5–6, Jer. 7:9—the same סוֹף פסוק sometimes only corresponds to the colon, semi-colon, or even the comma. Likewise, a verse sometimes contains a complete sentence, but is not divided into true clauses; and so the אֶתְנָח will not even correspond to a comma, as is seen in the first verse of Genesis.

CLXXXV.

The definition therefore of the function of the various disjunctive accents should be conceived as follows:

The אתנח divides the verse into two clauses [*membri*], real or apparent;

The סגול divides the first clause into two phrases [*incisi*];

The זקף distinguishes the different phrases, both in the first and second clauses;

The טפחא marks the most detached [*staccata*] word existing in a phrase ending with one of the two Kings סלוק and אתנח;

The רביע forms a semi-phrase [*semi-inciso*] within the final phrase of one of the other three Princes סגול, זקף, and טפחא;

The four Prefects זרקא, פשטא, תביר, גרש indicate a lesser division before a greater one marked by a Prince: The זרקא precedes the סגול; the פשטא comes before the זקף; the תביר occurs by the טפחא; and the גרש and לגרמה, by the רביע;

The גרש and לגרמה, as minimal disjunctives, also mark a super-light separation before the other three Prefects.

CLXXXVI

The following verse (Gen. 24:30) can serve as an example of the function of all the disjunctive Accents:

וַיְהִ֣י ׀ כִּרְאֹ֣ת אֶת־הַנֶּ֗זֶם וְֽאֶת־הַצְּמִדִים֮ עַל־יְדֵ֣י אֲחֹתוֹ֒
וּכְשָׁמְע֗וֹ אֶת־דִּבְרֵ֞י רִבְקָ֤ה אֲחֹתוֹ֙ לֵאמֹ֔ר כֹּֽה־דִבֶּ֥ר אֵלַ֖י הָאִ֑ישׁ
וַיָּבֹא֙ אֶל־הָאִ֔ישׁ וְהִנֵּ֛ה עֹמֵ֥ד עַל־הַגְּמַלִּ֖ים עַל־הָעָֽיִן ׃

Now, when he (Laban) saw the pendant and the bracelets on his sister's arms;

And he heard the words of Rebecca his sister, namely: Such and such that man spoke to me:

He went to the man, and here (i.e., and he found that) he was standing by the camels, next to the spring.

Here, the אתנח divides the verse into two clauses, the first of which expresses the motives that acted upon the will of Laban, and the second, the action that was the consequence of them.

The סגול divides the first clause into two phrases, expressing the two motives; that is to say, the things that Laban saw and the things that he heard. The first phrase is divided by רביע into two semi-phrases, the first of which is further divided by לגרמה, and the second by זרקא. The second phrase is divided by זקף into two semi-phrases, the first of which is further divided first by רביע, then by פשטא, and finally by גרש; and the second is subdivided by טפחא. The second clause is divided by זקף into two phrases, the first of which is subdivided by פשטא, and the second is subdivided first by טפחא, then by תביר.

CLXXXVII.

The greater or lesser degree of division indicated by each disjunctive accent is usually expressed by the Grammarians by a proportionate number of lines placed between the words. For example, ||| גּוֹי | וּקְהַל גּוֹיִם || יִהְיֶה מִמֶּ֫ךָ *A nation | and an assembly of nations || will be formed from you* ||| [Gen 35:11]. The תביר has here a disjunctive value = 1; the טפחא, which is more disjunctive than the תביר, has a value = 2; and the אתנח, which is more disjunctive than the טפחא, has a value = 3; that is to say that the תביר separates the word גוֹי from the following as 1, the טפחא splits גוֹיִם from the following as 2, and the אתנח divides the word מִמֶּךָ from the following as 3, indicating a greater division than the two preceding. Likewise,

|||| וַיָּבֹ֨א | יִתְרוֹ חֹתֵן מֹשֶׁה || וּבָנָיו וְאִשְׁתּוֹ ||| אֶל־מֹשֶׁה

Came | Jethro, father-in-law of Moses || with his sons and his wife ||| to Moses |||| [Exod. 18:5].

Here the תביר = 2, טפחא = 3, and the אתנח = 4, the שני גרשׁין being equivalent to the גרשׁ (§ 190), although it is the least of the disjunctives, still has a disjunctive value here = 1.

|||| כְּנַ֫עַן || בְּיָדוֹ | מֹאזְנֵי מִרְמָה ||| לַעֲשׁוֹק אָהֵב

The trader || has in his hand | a balance of deceit ||| he loves to oppress |||| [Hosea 12:8].

Here the טפחא = 3, although the תביר = 1; the רביע, which is more disjunctive than תביר, and less than טפחא, = 2.

|| וַיִּגַּשׁ אֵלִיָּ֫הוּ | אֶל־כָּל־הָעָם |||| וַיֹּאמֶר ||| עַד־מָתַ֫י | אַתֶּם פֹּסְחִים ||||| עַל־שְׁתֵּי הַסְּעִפִּים

Elijah drew near | to all the people |||| and said ||| until when | will you hop || on two branches [1 Kings 18:21].

Here the רָבִיעַ = 4, since it is followed by the פַּשְׁטָא, which is less disjunctive than it, but more disjunctive than the following גֶרֶשׁ, and also the following זַרְקָא; therefore, if the גֶרֶשׁ = 1, the זַרְקָא = 2, the פַּשְׁטָא = 3, the רָבִיעַ must = 4, and the סָגוֹל = 5.

When one wants to determine with lines the value of all the disjunctive accents of a verse, one should begin with the smallest accent and continue gradually to the greater ones, from those in the same phrase, to those in the same clause, and finally to those of the other clauses in the same verse.

CLXXXVIII.

The lines can be substituted by numbers, for example:

וַיָּבֹא (1) יִתְרוֹ חֹתֵן מֹשֶׁה (2) וּבָנָיו וְאִשְׁתּוֹ (3) אֶל־מֹשֶׁה (4)

and the numbers can be substituted by Hebrew letters, for example:

וַיָּבֹא (א) יִתְרוֹ חֹתֵן מֹשֶׁה (ב) וּבָנָיו וְאִשְׁתּוֹ (ג) אֶל־מֹשֶׁה (ד)

In such a manner, the value of the various disjunctive accents of any phrase, clause, or verse, can be expressed with the short formula אבג"ד.

The accents of the text כְּנַעַן בְּיָדוֹ [§ 187] would be expressed with the formula באג"ד; those of the text וַיִּגַשׁ אֵלָיו [§ 187] with the formula אדגא"בה; and so forth.

CLXXXIX.

Such an abundance of more or less disjunctive accents—the need for which is unknown in European languages—is not a quirk of the ancient Rabbis, but is required by the nature of Hebrew syntax. This, for all its simplicity and naturalness, is actually rather complex, and it greatly abounds in parenthetical clauses inserted within the main clause; that is to say, it is extremely rich in parentheses. The following verses will serve as examples:

וַיָּבֹא יִתְרוֹ חֹתֵן מֹשֶׁה (וּבָנָיו וְאִשְׁתּוֹ) אֶל־מֹשֶׁה

Jethro, father-in-law of Moses (with his sons and his wife) came to Moses.

ויתן אל משה (ככלתו לדבר אתו֒ בהר סיני֙) שני לוחות העדֻת

*He gave to Moses (having finished speaking with him on Mount Sinai) the two
tablets of the Law.* [Exod. 31:18]

והי֛ו הדברים האלה (אשר אנכי מצוך היום) על לבבך :

These things (that I command you today) shall be upon your hearts. [Deut. 6:6]

והיו העצים (אשר תכתב עליהם֒) בידך לעיניהם :

These sticks (on which you will write) shall be in your hand before there eyes.
[Ezek. 37:20]

כל החיה אשר אתך֙ מכל בשר (בעוף ובבהמה ובכל הרמש
הרמש על הארץ) הוצא אתך֙

*All the animals that are with you, from every species of flesh (of the birds,
quadrupeds, and every reptile crawling on the earth) take out with you.* [Gen. 8:17]

ויצא מלך סדם֒ לקראתו֙ (אחרי שובו֒ מהכות֒ את כדרלעמר
ואת המלכים אשר אתו֒) אל עמק שוה הוא עמק המלך :

*The King of Sodom went out towards him (after his returning from having defeated
Chedorlaomer and the Kings who were with him) in the valley of Shaveh, now the royal
valley.* [Gen. 14:17]

Now the end of every parenthetical clause is marked by an accent
more disjunctive than that of the word before the parenthesis; and its
beginning (if it is long enough to require more than one disjunctive) is
indicated by an accent less disjunctive than that of the word before the
parenthesis. So, in the fourth example, the word עליהם has תביר, greater
than the גרש of העצים, since אשר תכתב עליהם is a parenthetical
clause, and the main clause is והיו העצים בידך לעיניהם, that is to say:
The sticks, on which you will write, shall be in your hand before their eyes. If the word
העצים had been marked by רביע, greater than the תביר of עליהם, this
would indicate that the parentheses should embrace the words
אשר תכתב עליהם בידך, and the sense of the text would be: *The laws, on
which you will write with your hand, shall be before their eyes.*

CXC.

Several of the disjunctive accents sometimes (according to fixed rules) take
a different shape.

סְגוֹל, when it would not be preceded by זַרְקָא, i.e., when it should fall on the first word of the verse, changes to שַׁלְשֶׁלֶת.

זָקֵף, when it would not be preceded by פַּשְׁטָא or מֻנַּח, changes to זָקֵף גָּדוֹל.

פַּשְׁטָא falling in a short word, which is not preceded by a conjunctive accent, changes to יְתִיב.[27]

גֶרֶשׁ sometimes transforms into שְׁנֵי גְרִישִׁין, sometimes into תְּלִישָׁה גְדוֹלָה, and sometimes into פָּזֵר, all according to fixed rules.

When פַּשְׁטָא would be repeated three times, without an intervening greater disjunctive, the second of the three פַּשְׁטָא changes to רְבִיעַ; in which case the רְבִיעַ separates less from the פַּשְׁטָא that precedes, but more from the פַּשְׁטָא that follows it (§ 191); e.g.,

הֵן גְּבִיר (1) שַׂמְתִּיו לָךְ (3) וְאֶת כָּל אֶחָיו (2) נָתַתִּי לוֹ (1) לַעֲבָדִים (4)

Behold, superior (1) I have made him to you (3) and all his brothers (2) I have given to him (1) as servants (4). [Gen. 27:37]

In addition to this, several accents are sometimes met repeated within a single word; e.g. טֶרֶם יִשְׁכָּבוּ. This duplication of accents seems to be of secondary institution. In words with penultimate stress marked with one of the accents placed at the end [postpositive] (these are זַרְקָא, סְגוֹל, פַּשְׁטָא, and תְּלִישָׁה קְטַנָּה), some Punctuators, intent on removing all ambiguities in reading, added another accent above the letter on which the stress should fall. The modern editions do not usually follow this practice, except for with פַּשְׁטָא, e.g., מִמַּעַל.

CXCI.

Every time that a disjunctive accent is repeated two or more times, without the intervention of a greater disjunctive, the disjunctive value of the repeated accent decreases proportionally to the number of repetitions. For example,

נִבְקְעוּ (2) כָּל־מַעְיְנוֹת (1) תְּהוֹם רַבָּה (3)

Burst open (2) all the fountains (1) of the great abyss (3). [Gen. 7:11]

---

[27] יְתִיב occurs only when the stress falls on the first syllable (as is the case with short words).

וַתֵּצֵא יָעֵל לִקְרָתוֹ (4) וַתֹּאמֶר לוֹ (3) לֵךְ וְאַרְאֶךָּ (2) אֶת־הָאִישׁ (1)
אֲשֶׁר אַתָּה מְבַקֵּשׁ (5)

Yael came out towards him (4) *and said to him* (3) *come so I might show you* (2)
the man (1) *whom you seek* (5). [Judg. 4:22]

יַעַן (1) אֲשֶׁר שָׁלַחְתָּ מַלְאָכִים (3) לִדְרֹשׁ (2) בְּבַעַל זְבוּב (1)
אֱלֹהֵי עֶקְרוֹן (4)

Because (1) *you sent messengers* (3) *to consult* (2) *with Beelzebub* (1) *God of
Ekron* (4)... [2 Kings 1:16]

CXCII.

Several times it happens that the Accents offer a division divergent from
the logical division of the discourse. This occurs

a) in poetic pieces, where the symmetry of the hemistiches sometimes
calls for a break not expected by the meaning; e.g.,

המה ראו מעשי יי	*They saw the works of God,*
ונפלאותיו במצולה	*And his wonders in the deep waters.*

PSALM 107:24.

where the meaning would require that the word ונפלאותיו and his wonders
be placed in the first, rather than the second hemistich. Likewise,

על־כן יצאתי לקראתך	*Therefore I have come forth to meet you,*
לשחר פניך ואמצאך :	*Seeking your face, and I found you.*

PROV. 7:15.

where לשחר פניך *seeking your face* clearly belongs to the first [half of the]
verse. Likewise,

מה־יפית ומה נעמת	*Oh! how beautiful, oh! how sweet you are,*
אהבה בתענוגים :	*Love, among the delights.*

CANT. 7:7.

that is to say: *How you are, Love, sweet and beautiful among all the delights*, as Ibn
Ezra interprets, where the word אהבה *Love* belongs to the first [half of
the] verse.

b) in prose, due to a certain symmetry between the two parts of the
sentence, intended to give respite to the chanter. This only happens if the
meaning of the sentence is obvious, and it could not produce ambiguity; for
example,

בְּעֶצֶם הַיּוֹם הַזֶּה בָּא נֹחַ וְשֵׁם וְחָם וָיֶפֶת בְּנֵי נֹחַ
וְאֵשֶׁת נֹחַ וּשְׁלֹשֶׁת נְשֵׁי בָנָיו אִתָּם אֶל הַתֵּבָה ׃

On that very day went Noah, and Shem, Ham, and Japhet, sons of Noah,
And Noah's wife, and the three wives of his sons with him, into the ark.

GEN. 7:13.

a sentence which is not strictly divisible into two parts. The accent אתנח, which divides it into two, separates the words *into the ark* from the first part, to which it refers, in meaning, equally as much as it does to the second part. The same is found in the text:

אֶת צֹאנָם וְאֶת בְּקָרָם וְאֶת חֲמֹרֵיהֶם
וְאֵת אֲשֶׁר בָּעִיר וְאֵת אֲשֶׁר בַּשָּׂדֶה לָקָחוּ ׃

Their small and large livestock, and their asses,
And that which was in their cities, and that which was in the field, they took.

GEN. 34:28.

c) for several prudent reasons pointed out at the end of § 8; e.g., in the text of שְׂרָפִים עֹמְדִים מִמַּעַל לוֹ (Isaiah 6:2), where in place of the literal sense, which is: *The seraphs were standing above him*, the accents give the following meaning: *The seraphs, who stand on high, are his*, i.e., *they are at his service*. Likewise in the text וְהָאַלְמָנָה אֲשֶׁר־תִּהְיֶה אַלְמָנָה מִכֹּהֵן יִקָּחוּ (Ezek. 44:22),[28] instead of expressing the natural sense, which is: *The widow, who is the widow of a priest, they (the priests) may take as a wife*; the accents express the Talmudic interpretation (Kiddushin fol. 78), which is: *The widow, whoever is a widow, some of the priests (that is to say, all, except for the head Pontiff) may take as a wife*; an interpretation intended to remove the contradiction between Ezekiel, which prohibits priests to marry widows, except widows of other priests, and the Pentateuch, which forbids only the high Priest from marrying a widow (Lev. 21:14). Likewise in Zechariah (4:10), the Pointers wanted (as the Targumist also wanted) the words *these seven* (שִׁבְעָה אֵלֶּה) to refer to what precedes rather than to what follows; this had the purpose of removing from the ears of the people a symbolic expression that would have been found monstrous, since it attributed to God seven eyes.

d) due to the obscurity and ambiguity of any text in which the Pointers, or the ancient Rabbis who fixed the reading of the Holy Books

---

[28] The Leningrad Codex has here אֲשֶׁר תהיה, with no overall syntactic difference.

(§§ 142, 143), adopted an interpretation different from that which would be the most correct in our judgment. Of this not a few examples will be found here and there in my Commentaries on the Pentateuch and on the Prophets. As much as Ibn Ezra warns against allowing any interpretation that is contrary to the Accents, it is most certain that there is no Hebrew Commentator, including Ibn Ezra himself, who does not provide some interpretations contrary to the division of the Accents. Anyone who wants to be sure of this has only to compare the following citations. It should be noted that since the very detailed laws of the Accents have been exactly known to extremely few of the Commentators, I have collected only those interpretations whose contrast with the Accents is clear, and so could be realized by anyone who had even a superficial knowledge of Hebrew Accentuation; omitting many of them whose aversion to the Accents can only be exposed through a profound understanding of their laws. These are therefore some of the places in which the principal Hebrew Commentators, listed in chronological order, have deviated from the division indicated by the Accents.

Moses ha-Cohen, according to Ibn Ezra, Psalm 139:14.

Rashi, Lev. 23:16. Isaiah 1:9. Jeremiah 6:29.

Rashbam, Genesis 30:33; 41:57. Exodus 14:30. Deut. 32:12.

Ibn Ezra, Gen. 13:13; 25:25; 30:33; 41:57. Num. 12:6; 26:10. Deut. 6:7; 16:6; 32:5.

Joseph Kimḥi, according to his son David, Isaiah 27:4.

Naḥmanides, Gen. 7:23; 36:11. Lev. 1:2. Deut. 32:5.

Rabbi Baḥya [ben Asher ben Halawa], Deut. 32:5.

Ḥazzekuni [Hezekiah ben Manoah], Gen. 37:19; 47:6; 49:27.

[Joseph] Albo, in his Ikkarim (Tractate 2, Chap. 3), Isaiah 10:15.

[Isaac] Abravanel, Gen. 3:10; 10:21; 14:23; 17:13; 18:21. Isaiah 8:19.

Obadiah Sforno, Gen. 9:5; 49:22. Exodus 15:10. Num. 10:36. Deut. 33:26.

[Moses] Mendelssohn, Gen. 24:32; 30:38; 47:26.

[Naphtali] Hartwig Wessely (in the beginning of רוח חן), 2 Sam. 23:3.

David Kimḥi, more straightforward than Ibn Ezra, at verse 12 of Chap. 12 of Hosea wrote openly that the exegetical meaning of the sacred Text does not follow the Accents of the Pointing: אין כל הפירושים הולכים אחרי טעמי הנקוד.[29] See also the same Commentator on Isaiah

---

[29] "Not all interpretations follow the accents."

45:8, 24. Likewise Abravanel, on Isaiah 8:19, says openly that it is necessary to interpret that text against the intention of the author of the Accents: ועם היות שבעל הטעמים ימאנהו, נכון לפרש וכו'.[30] And in an era before all of these writers, one of the Geonim (1), according to Ibn Ezra in the beginning of מאזנים, wrote that there were in the sacred Scripture ten verses tightly bound to the following, and therefore divided by the Pointers without reason.

e) due to errors of the copyists or editors; e.g.,

ויֹּאמר אליו *And he said to him:*

אברהם ויֹּאמר הנני : *Abraham, and he said: Here I am.*

Where it should be read:

ויֹּאמר אליו אברהם *And he said to him: Abraham!*

ויֹּאמר הנני : *And he said: Here I am.* [Gen. 22:1]

as in fact is read in the membranous [vellum or parchment] manuscript of the Pentateuch owned by me, without a date, but written not later than 1411. Likewise:

אל־המדבר *Into the wilderness,*

אשר־הוא חנה שם הר האלהים : *Where he encamped, at the mountain of God.*

Where it should be read:

אל־המדבר אשר־הוא חנה שם *Into the wilderness where he was encamped;*

הר האלהים : *That is, at the mountain of God.* [Exod. 18:5]

as was read in the Bible manuscript possessed by Mendelssohn.[31]

A grave error is met in many of the more correct Bibles in 2 Samuel 15:34, where we read:

ואמרת לאבשלום עבדך *And you will say to Absalom your servant:*

אני המלך אהיה *I, O King, will be.*

where the word עבדך should have (as in the Mantua Bible) קדמא, a non-disjunctive accent, instead of זקף; i.e.,

---

[30] "Though the pointer denies it, it is correct to interpret [in this way]."

[31] The latter is also the reading found in the Leningrad Codex.

וְאָמַרְתָּ לְאַבְשָׁלוֹם   *And you will say to Absalom:*
עַבְדְּךָ אֲנִי הַמֶּלֶךְ אֶהְיֶה   *Your servant, O King, I will be.*[32]

Another clear error is encountered in the majority of Bible editions in 1 Sam. 14:41, where we read:

וַיִּלָּכֵד יוֹנָתָן וְשָׁאוּל וְהָעָם   *Jonathan, Saul, and the people were taken;*
יָצָאוּ :   *They went out.*

instead of

וַיִּלָּכֵד יוֹנָתָן וְשָׁאוּל   *Jonathan and Saul were taken;*
וְהָעָם יָצָאוּ :   *And the people went out* (that is, *were excluded*).[33]

as is read in the Bible manuscript from 1347 possessed by Rabbi M. S. Ghirondi, which is number 39 of the foreign Codices collated by De Rossi.

(1) It is probable that this Gaon was the famous Saadiah, since for two of these Texts (Jer. 17:11, Hosea 4:10), the interpretation that Ibn Ezra attributes vaguely to one of the Geonim, is explicitly attributed to Saadiah by Kimḥi.[34]

CXCIII.

Despite everything that was said in letter *d* of the preceding §, it cannot be denied that most of the time we discern in the application of the Accents, and in the Pointing in general, an admirable profundity, and a very acute understanding of the literal sense of the sacred Text; so that the Pointers should rightfully be regarded by every scholar of the sacred Scripture as the most excellent of Commentators; and nothing is more false than what Louis Cappel wrote in his *Arcanum punctationis revelatum*, that *Accentus si una litura expungerentur, nihil inde detrimenti metuendum.*[35] In support of my opinion, I am pleased to adduce an example taken from an expression in one of the first texts of Genesis, an expression that was misunderstood by all of the

---

[32] Once again, this is the reading of the Leningrad Codex.

[33] Once again, this is the reading of the Leningrad Codex.

[34] SDL is certainly correct, that Ibn Ezra is referring to Saadiah. On this and more on Ibn Ezra's view on the accentual system, see A. Sáenz-Badillos, "Abraham ibn Ezra: Between Tradition and Philology," in *Zutot 2002*, ed. S. Berger, M. Brocke, and I. Zwiep (Dordrecht, 2003), pp. 85–94 (esp. n. 13).

[35] "If one mark of the accent were erased, one ought not to fear any detriment." (translation Stephen Wheeler.)

Commentators and Translators, but correctly understood by the Pointers. This is the expression לְמִינוֹ in the text עֵץ פְּרִי עֹשֶׂה פְּרִי לְמִינוֹ (Gen. 1:11), translated by all: *Fruit trees, producing fruit according to its own kind.* Everyone sees that this expression *according to its own kind* is insignificant and superfluous, but no one has been able to doubt that the word לְמִינוֹ could have another meaning than this. However, from examination of all the texts where we meet לְמִינָה, לְמִינֵהוּ, לְמִינוֹ, it appears that this word is an expression, an idiom of the Hebrew language, possessing a meaning rather different than that which it should mean grammatically. This form means *of whatever kind, of every kind.*[36] So אֶת־הַנֵּץ לְמִינֵהוּ, אֵת כָּל־עֹרֵב לְמִינוֹ, אֶת־הָאַרְבֶּה לְמִינוֹ, הָאֲנָפָה לְמִינָהּ (Lev. 11:15, 16, 19, 22) mean *of any kind.* Likewise תוצא הארץ נפש חיה למינה בהמה ורמש וחיתו ארץ למינה (Gen. 1:24) means: *Let the earth produce animals of every kind, cattle, reptiles, and wild beasts of every kind.* Likewise למינה תהיה דגתם (Ezek. 47:10) means: *Of every kind, of various kinds, will be the fish.* Similarly, the Talmudists (Jerus. Talmud Shekalim, ch. 6) interpret this text with the words למיני מינים תהיה דגתם *Of a great many kinds will be their fish.*

Now the pointers, placing over עֵץ פְּרִ֜י a גֶּרֶשׁ, a lesser disjunctive, and over עֹשֶׂה פְּרִ֖י a פָּשְׁטָא, a greater disjunctive, making use of the formula אב"ג [see § 188], indicate with this that the word לְמִינוֹ refers not only to עֹשֶׂה פְּרִי (*producing fruit according to its own kind*), but also to עֵץ פְּרִ֜י (*fruit trees of every kind*, i.e., *various fruit trees*), and that the words עֹשֶׂה פְּרִי form a parenthesis: *fruit trees (i.e., fructiferous ones) of every kind.* If they had thought it should be translated: *producing fruit according to its own kind,* they would have employed the formula בא"ג, placing the פָּשְׁטָא over עֵץ פְּרִי, so: עֵץ פְּרִי֜ עֹשֶׂה־פְּרִי לְמִינוֹ .

---

[36] Many modern translations, including the *NJPS* and *NRSV*, have adopted this translation.

APPENDIX VI.

On the secondary Pointing, in illustration of § 147.

CXCIV.

It appears from the ancient Grammarians that mobile שוא was generally not pronounced as it is by us, as short *e*, but was commonly pronounced as short *a*; when it was followed by a guttural letter, it was given a sound similar to the vowel of the guttural; and when it was followed by Yod, it was pronounced as short *i*. Therefore it happened that some Punctuators, wanting, for the benefit of less learned readers, to indicate that a certain שוא, which for whatever reason might have been judged silent, was mobile, often changed it to חטף פתח, representing precisely short *a*, i.e., roughly the sound of mobile שוא. From this derives the חטף פתח:[37]

a) of a letter followed by a second identical one, e.g., חַצְצֹן, הַלְלוּ, רְבְבוֹת; intended to avoid reading them רְבְבוֹת, חַצְצֹן, הַלְלוּ, with silent שוא, since it is preceded by פתח, or by חירק not followed by Yod [see § 167 *b*]; and because the law that makes mobile the שוא under a letter followed by another identical one, is not found among the ancient Grammarians:

b) of a letter that should have דגש, e.g., הַצְפַרְדְעִים, הַמְשַלֵחַ, וַתְּאַלְצֵהוּ, originating from the opinion of some Punctuators, that the שוא of a letter that should have דגש, is often times to be pronounced mobile, as it should if the letter had דגש (As a rule, [Solomon] Hanau considers mobile every שוא under a letter which should have דגש (1)):

c) following an initial וּ, e.g., וּתְבַקְשִׁי, וּשְׁמַע, וּשָׂדֶה, וְזָהָב, וְלַהַבְדִּיל, originating from the opinion that such a שוא was fundamentally not mute (since it was primitively mobile, and the following letter did not take דגש lene), and can therefore, out of necessity due to the chant, be made mobile:

d) following another vowel which has been substituted for שוא, e.g., הַבְרָכָה, סְבְבֵי, נְדְרוּ, מְשְׁכוּ; based on the opinion that such a שוא is also fundamentally not mute, since it was primitively preceded not by a vowel,

---

[37] The following examples rarely agree with the better manuscripts, like the Leningrad Codex. See the discussion of this phenomenon in *Gesenius-Kautsch-Cowley*, § 10g.

but by another שוא (מְשֹׁךְ, נְדֹר, סְבַךְ, (הַבְרָכָה), and is not followed by דגש
lene (Hanau consistently considers mobile every שוא following an initial וֹ,
or following any other vowel substituting for שוא, to which he gives the
epithet 'light' [lene], תְּנוּעָה קַלָּה):

as well as the חטף קמץ of לֶקָחָה, וּצְעָקִי, וּסְעָדָה. Here we do not
find חטף פתח, due to the fact that the שוא is followed by a guttural with a
kamets, formerly having the sound of a short kamets. In לֶקָחָה, the חטף
indicates that the שוא is mobile, since the ק does not have dagesh, as it
should.

Extremely rarely we find a שוא not preceded by a light vowel made
mobile in this way, always due to the chant (§ 144 d. 1), e.g., הִתְמַלֵּךְ,
יִצְחַק־לִי.

Not of secondary institution is the חטף פתח under the ר of
וַאֲבָרֲכָה מְבָרֲכֶיךָ and the like, nor that under the כ of תֹּאכֲלֶנָּה and the
like; but rather, I believe that the first stems from the ר being a semi-
guttural letter, and the second comes from the guttural quality of כ, a letter
not without an affinity with ח; or else from a tendency to somehow
preserve in long words the primitive vowel, by which from תֹּאכַל one says
תֹּאכֲלֶנָּה rather than תֹּאכְלֶנָּה, as from אֶכְתֹּב one says אֶכְתֳּבֶנָה; from תְּקֹב,
תְּקֳבֶנּוּ; from שִׁבֹּלֶת, שִׁבֳּלִים; from צִפֹּר, צִפֳּרִים; from כֻּתֹּנֶת, כֻּתֳּנוֹת; from
קָדְקֹד, קָדְקֳדוֹ; and why from אֶשְׁקֹט is written אשקוטה (Isaiah 18:4), and
from אֶשְׁקֹל, אשקולה (Ezra 8:25).

(1) In תֵּרָצְחוּ, where the צ does not have דגש, a חטף פתח would likewise have
been expected under the same צ; but since this was followed by a guttural
accompanied by the vowel u, the preceding שוא would not have had the sound
of חטף פתח among the ancients, but rather was pronounced as a half u.

CXCV.

The semi-accent (מֶתֶג) of primary institution only appears in a simple
[open] syllable, and is always preceded by a vowel, e.g., וְאָמַרְתָּ לְיַעֲקֹב.
Some Punctuators added many of these—contrary to the primitive purpose
of the semi-accent—with which they indicated a secondary stress [semiposa]
in the third syllable before the accent, even if it was a mixed [closed]
syllable, provided that the word was marked with a disjunctive accent; a

secondary stress probably introduced by some public readers or chanters of the Bible, for the purpose of being better able to chant the disjunctive accent; e.g., וּמִכְנָסֵי־בַד ,יִזַּל־מַיִם ,נֶתַחכְּמָה ,הִתְיַצְּבוּ ,וַיִּשְׁמְעוּ, וּמִשְׁנֶה־כֶּסֶף. Such a semi-accent is called by the old Grammarians גַּעְיָא כְבֵדָה *heavy roar*, since it appears in heavy syllables, that is to say, mixed [closed]. In such cases the semi-accent does not indicate in the least that the following שוא is mobile.

Other times some Punctuators added the semi-accent after a light vowel (§ 194) followed by שוא, with the aim of making it mobile; for example, עַרְבוֹת, חַרְבוֹת, חַסְדֵי. In this last word (according to [Abraham de] Balmes and an anonymous person cited by [Jedidiah] Norzi [in *Minḥat Shai*], Num. 10:36), the ע always has a semi-accent, except in מֵעַרְבוֹת (Deut. 34:1); this means that שוא preceded by a light vowel was regarded by the Punctuators as anceps, being made mute or mobile according to what best suits the pronunciation or chanting of a particular word; therefore in עַרְבוֹת and בְּעַרְבוֹת, words lacking a semi-accent, they added it to the ע, making the שוא mobile; in מֵעַרְבוֹת however, where the מֵ is capable of receiving the secondary stress, they omitted it under the ע, and made the שוא mute.

Also, the same שוא, when it is initial (especially in a word marked with a disjunctive accent), and two or more syllables away from the stress, is sometimes prolonged by the Chanters due to the chant, and transformed into a true vowel; and in these cases the Punctuators have added to it the semi-accent; e.g., שְׁלָמִים, מְסִבָּלִים, מְשַׁקֵּדִים, סְלַח־נָא, שְׁלַח־נָא. Such a שוא is called שְׁוָא גַעְיָא, and the ancient Grammarians report that it has the sound not of חטף פתח, but of פתח. Some Punctuators distinguished this semi-accent, placing it to the right of the שוא (שְׁלַח־נָא), a usage disapproved of by Ḥayyuj.

This right-side semi-accent was also added by some to every interrogative He pointed with פתח or סגול (when the word did not already contain a regular semi-accent, e.g., הַאֲחֵיכֶם), perhaps to distinguish it from Demonstrative He, e.g., הֶהָשֵׁב ,הָאֵלֶךְ ,הָעוֹד ,הָאִם ,הָהוּא ,הָאַף, הַבְּרָכָה ,הַמְכַסֶּה.

CXCVI.

It is well known that mixed [closed] syllables containing quiescent Vav or Yod, like those found in the words תָּקִים, תָּקוּם, are necessarily accented

(§ 121 *l*); and that they therefore do not tolerate a following מַקֵּף; and so, when they are obliged to tolerate it, they take, in compensation for the lost accent, a semi-accent, e.g., הִשְׁאִיר־לוֹ, בֵּית־אֵל. Nevertheless, some examples are met in which, contrary to this rule, the semi-accent is on the simple [open] syllable that precedes the mixed one containing the quiescent letter. So תָּקוּם־אִתָּךְ (Isaiah 54:17), and in some editions הֶעָרִים־הָאֵלֶּה (Deut. 19:5),[38] הָעִיר־הַהוּא (ib. 22:18).

Ben-Asher and Ben-Naphtali differed on this matter. In my membranous [vellum or parchment] Pentateuch (§ 192, 197), for the words יָשִׁיר־מֹשֶׁה (Exodus 15:1) the following Note is read: יָשִׁיר, נפתלי טעמא למעלה, אשר טעמא למטה, that is to say: The word יָשִׁיר is controversial: Ben-Naphtali wants it stressed on the penult (יָ֫שִׁיר); Ben-Asher wants it stressed on the ultima (יָשִׁ֫יר). In the text, the semi-accent is found duplicated, that is to say, under the Yod and under the Shin.

Norzi ([*Minḥat Shai,*] Deut. 20:15) found just the opposite in a Codex containing the Variants of those two ancient Punctuators; he found recorded according to Ben-Asher הַגּוֹיִם־הָאֵלֶּה, and according to Ben-Naphtali הַגּוֹיִם־הָאֵלֶּה (1). One of the two Codices must be mistaken, mine, or that of Norzi. It is, however, more likely that the error is in his rather than in mine; because it is much easier in a long Catalogue of Variants to put in the wrong place the little line which is the semi-accent, than it is in a short Masoretic Note to write one word for another.

(1) The final syllable of the word הַגּוֹיִם does not, in actuality, contain a quiescent letter; it is to be regarded, however, as if it contained one, since it is missing the Yod of the plural, which must necessarily be inferred, as in צַדִּיקָם and the like.

CXCVII.

It is well known that the final He that is found in a word strictly joined to the following, in such a way that it can be considered part of it, is considered (if it is preceded by פתח, קמץ, or סגול) not quiescent, but otiose, and as if non-existent, so that the following letter is regarded as immediately preceded by a short, unaccented vowel, and therefore takes

---

[38] The *metheg* is lacking here in the Leningrad Codex.

dagesh; for example, מַה־זֶּה (= מַזֶּה Exod. 4:2), מַה־לָכֶם (= מַלָּכֶם Isaiah
3:15), נָתַתָּה לִּי (1).

Now some Punctuators used such a דגש even after the other gutturals
pointed with שוא. So the anonymous שַׁעֲרֵי נִקּוּד:

> בזאת ישתנה אחה"ע להדגיש אות שלאחריו אף על פי שאין
> האות בג"ד כפ"ת בכמה מקומות, כגון יַאְלָם, וַיֶּאְסֹר, לֶאְסֹר,
> ואין לפרש במה הדבר תלוי, וגם כל שני חטפים, והראשון
> באות אחה"ע, אות שאחריה שבה חטף דגישה אפילו אינה
> אות בג"ד כפ"ת, כגון יֶחְמְרוּ, יַעְלְזוּ, יֶחְשְׁכוּ וכן כל דוגמתם :

That is: "The gutturals have the property of producing in many cases
דגש in the following letter, even if it is not a בג"ד כפ"ת, e.g., וַיֶּאְסֹר, יַעְלָם,
לֶאְסֹר; one cannot explain on what it depends. Also, in every case of two
successive שוא, the first of which is a guttural, the letter that follows it,
pointed with שוא, takes a dagesh, without it being a בג"ד כפ"ת letter; e.g.,
יֶחְשְׁכוּ, יַעְלְזוּ, יֶחְמְרוּ, and all the similar ones."

In fact, in several Codices of the Public Libraries of Hamburg, Cassel,
and Erfurt, one meets דגש in the words יַעְלָם (Gen. 36:5), יַעְקֹב, יַעְזֵּר (Jer.
9:3), מַחְלוֹן, רֶעְמָה (see Gesenius, *Lehrgeb.*, p. 91). Also the Codex owned by
me (§ 192)—containing the Pentateuch plus the Targum of Onkelos, the
five Megillot, the Haftarot, and the book of Job—has דגש in the words
נֶחְקַר, וְטַעְמוֹ, לַחְמוֹ, הֶחְסִיר, וַתַּחְמֹל, וַתַּחְמְרָה (Num. 32:35), יַעְזֵּר, יַעְלָם,
יֶחְשְׁכוּ, etc. It seems to have been the custom of some readers to
pronounce with a certain amount of emphasis, as if doubled, consonants
preceded by an unvocalized guttural; and in truth, the aspirate letters, as
pronounced by the Orientals, require a certain vehemence in the emission
of the breath, which cannot help but transmit some of the emphasis to the
consonant that follows.

Even the ר, since this is considered a semi-guttural in the triliteral
languages, has been able to give rise to such emphasis, and therefore to
דגש; for example, חַרְצֻבּוֹת, בַּרְזֶל, גַּרְזֶן. Sometimes this same emphasis was
made felt not after, but before the guttural, if the guttural was not followed
by another consonant, and if the preceding consonant was pointed with
שוא; e.g., נִטְמְאוּ, יִמָּלְאוּ, יִשְׁמְעוּ, נִמְצְאוּ, נִבְלְעוּ, and in my Codex.
Analogous to this דגש is that of קוּמוּ סְעוּ, קוּמוּ צְאוּ, which, however,
seems to be of primary institution, since it is recorded in the Masorah. I call
all of these דגש *emphatic*.

The דגש of עִנְבֵי, עִקְבֵי, עֶשְׂבוֹת, עַצְרוֹתֵיכֶם, הַרְעִימָה, הִרְאִיתֶם, known as 'euphonic' (and probably of primary institution), is perhaps also such, that is to say, that it indicates an emphasis occasioned by the guttural.

A few Codices exhibit some initial דגש outside of any rule, probably emphatic, and deriving from the eccentricity of some ancient readers; e.g., in the above-mentioned [Codex] of mine לְקְטוּ (Exod. 16:16), זֶה (ib. 16:32). Probably of like origin is the דגש of לֹא (Gen. 19:2; 1 Sam. 8:19), and of יָה (Psalm 94:12, 118:5, 18), although it is also more ancient and of primary institution, being recorded by the Masoretes.[39]

(1) Likewise in Italian, the Crusca[40] observes that "*A ciascuno, A lui, A me*, reduplicate the consonant in pronunciation, and from two distinct written items, the pronunciation confusing them, are made one: *acciascuno, allui, ammè*."

So in the same way, even when writing joins two words, the first of which ends in a vowel, and the second begins with a consonant, the consonant of the second is normally doubled; e.g., *dabbene*, for *da bene*; *laddove*, for *là dove*; *vieppiù*, for *vie più*.[41]

CXCVIII.

Of a totally different nature is the דגש that in some Codices is found in an initial letter which is identical to the final letter of the preceding word, e.g., בֶּן־נוּן, נָתֵן נְשָׁמָה, וְכָל־לָשׁוֹן (a דגש adopted by יהב"י [Jekuthiel ha-Cohen ben Judah] and by [Wolf] Heidenhim);[42] as well as in a letter preceded by another one homogeneous to it, either because they are both liquids, or because of the affinity that some linguals have with the sibilants; e.g.,

---

[39] Indeed, the occurences of last two examples, לֹא and יָה, are found in the Leningrad Codex, unlike the preceding examples from SDL's own manuscript.

[40] Perhaps SDL is referring to the *Dizionario della lingua italiana*, published by the Accademia della Crusca in Padua, 1827–30. The Accademia was, and in fact remains, a well-known linguistic society dedicated to the study and proper usage of the Italian language. They have been producing dictionaries since 1612.

[41] For a description of this process in modern Italian, known as *raddoppiamento sintattico* or *rafforzamento sintattico*, see Martin Maiden and Cecilia Robustelli, *A Reference Grammar of Modern Italian* (Chicago, 2000), pp. 10–13.

[42] Recall that Heidenheim published Yahbi's *Ein ha-Kore* in his edition of the Torah, *Ḥumash Me'or Enayim* (Rödelheim, 1818–21).

מִבְּכֹרוֹת־צֹאנוֹ ,שִׁכְבַת־זֶרַע ,כָּל־מְלָאכָה ,מַמְלְכוֹת (Gesenius, loc. cit.),
כָּבֵד זֶה (in my above-mentioned Codex). This is based on the opinion of
some ancient Grammarians (among them [Jonah] Ibn Janaḥ; see [Kimḥi's]
Michlol fol. 95), who, by example of the Arabs, claimed that consonants
followed by identical or homogeneous ones could be elided, assimilating to
them, for example, pronouncing *binnùn* instead of *bin-nun* (בֶּן־נוּן), *ittellì*
instead of *itten-lì* (יִתֶּן־לִי), *ennamalà* for *el-nemalà* (אֶל־נְמָלָה); an affectation
rightly reproved by Kimḥi.

CXCIX.

It is well known that in the form וִילְלַת (Jer. 25:36), the חִירק proper to the
Yod has been shifted to the preceding Vav, which should have Schwa:
וְיִלְלַת. Likewise, Kimḥi read, and some editions still read, וִיחֵלוּ (Job 29:21)
instead of וְיִחֵלוּ. Such a regression of the חִירק of the Yod was
consistently adopted by Ben-Naphtali, who punctuated, for example, וִיתֵּן,
בִּיזְרְעֵיל ,לִישְׂרָאֵל, in place of לְיִשְׂרָאֵל ,וְיִתֵּן, etc., cases in which Ben-
Asher, on the contrary, preserved the initial שׁוא, probably because
quiescent Yod cannot regularly appear in a mixed [closed] syllable.

Our printed books have preserved two examples of Ben-Naphtali's
Orthography in the words בִּיקְרוֹתֶיךָ (Psalm 45:10), כִּיתְרוֹן (Eccles. 2:13).[43]
In this last word, it is without a doubt an error to make the שׁוא mobile, as
Norzi would like.

Such an Orthography supposes that through a softening of
pronunciation very common in Languages (§ 102), the Yod accompanied by
the vowel *i* had lost its consonantal sound, so that instead of being
pronounced *yi*, it was pronounced (as C. B. Michaëlis also believed, *Lum. syr.*
§ 8) simply *i*. This statement is supported

a) by the Orthography of the Syrians and the Arabs, who write *Isaac*
and similar names with an initial א (Syr. אִיסְחָק, Arab. אֲצְחַק);

b) by the Biblical אִישִׁי (1 Chron. 2:13), equivalent to יִשַׁי;

c) by the סגול under the א of the Future, e.g., אֶפְקֹד instead of
אִפְקֹד, intended (in the opinion of Kimḥi, Michlol fol. 20) to prevent the
first person from being confused with the third (יִפְקֹד); an opinion greatly

---

[43] In the Leningrad Codex, the so-called Ben-Naphtali orthography is found in
this example from Ecclesiastes 2:13, but not in Psalm 45.

supported by the observation that the forms אֶתְחַבַּר, אֶשְׁתּוֹלְלוּ, אֶגְאַלְתִּי, have סֶגוֹל, while הִתְפַּקַּד, הִפְקִיד, הִתְחַבַּר, and the like consistently have חִירֵק in the initial letter, a guttural, a fact which disproves the opinion of Elijah Levita, who believes that the א has סֶגוֹל because it is a guttural;

d) by the analogy of initial וּ, which is pronounced *u* by everyone, and not *vu*.

e) by the meaningless דָגֵשׁ of the plurals עֲנָיִים, צָיִים, אָיִים, and the like, which do not seem intended for anything except to prevent the elision of one of the two *i*'s, that is to say, that it is pronounced *tsi-yim*, rather than *tsiyyim*, with a doubled *Y*; if the Yod did not have dagesh, *tsi-im* might have been pronounced in a single syllable, צִים, as in fact it was sometimes pronounced and written (Num. 24:24), (for this reason the Patronymics have both of these plurals, one with a single *i*, עִבְרִים, the other with two *i*'s, but with dagesh in the Yod, עִבְרִיִּים). If Yod pointed with חִירֵק was pronounced *yi*, there would not be any need for the דָגֵשׁ to avoid the elision of one of the two *i*'s (1);

f) by the meaningless דָגֵשׁ of הַיֵּיטַב (Lev. 10:19), which likewise appears intended only to make the Yod felt, and to prevent the word from being confused with הַאֵיטַב.

(1) This דָגֵשׁ, necessary in the masculine plural, was afterwards, by analogy, extended to the feminine singular and plural; e.g., עֲנִיָּה, עֲנִיּוֹת.—According to Gesenius (*Lehrg.*, p. 522), the Yod of the Patronymics inherently has dagesh, as it does in Arabic. I find, however, that it does not have dagesh in Aramaic.

CC.

Also any non-quiescent final Yod, for example, that of פָּנַי, גּוֹי, has naturally lost its consonantal sound, and is pronounced simply *i*, forming with the preceding vowel a compound vowel, or diphthong (*goi, panài*); and it is therefore that some Punctuators added to it a חִירֵק: פָּנִי. That such a Yod was pronounced as a vowel *i*, rather than as a consonant, is confirmed by the universal judgment of the Hebrews, Syrians, and Arabs, and by a large number of Grammarians, with the exception of Gesenius and Shalom ha-Cohen, who teach that they should be pronounced *goy, panay*, with a consonantal *y*.

Likewise, non-quiescent final Vav, e.g., that of פָּנָיו, גֵּו, וָו, is pronounced as *u* by the majority of Hebrews, as well as by the Syrians and the Arabs, and by many Grammarians; however, it is pronounced as *f* (German *v*) by the German Hebrews, and therefore by [Johann] Reuchlin and [Sebastian] Münster, and it is pronounced as a consonantal *v* (German *w*) by Gesenius and Shalom ha-Cohen; it is because of this that some Punctuators (probably Germans) tended to add שוא to such final Vav's: פָּנָיו.

I assume, with Gesenius, the greater part of non-quiescent final Yod's and Vav's to have been primitively consonants; I believe, however, that their pronunciation was naturally softened and made into a vowel by the ancient Hebrews, as well as by the Syrians and the Arabs.

However, in the words פִּיו, אָחִיו, אָבִיו, it does not seem to me that the Vav was ever a consonant, and I believe that these words were primitively pronounced פִּיהוּ, אָחִיהוּ, אָבִיהוּ, as is still read in several scriptural passages, and which is analogous to the primitive Chaldean אֲחוּהִי, אֲבוּהִי (§ 126).

If this is true, it proves that already in Biblical times, the final Vav lost its consonantal sound; since in these words, where consonantal *V* had never been present, such an orthography (פִּיו, אָחִיו, אָבִיו) would not have been used, if [final] Vav had not already been pronounced as a vowel *U*.

It will be said: If non-quiescent final Yod and Vav had a vowel sound, they would not prompt a דגש in a subsequent בגד כפת letter, as happens in יָדָיו תְּבִיאֶינָה, גּוֹי גָּדוֹל, and the like.

But here it must be considered that, although the words *goi, yadau,* and the like terminate in the vowels *i* and *u*, these do not have the status of bare and simple vowels, but rather form part of a compound vowel, or diphthong. Now no one will deny that a simple vowel and a compound vowel can, as rather different creatures, have different influences on the initial consonant of the subsequent word.

Diphthongs also occur in the middle of a word, in which case the Vav and Yod are pointed with שוא, for example, לַיְלָה *lai-la*. In this case, however, the diphthong is not followed by דגש; for example, עָלַיְכִי, בֵּיתָה, הַמָּוְתָה, with the exception of the lone form שַׁלַוְתִּי [Job 3:26]. The same circumstance applies to קַו־תֹהוּ (Isaiah 34:11), where the מקף joins the two words into one; and to שָׁלוּ בָהּ (Ezek. 23:42), אֲדֹנָי בָּם (Psalm 68:18), where the second word is monosyllabic, and so the two words, even without מקף, behave almost as if one (1).

It does no good to object by saying that in בַּיְתָה etc., the Yod and the Vav were originally vocalized (מָוֶת, עָלֶיךָ, בַּיִת), and hence are not equivalent to קָרְ־תֹהוּ etc. This is because Biblical Chaldean has the forms לְהֵיתָיָה, הֵיתִיו, הֵיתִי, with no dagesh in the ת, even though the first radical, here represented by the Yod, is fundamentally unvocalized in the verbal form אַפְעֵל, to which these three words belong. And since the rules for דגש lene are the same in Biblical Chaldean as in Hebrew, it can be inferred from this that the absence of דגש in בַּיְתָה etc. does not derive from the fact that the letters, which here are at the end of a syllable, primitively began them, but rather there is a law by which a diphthong is not able to prompt דָּגֵשׁ in a following בגד כפת letter, except when it [the diphthong] is word final.

(1) Two words not joined by מקף can, when one of them is monosyllabic, be considered as a single word, as happens in the case of regression of the accent (see § 123, note 2), but can also, as happens in most cases, be regarded as two distinct words. So the fact that in גֵּו כְּסִילִים, דָּמָיו בּוֹ, עֵשָׂו בָּא, גּוֹי גָּדוֹל and the like, where one of the two words is monosyllabic, the בגד כפת letter takes a dagesh after the diphthong, without it being considered as if it were in the middle of the word, does not prove in the least that in אֲדֹנָי בָּם, שָׁלֵו בָּהּ the two words cannot have been considered by the Pointers as if joined and forming a single word.

BIOGRAPHICAL APPENDIX

The following biographies were compiled from the content of this book, from comprehensive reference works like the *Jewish Encyclopedia*, the *Encyclopaedia Judaica*, and the *Catholic Encyclopedia*, national biographies like the *Allgemeine Deutsche Bibliographie, Neue Deutsche Biographie, Dizionario Biografico degli Italiani, Dictionnaire de Biographie Française, Biographie Universelle, Oxford Dictionary of National Biography*, and *Nieuw Nederlandisch Biografisch Woordenboek*, from information given by authors in their own publications, and from a number of other more focused studies. The publication details of the scholars' works have all been checked in library databases and, whenever possible, by examining the books themselves. Details occasionally disagree with those of other reference works, but pains have been taken to ensure that they appear correctly here. Within an entry, an asterisk (*) before a name indicates that there is a separate entry for this person.

Following each biographical entry is a list of the sections or paragraphs in which the authors are mentioned. In these lists, which serve as an index, I make a distinction between a textnote (n.) an a translator's footnote (fn.). When an author is cited in the main body of a paragraph, as well as in a textnote or footnote to that paragraph, I give only the paragraph number.

Aaron ben Joseph (Ha-Rishon; ca. 1255–ca. 1320), Crimean Karaite philosopher, physician, and poet. A prominent and renowned Karaite scholar, he wrote an important commentary on the Torah entitled *Mivhar* (Koslov, 1834/35), and the *Seder Tefillot* (Venice, 1525–29), which became the standard Karaite prayer book. In addition, he wrote an unfinished grammar entitled *Kelil Yofi*, which was later completed by Isaac Tishbi (Constantinople, 1581; Koslov, 1847). (**§ 17**)

Aaron Moses ben Tzvi Hirsch (18th c.), Hebrew grammarian. A native of Lemberg (Lvov), among his grammatical works is the *Ohel Moshe* (Zolkiew, 1765; Salzbach, 1771), which follows *David Kimhi's *Sefer ha-Zikkaron*, and criticizes the work of *Solomon Hanau. (**§ 36**)

Abendana, Jacob (1630–95), Dutch-Sephardic rabbi and scholar. Rabbi of the Spanish Jews in London, he translated *Judah ha-Levi's *Kuzari* into Spanish (Amsterdam, 1663) and, along with his brother Isaac, published an annotated edition of *Solomon ben Melech's *Michlal Yofi* (Amsterdam, 1660/61; 2nd ed., 1684–85). (§ 33)

Abraham ben David ha-Levi (Abraham ibn Daud, Abram ben Dior; 1110–80), Spanish Jewish astronomer, historian, and philosopher. In 1161, he wrote the influential historical work *Sefer ha-Kabbalah*, oriented against Karaism (Mantua, 1514); a critical edition with an English translation was made by Gerson D. Cohen (Philadelphia, 1967). (§ 12 n. 1)

Abraham (Vita) de Cologna (1754/55–1832), Italian rabbi and politician. While rabbi at Mantua, he was elected a member of Parliament in the Napoleonic kingdom of Italy, and in 1806 to the assembly of notables in Paris. He held the title of *Chevalier* in the Order of the Iron Crown (*Couronne de Fer*), founded by Napoleon in 1805. SDL writes in his autobiography that while still a teen, he visited with Cologna, whose work had inspired his love for Hebrew grammar as a child. Cologna had become blind in his old age, and SDL would read to him or take dictation. SDL continues, however, that he soon became disgusted with Cologna's egotism and phoniness, and consequently ceased his visits. (§ 42 n. 3)

Abravanel, Isaac (1437–1508), Portuguese Jewish exegete, philosopher, and statesman. Once treasurer to the King of Portugal, he was forced to flee to Spain in 1483, where he soon entered the service of Ferdinand and Isabella of Castille. Despite his royal connections, he was forced to flee to Italy in 1492, where he spent the rest of his life. He was a prolific writer, having produced commentaries on the all of the Torah and Prophets, the Passover Haggadah, and on the Mishnaic tractate Avot, as well as a number of other religious and philosophical works. His Biblical commentaries were extremely popular and influential. This holds true even among Christian scholars, probably because of Abravanel's tolerant attitude towards early Christian commentators like *Jerome and *Nicholas of Lyra. (§§ 36 n. 1; 92; 102; 192)

Abu al-Faraj Harun (Aaron ben Jeshua of Jerusalem; 11th c.), grammarian and lexicographer. A Karaite living in Jerusalem, his works include the Hebrew grammar *Al-Kitāb al-Mushtamil* and a commentary to the Pentateuch. Recent research suggests that he was also the author of the work *Hidāyat al-Qāri*, which was translated into Hebrew, possibly by *Menahem ben Nataniel, as *Horayat ha-Kore* (see § 13). His work was highly praised by *Abraham ibn Ezra, *Judah ibn Bal'am, and *Jonah ibn Janah. **(§ 11 fn. 17; 13 fn. 34)**

Acurense, Joseph (Joseph Aqouri; 17th c.), Maronite Patriarch. The successor of Patriarch *George Amira in 1644, he was also the author of a Syriac grammar, *Grammatica linguae syriacae* (Rome, 1647), referred to by SDL as "the most authoritative of all" (§ 132, note 3). **(§ 132 n. 1, n. 3; 134; 136; 175)**

Adonim ben Tamim (Dunash ibn Tamim, Abu Sahl; ca. 980–after 955), North African scholar. He wrote a now lost comparative study of Hebrew and Arabic (quoted by *Ibn Ezra and others), along with other scientific and exegetical works. **(§ 11)**

Adonim the Levite of Fez see Dunash ben Labrat.

Agius de Soldanis, Giovanni Pietro Francesco (1712–70), Maltese linguist and folklorist. The first curator of the Public Library of Malta (founded in 1760), he published a history of the island of Gozo (the island neighboring Malta), a Maltese dictionary, and a grammar of Maltese (one of the earliest) entitled *Della lingua Punica presentamente usata dai Maltesi* (Rome, 1750). From the title of his grammar, it is clear that he promoted (as others would later) the false notion that Maltese, actually a dialect of Arabic, descended from Punic (Phoenician). **(§ 52 n. 3)**

Agostini, Giovanni degli (1701–55), Italian literary historian. A native of Venice, he wrote the *Notizie istorico-critiche intorno la vita e le opere degli scrittori viniziani* (Venice, 2 vols., 1752–54) which covers Venetian writers from the period 1074–1591. In this work he is critical of the work of *Sansovino. **(§ 19 n. 1)**

Albo, Joseph (15th c.), Spanish Jewish theologian. He is best known for his treatise on the fundamentals of Jewish faith, *Sefer ha-Ikkarim*, completed in 1425. **(§ 192)**

Alfasi, Isaac ben Jacob (1013–1103), North African Jewish Talmudist. A native of Algeria, he later settled in Fez (hence his surname), then Spain. He gained fame from his very important work *(Sefer ha-)Halachot*, which essentially presented all of the Halachah of the Talmud in abridged form.

The work was praised by *Maimonides. It was first printed in Constantinople (1509), then Venice (1521). The second edition, upon which the many subsequent printings were based, included the first printing of the Tosefta, as well as other addenda. *Judah ha-Levi is counted among Alfasi's many students. (§ 81)

Alighieri, Dante (1265–1321), Florentine poet and author. Most famous for his *Divine Comedy* (from which SDL quotes), he also wrote *De vulgari eloquentia* (1303–4), a treatise in Latin on vernacular language in Italy. (§§ 43; 72 n. 1)

Almoli, Solomon ben Jacob (late 15th–early 16th c.), Sephardic Jewish physician and grammarian. He wrote a grammatical work on the Hebrew schwa entitled *Halichot Shwa* (Constantinople, 1519). He also wrote the popular *Pitron Ḥalomot*, a work on dream interpretation in the Talmud (Salonika, 1516; Constantinople, 1518), as well as introductions to *Elisha ben Abraham's *Magen David* (Constantinople, 1517) and the second edition of *David ibn Yaḥya's *Leshon Limmudim* (Constantinople, 1542). He also helped to publish *Abraham ibn Ezra's *Yesod Mora* (1530) and *Safah Berurah* (1530), at his own expense. (§ 17)

Altaras, David ben Solomon (1675–1714), Italian rabbi and editor. He wrote *Kelalei ha-Dikduk*, a Hebrew grammar, which was printed at the front of the Venice edition of the *Mikra'ot Gedolot* (1675–78). (§ 34)

Alting, Jacob (1618–79), German Protestant theologian and Hebraist. A native of Heidelberg, he studied theology and Oriental languages at Gröningen, Utrecht, Leiden, and Oxford; in England he was ordained a priest of the Anglican Church. He spent his entire teaching career in Gröningen, where he was professor of Oriental languages and (towards the end of his career) of theology. His Hebrew grammar *Fundamenta punctationis linguae sanctae* (Gröningen, 1654; many subsequent editions) was quite widely used, and is notable for being the first to deal with the structure of the syllabie. (Preface; §§ 18; 20 n. 1; 22; 29; 35; 170)

Ambrogio, Teseo (1469–1540), Italian Orientalist. A professor at Bologna, he was the first European scholar to learn and teach Syriac. He treats Syriac briefly in his *Introductio ad chaldaicam linguam, syriacam, atque armenicam, et decem alias linguas* (Padua, 1539), the first book in which Syriac, and several other languages, were printed with movable type. (§ 43 n. 3)

Amira, George Michael (1568?–1644), Maronite Patriarch. A native of Lebanon, he studied at the Maronite College at Rome (1583–95), and was later appointed Patriarch (1633). He published the most important Syriac grammar of the sixteenth century, *Grammatica syriaca, sive chaldaica* (Rome, 1596), as well as an edition of the Syriac New Testament. (§§ 114 n. 1; 128; 131; 132 n. 3; 134; 136; 139 n. 1; 176; 177; 178)

Anan ben David (8th c.), Babylonian Jew. He was the founder of the Ananite sect of Judaism. The Ananites (his immediate followers) were few in number and were eventually absorbed into the larger Karaite movement. Anan was subsequently regarded by the Karaites as their founder. (§ 4)

Aquila, Anotonio dell' (17th c.), Italian priest and scholar. He was the author of an Arabic grammar entitled *Arabicae linguae novae, et methodicae institutiones* (Rome, 1650), in which, like *Masclef later did for Hebrew, he taught the reading of Arabic words using the vowels that correspond to the name of each letter. His grammar was published by the Congregation of the Propaganda, suggesting that Aquila may have been affiliated with the Collegium Urbanum in Rome. (§ 30 n. 2)

Archivolti, Samuel (ca. 1516–1611), Italian Jewish author, grammarian, and poet. In addition to numerous poems, piyyutim, and other scholarly works, he wrote a grammar entitled *Arugat ha-Bosem* (Venice, 1602; Amsterdam, 1730). The last part of this grammar was translated by *Johannes Buxtorf II, who appended to it his Latin translation of *Judah ha-Levi's *Kuzari* (Basel, 1660). (§§ 18 n. 2; 33; 42)

Assemani, Giuseppe Simone (Josephus Simonius Assemanus; 1687–1768), Syrian Maronite priest and Vatican librarian. He is responsible for collecting the manuscripts which subsequently formed the basis of the famous Vatican collection. His monumental work *Bibliotheca orientalis Clementino-Vaticana* (4 vols., Rome, 1719–28) is the most comprehensive treatment of Syriac literature ever undertaken. Much of his other work was destroyed by a fire in his apartment in 1768. (§§ 6; 114 n. 1)

Aurivillius, Karl (1717–86), Swedish Orientalist. A professor of Oriental languages at Uppsala and Sweden's foremost Orientalist of the eighteenth century, he wrote the massive *Dissertationes ad sacras literas et philologiam orientalem pertinentes* (Göttingen, 1790). This included a preface by *J. D. Michaëlis. He had studied with *C. B. Michaëlis at Halle in the early 1740s, as well as with *Johann Tympe at Jena, and *Étienne Fourmont in Paris, and *Albert Schultens at Leiden. (§§ 25; 27)

Aurogallus, Mattaeus (1490–1543), German Christian Hebraist. A professor at Wittenberg, his work includes a Hebrew grammar, printed right to left, entitled *Compendium hebreae chaldeaeque grammatices* (Wittenberg, 1525; 1539); this work also includes an edition of the Hebrew text of Daniel. Also noteworthy is the assistance he gave to Martin Luther in his translation of the Old Testament. (§ 20)

Bacon, Francis (Baron of Verulam; 1561–1626), British philosopher, statesman, and scientist. His first work was the *Advancement of Learning* (London, 1605), which was later revised and expanded in a Latin edition entitled *De dignitate et augmentis scientiarum* (London, 1623). (§ 101 n. 1)

Baḥya ben Asher ben Halawa (d. 1340), Spanish Jewish exegete and Kabbalist. His principal work was a commentary on the Torah, finished in 1291 and first published in 1492 (Naples). In it he made significant use of the Kabbalah as a means of interpretation. His commentary achieved wide popularity, a fact to which its ten supercommentaries are a testament. He also wrote several other popular works on religion, morality, and Kabbalah. (§ 192)

Baḥya ben Joseph ibn Paquda (11ᵗʰ c.), Spanish Jewish dayyan and philosopher. In 1040, he wrote *Kitāb al-Hidāyah ilā Farā'iḍ al-Qulub*, the first Jewish system of ethics, translated into Hebrew by *Judah ibn Tibbon as *Ḥovot ha-Levavot*. This work, which became quite popular in its Hebrew form, was largely modeled on Muslim works on philosophy and mysticism and Arabic Neoplatonism. (§ 92)

Balmes, Abraham ben Meir de (1440–1523), Italian Jewish physician, philosopher, grammarian, and translator. His *Mikne Avram*, written at the urging of the famous printer Daniel Bomberg, was published in Hebrew and Latin (Venice, 1523). In this lengthy work, widely used by Christian Hebraists, he attempts to treat Hebrew grammar philosophically, and refutes the opinions of *David Kimḥi; he was also the first to treat syntax as a special part of the grammar. He died just before its completion, and the final chapter was completed by *Kalonymus ben David. He had been given special permission by the Pope to study at the University of Naples, and, according to *Gedaliah ibn Yaḥya, had taught at the University of Padua. (§§ 9 n. 1; 12 n. 1; 13; 14; 17; 18; 151; 158; 195)

Bar Hebraeus, Gregorius (Abulfaraj; 1226–1286), Syrian Orthodox catholicos, historian, philosopher, grammarian, and Biblical commentator. One of the leading scholars of his time, he produced a large body of work on a wide range of topics, much of it still unpublished. SDL refers to his work on grammar, *Ktābā d-Ṣemḥe* 'The Book of Rays'. Because of his surname, many have thought him to have been the son of a Jew, however, there is no evidence for this, and the Latinized Bar Hebraeus, 'Son of a Hebrew,' may be a misunderstood (and misleading) rendering of the Syriac *Bar Ebrāyā*. (§ 6)

Bartolocci, Giulio (1613–87), Italian Christian Hebraist and bibliographer. His famous *Bibliotheca Magna Rabbinica* (4 vols.; Rome, 1675–93) was one of the first attempts to give a comprehensive account of Jewish literature. In this bibliographical work, which served as the basis for *Wolf's *Bibliotheca*, he occasionally presents Hebrew and Aramaic texts in full (with Latin translation), and provides biographies of some of the more important authors. The last volume was edited by *Carlo Imbonati, who also added a fifth volume to the series. (§ 17)

Bassan, Jacob (Jacob Babani, Bassani, Basan; d. 1769), German Sephardic rabbi. Rabbi of the Spanish and Portuguese communities of Hamburg, he wrote the grammatical work *Yashresh Ya'akov* (Nuremberg, 1767/68). (§ 37)

Bazzarini, Antonio (1782–1850), Italian scholar. He wrote the *Dizionario enciclopedico delle scienze, lettere, ed arti* (Venice, 1830–37), for which he became well known. He wrote a smaller encyclopedia, a dictionary of Italian, and a Latin-Italian Italian-Latin dictionary. (§ 70 n. 1)

Bedersi, Jedaiah ben Abraham (Ha-Penini; 1270–1340), Jewish Provençal poet, physician, and philosopher. He wrote his *Iggeret Hitnatselut* (Venice, 1545; first printed separately 1809; reprinted Warsaw 1882), a defense of science and philosophy, in response to a 1305 ban on the study of these fields proclaimed by the Spanish Rabbi Solomon ben Abraham Adret in Barcelona. (§ 14 n. 2)

Bellarmino, Saint Roberto Francesco Romolo (Robert Francis Romulus Bellarmine; 1542–1621), Italian Jesuit theologian, cardinal and writer. In addition to a distinguished career in the Church, which included a professorship in theology at the Roman College and role in the trial of Galileo, he wrote a Hebrew grammar called *Institutiones linguae hebraicae*

(Rome, 1578; several subsequent editions). He was canonized in 1930. **(§ 20)**

Ben-Asher, Aaron ben Moses (10th c.), Tiberian masorete. The last in the line of an important family of masoretes in Tiberias, he was responsible for pointing the Aleppo Codex (ca. 930), today considered the most authoritative Masoretic Bible manuscript. He also wrote a treatise on vocalization and pronunciation entitled *Dikdukei ha-Te'amim*, first published in the Bomberg Rabbinic Bible (Venice, 1517–18). **(§§ 9; 10; 147; 196; 199)**

Ben-Naphtali, Moses ben David (9th–10th c.), masorete. Presumably he lived in Tiberias, roughly contemporary with *Aaron ben Moses ben Asher. Nothing is known about him apart for his name. There survives a list of minor variants (about 850) from the readings of Ben Asher, with regard to the vowels and accents, attributed to Ben-Naphtali. There are no systematic differences, suggesting that they do not stem from two different masoretic "schools", as once thought. **(§§ 9; 10; 147; 196; 199)**

Benjamin Simeon ha-Levi (d. before 1773), Jewish Hebrew grammarian. He wrote a short Hebrew grammar entitled *Da'at Kedoshim* (London, 1772/73); the *Jewish Encyclopedia* (in the incorrectly titled entry "Benjamin, Simeon") calls this one of the earliest works by an Ashkenazic Jew in England. The title page of his grammar calls him "Benjamin Simeon ha-Levi of blessed memory, from Amsterdam". Nothing more is known of the author. **(§ 37)**

Benveniste, Samuel (d. after 1356), Spanish Jewish physician and translator. A physician to the brother of King Pedro IV of Aragon, he was a familiar in the royal court. He translated into Hebrew a treatise on asthma by Maimonides and, probably, Boethius' *De consolatione philosophae*, a popular medieval work. SDL attributes to him some grammatical study in which he is critical of *David Kimḥi; I have not been able to find any reference to a grammatical work of his, so most likely his criticisms are mentioned within his works on other topics. **(§§ 14; 17)**

Biancuzzi, Benedetto (Biancuccio, Blancuccius, Blancutius; late 16th–early 17th c.), Italian Hebraist. A Roman and a teacher of Hebrew, he wrote a grammar entitled *Institutiones in linguam sanctam hebraicam* (Rome, 1608). **(§ 21)**

Blomfield, Edward Valentine (1788–1816), English classicist. A promising classical scholar who died quite young, he is best known for his translation (from German) of *Matthiae's Greek grammar, *A Copious Greek Grammar* (Cambridge, 1818; 4th ed., London, 1832). (§ 53 n. 1)

Bochart, Samuel (1599–1667), French Orientalist. He earned renown with his historical work *Geographia sacra*, which appeared in two parts, *Phaleg* (Caen, 1646) and *Chanaan* (Caen, 1651). Also well known was his massive study on the animals of the Bible, *Hierozoicon* (London, 1663). These works, along with several others smaller ones, were published together as *Opera omnia* (Leiden, 1675). (§ 57 n. 1)

Böschenstein, Johann (1472–1540), German Christian Hebraist. Many scholars claim that he was the child of Jewish parents, though he denied this charge. His very short Hebrew grammar *Elementale introductorium in hebreas litteras teutonice et hebraice legendas* (Augsburg, 1514)—containing a sketch of the alphabet and punctuation, along with some reading selections—was one of the earliest made by a Christian. Other publications include a Latin translation of a grammar of *Moses Kimḥi, entitled *Rudimenta hebraica* (1520). (§ 20)

Bouget, Jean (Joanne Bouget, Bougetius; 1692–1775), French Catholic Hebraist. A professor of Hebrew at the Collegium Urbanum in Rome (the seminary of the Propaganda), he was also part of the court of Pope Benedict XIV (as *cameriere segreto*). His works on Hebrew include *Brevis exercitatio ad studium linguae hebraicae* (Rome, 1706), *Grammaticae hebraeae Rudimenta* (2nd ed., Rome, 1717; 3rd ed., 1740), and *Lexicon hebraicum et chaldaico-biblicum* (Rome, 1737). (§ 23)

Briel, Judah Leon ben Eliezer (Brieli; ca. 1643–1722), Italian rabbi and exegete at Mantua. A halachic authority, he composed various religious writings, in addition to a Hebrew grammar entitled *Shefer Kelalei Dikduk* (Mantua, 1729/30; 1769), his only published work. (§ 42)

Buxtorf, Johannes (1564–1629), Swiss Christian Hebraist and lexicographer. Considered one of the founders of Hebrew and Rabbinical studies among Christian scholars, he held the chair in Hebrew at Basel for many years. He published numerous lexicographic, grammatical, and bibliographical works, among which are *Epitome Grammaticae hebraeae* (Basel, 1605), *Thesaurus grammaticus linguae sanctae* (Basel, 1609), *Lexicon hebraicum et chaldaicum* (Basel, 1607), *Bibliotheca Rabbinica* (Basel, 1613), and *Grammaticae chaldaicae et syriacae libri III* (Basel, 1615). He also printed the sixth Rabbinic

Bible in 1618–19, to which he published a supplemental study of the Masorah, *Tiberias, sive, Commentarius Masorethicus* (Basel, 1620). Many of his works went through several subsequent editions, often revised and published by his son, *Johannes Buxtorf II. (§§ 10 n. 1; 18 n. 2; 21; 43 fn. 107; 133; 153; 176)

Buxtorf, Johannes II (1599–1664), Swiss Christian Hebraist and lexicographer. The son of *Johannes Buxtorf, he continued the legacy of his father, whose chair he took over at the University of Basel. In addition to several original works on Hebrew grammar, he completed and published his father's *Lexicon chaldaicum, talmudicum et rabbinicum* (Basel, 1639), and revised and republished many of his father's other works. He also translated various Hebrew authors into Latin, including *Maimonides, *Judah ha-Levi, and *Samuel Archivolti. (§ 18 n. 2)

Calasio, Francesco Mario di (Calasius; ca. 1550–1620), Franciscan friar and Hebraist. He wrote the *Canones generales linguae sanctae* (Rome, 1616), in addition to a Hebrew dictionary and concordance. (§§ 21; 157)

Calcio, Ignazio (Ignatius Calcius; 18th c.), Italian Hebraist. A professor of Hebrew, he wrote a grammar entitled *Linguae sanctae rudimenta in usum tironum versibus concinnata accedit exercitatio grammatica* (Naples, 1753). (§ 29)

Calimani, Simone (Simḥah) ben Abraham (1699–1784), Italian rabbi and author. He edited a large number of books in his position as corrector at the Hebrew printing office of Venice. Among his own works was a Hebrew grammar called *Kelalei Dikdukei Leshon Ever*, inserted at the end of the Bible printed at Venice (1739; reprint, Bnei Brak, 1995), and which appeared in an Italian translation as *Grammatica ebrea spiegata in lingua italiana* (Venice, 1751; Pisa, 1815). Also a poet and playwright, he composed a poem on the occasion of the wedding of *Moses Ḥayyim Luzzatto, SDL's great-great-uncle. (§ 42)

Caluso, Tommaso Valperga di (1737–1815), Italian astronomer, mathematician, Orientalist, and poet. In addition to teaching astronomy and Oriental languages at the University of Turin, he was also the director of Turin's observatory, and secretary, later president, of the Reale Accademia delle Scieze. Though most of his work focused on the sciences, he had a strong interest in languages, especially Hebrew and Coptic. In addition to a few other works on these languages, he wrote the short *Prime lezioni di Grammatica ebraica* (Turin, 1805; 2nd ed., 1826). The second edition contained corrections and a preface by *Vittorio Amadeo Peyron, who was probably a former student. (§ 29)

Cappel, Louis (Ludovicus Cappellus; 1585–1658), French Christian theologian and Hebrew scholar. A professor of Hebrew and theology at the Reformed Academy of Saumut, he gained fame via his books *Arcanum Punctationis Revelatum* (Leiden, 1624) and *Critica Sacra* (Paris, 1650). In the former, which was published by *Thomas Erpenius, he proved that the Hebrew pointing must date from after the Christian era; in the latter, he proved that the consonantal text had not been transmitted without errors. (§§ 9 n. 1; 18 n. 2; 193)

Caspi, Joseph ben Abba Mari (1279/80–1340), philosopher, Biblical commentator, and grammarian. A wealthy man who lived variously in France, Spain, Egypt, and Morocco, he wrote a lost commentary on the grammar of *Jonah ibn Janah, a dictionary entitled *Sharsherot Kesef*, in addition to numerous other works. (§ 17)

Castell, Edmund (1606–85/86), English Orientalist. His major work was the *Lexicon heptaglotton* (2 vols., London, 1669–86), a project which ruined him financially. *Johann David Michaëlis extracted and published the Syriac portion of this lexicon, which appeared as *Lexicon syriacum* (Göttingen, 1788). Castell also contributed to the great Polyglott Bible of Brian Walton, serving as his chief assistant. He was, from 1666, a professor of Arabic at Cambridge, though he had very few students and did not spend much time there. (§§ 132 n. 3; 136; 139)

Castiglioni, Vittorio (Yitshak Hayyim Castiglioni; 1840–1911), Italian rabbi, writer, and translator. A native of Trieste, he was a cousin and pupil of SDL, and eventually became chief Rabbi of Rome (1904–11). His own original work includes *Pe'er Adam* (Krakow, 1892), on the theories of Darwin, and other smaller works on Judaism and the natural sciences. He encouraged the publication of some of SDL's works, most notably his collected letters (*Iggerot Shadal*, ed. E. Graeber, Pszemysl, 1882–94; reprint, Jerusalem, 1966/67). He also collected and published the writings of Rachel Luzzatto, SDL's cousin, based partly on previous work done by SDL. His Hebrew translation of SDL's *Prolegomeni* appeared in two parts, in *Yad Shadal* (1895) and *Otsar ha-Sifrut* (1896) (see above, Translator's Preface, p. xv).

Cellarius, Christoph (Keller; 1638–1707), German Christian philologist, historian, and geographer. He taught in several places, most notably Zeitz, before ending up as professor of rhetoric (*Beredsamskeit*) and history at Halle. He wrote *Grammatica hebraea in tabulis synopticis, cum consilio 24 horis perdiscendi linguam sanctam* (Zeitz, 1684), intended to teach one Hebrew in 24 hours, as well as works on Syriac, Arabic, and Samaritan. (§ 23)

Cellérier, Jacob Elisée (1785–1862), Swiss priest and Bible scholar. A professor of Hebrew and Bible at the Geneva Academy (now the University of Geneva), his best-known work was probably the *Manuel d'herméneutique biblique* (Paris, 1852; English trans., New York, 1881). He also published a free translation of *Gesenius' *Hebräische Grammatik*, entitled *Élémens de la grammaire hebraïque, suivis des principes de la Syntaxe de Gesenius* (Geneva, 1820; 2nd enlarged ed., 1824). (§ 29)

Chelm, Solomon ben Moses see Solomon ben Moses Chelm.

Chevalier, Antoine Rodolphe (Cevallarius; 1507–72), French Protestant Hebraist. Having fled France for England, he taught French to Princess Elizabeth, the future queen. In England he also taught Hebrew to *Joannes Drusius. Later he taught Hebrew in Strasbourg and Geneva, and back in France, at Caen. He assisted Calvin with Hebrew translation, and his own Hebrew works include *Alphabetum hebraicum* (Geneva, 1566) and *Rudimenta linguae hebraicae* (Geneva, 1560?; 1567; several subsequent editions). (§ 20)

Cinquarbres, Jean (Johannes Quinquarboreus; 1514–87), French Orientalist. Before becoming a professor of Hebrew and Syriac at the Collège de France in 1554, he published his Hebrew grammar *De re grammatica hebraeorum* (Paris, 1546; 1549; 1556; 1582; 1588; 1609; 1621). To the 1582 edition was attached a short treatise, *De notis hebraeorum* by Jean Mercier. The 1609 and 1621 editions, published under the title *Linguam hebraicam institutiones absolutissimae*, included notes and additional material by Pierre Vignal and other scholars. An abridged version of the grammar appeared as *Institutiones in Linguam hebraicam* (Paris, 1559; 1582; 1609; 1621). He also translated several of the Targumic prophetic books into Latin. (§ 20)

Clénard, Nicolas (Nicolaes Cleynaerts; 1493/94–1542), Belgian grammarian. A teacher of Hebrew and Greek at Louvain, he published a popular Hebrew grammar entitled *Luaḥ ha-Dikduk, Tabula in Grammaticen hebraeam* (Louvain, 1529; several reprints), as well as a grammar of Greek.

After traveling to Spain and learning Arabic, he attempted, unsuccessfully, to foster peaceful dialogue between Christians and Muslims. (§ 20)

Cohen, Joseph see Joseph ben Joshua ben Meir ha-Cohen.

Cohen, Hananiah (Elḥanan Hai Coën, Graziadia Vita Anania Coen; 1750/51–1834), Italian rabbi and scholar. A prominent rabbi—he became chief Rabbi of Florence in 1825—he was the author of several pedagogical and grammatical works, including the grammar *Sha'arei Leshon ha-Kodesh* (Venice, 1808), a Hebrew-Italian and Italian-Hebrew dictionary entitled *Ma'ane Lashon* (Reggio, 1812), and a work on Mishnaic Hebrew entitled *Safah Eḥat* (Reggio, 1822). (§ 42)

Cohen, Shalom ben Jacob (Shalom ha-Cohen; 1772–1845), Polish Jewish Hebraist. A friend of *Naphtali Herz Wessely, he was the editor of *Ha-Me'assef* during its 1809–11 run, and founder of the Hebrew periodical *Bikkurei ha-Ittim* in 1821 (see § 41). He also authored a variety of works, including poetry, a play, and a guide to letter-writing. He published a Hebrew grammar intended for school use (in German with Hebrew characters), entitled *Torat Leshon Ivrit, Hebräische Sprachlehre* (in three parts; Berlin, 1802; 2nd ed., Dessau, 1807–9; Vienna, 1816). The grammar, which was based on *Judah Löwe ben Zeev's *Talmud Leshon Ivri*, was also published with improvements by *Wolf Mayer (Prague, 1816; six subsequent editions). (§§ 41; 200)

Condillac, Étienne Bonnot de (1715–80), French philosopher. Though unfinished, *La Langue des Calculs* was published posthumously, as part of the first complete edition of his writings (*Oeuvres complètes de Condillac*, vol. 23, Paris, 1798; reprint, Lille, 1981). (§ 43)

Dante see Alighieri, Dante.

Dantz, Johann Andreas (Danz; 1654–1727), German Protestant theologian and Hebraist. A professor of Oriental languages at Jena, he was a follower of the system of *Alting, and one of the foremost Hebraists of his time. His works include *Medakdek, sive, Litterator ebraeo-chaldaeus* (Jena, 1694), a follow-up work on syntax entitled *Turgeman, sive, Interpres ebraeo-chaldaeus* (Jena, 1694), and a *Compendium Grammaticae Ebraicae-Chaldaicae* (Jena, 1699; 1706). (§§ 18; 21; 24; 27; 123 n. 2; 170)

David ben Joseph ibn Yaḥya (1465–1543), Portuguese rabbi, grammarian, and philosopher. He was a cousin of *David ben Solomon ibn Yaḥya, and put out an abridged version of the latter's *Leshon Limmuduim* (Rome, 1540), which included an introductory poem by *Solomon Almoli. (§ 17 fn. 45)

David ben Solomon ibn Yaḥya (1440–1524), Portuguese Jewish grammarian and Bible commentator. He wrote a Hebrew grammar entitled *Leshon Limmudim* (Constantinople, 1506), as well as commentaries on the Bible, Maimonides, and Hebrew poetry. (§ 17)

De Rossi, Giovanni Bernardo (1742–1831), Italian Christian Hebraist. A professor of Oriental languages at Parma for more than fifty years, he possessed one of the most valuable collections of Hebrew books and manuscripts ever assembled. His *Mss. codices hebraici Biblioth* (3 vols., Parma, 1803) is a catalogue of the several thousand works in his collection, now housed in the Palatine Library at Parma. He wrote numerous other works on Hebrew, including *Synopsis institutionum hebraicarum* (Parma, 1807), and *Introduzione allo studio della lingua ebrea* (Parma, 1815). Also included in the Parma De Rossi collection is his (mainly received) correspondence with hundreds of other scholars including *Caluso (231 letters), *Gallicciolli (166 letters), *Jahn, *J. D. Michaëlis, *Peyron, and *Schnurrer. (§§ 9 n. 3; 11 n. 4; 13 n. 2; 14 n. 3; 17 n. 2; 29; 78; 192)

Dieu, Ludwig de (Louis, Lodewijk; 1590–1642), Dutch Christian Orientalist and minister. A student of *Erpenius at Leiden, he spent his career as a minister, mainly in Leiden. He was a specialist in Hebrew, Aramaic, and Persian, and published many works, mostly dealing with Biblical studies, including *Grammatica linguarum Orientalium Hebraeorum, Chaldaeorum et Syrorum inter se collatarum* (Leiden, 1628; Frankfurt am Main, 1688). **(Preface; §§ 21; 94; 106 n. 1)**

Dilherr, Johann Michael (1604–69), German Protestant theologian and songwriter. A professor at Jena, then at Nuremberg, he wrote *Atrium linguae sanctae Ebraicae* (Nuremberg, 1659) and *Peristylum linguae sanctae Ebraicae* (Nuremberg, 1660). (§ 27)

Dosa ben Eliezer ben Afsoi (late 4th–early 5th c. ?), Masorete. He is probably the earliest Masorete known by name. The Masorah of the total number of verses in the Bible is attributed to him. (§ 9 n. 3)

Drusius, Joannes (Van den Driesche; 1550–1616), Flemish Protestant Orientalist and exegete. A very distinguished scholar, his works include *De* *litteris Mosche Vechaleb* (Leiden, 1589; 1599; Franeker, 1608), *De recta lectione linguae sanctae* (Franeker, 1609), *De particulis Chaldaicis, Syriacis, Thalmudicis et Rabbinicus* (Franeker, 1609), *Alphabetum Ebraicum vetus* (Franeker, 1587; 1609), and *Grammatica linguae sanctae nova* (Franeker, 1612). He studied Hebrew with *Antoine Chevalier in London, where his family had moved for religious reasons. He became professor of Oriental languages at Oxford in 1572 (at the age of just twenty-two), in 1577 professor at Leiden, and in 1585 at Franeker, where he remained until his death. (§ 20)

Dubno, Solomon ben Joel (1738–1813), Russian Jewish grammarian, poet, and exegete. A student of *Solomon ben Moses Chelm, he eventually settled in Berlin, where he befriended *Moses Mendelssohn, whose son he tutored. Dubno collaborated on the commentary that accompanied Mendelssohn's edition of the Torah, and wrote the treatise *Tikkun Soferim*, attached to the same publication. (§ 38)

Dunash ben Labrat (Adonim ha-Levia?; mid 10th c.), Hebrew grammarian and poet. A student of *Saadiah Gaon, he was the first to apply Arabic poetic meter to Hebrew, laying the framework for medieval Hebrew poetry. He clashed with *Menaḥem ben Saruq, against whose dictionary *Maḥberet* he wrote a scathing response, and whose career he effectively ended. (§§ 11; 12 n. 3)

Duran, Profiat (Efodi, Isaac ben Moses ha-Levi; late 14th–early 15th c.), Catalonian Jewish philosopher and grammarian. He wrote a grammar, *Ma'ase Efod*, in 1403. First published only in 1865 (Vienna, as *Maase Efod*), it was edited by J. Friedländer and J. Kohn, and included Hebrew notes by SDL. Efodi was a critic of David Kimḥi. Efodi, the name with which he signed his works, is an acronym for אני פרופייט דוראן. (§§ 14; 17)

Efodi see Duran, Profiat.

Egidio da Viterbo (ca. 1469–1532), Italian cardinal, Christian Kabbalist, and scholar. A student and generous patron of *Elijah Levita, he also served as the latter's teacher of Greek and other secular literature. His interest in Hebrew stemmed mainly from his interest in the Kabbalah, a topic on which he wrote numerous works, most still in manuscript. He also translated, or sponsored translations of, many Jewish works, including the Zohar. He also maintained correspondence with *Johann Reuchlin. (§ 17)

Eichhorn, Johann Gottfried (1752–1827), German Christian Bible scholar. Considered one of the founders of the modern study of the Bible, he was a student of *Johann David Michaëlis, whom he succeeded at Göttingen. His works include *Allgemeine Bibliothek der biblischen Literatur* (10 vols., Leipzig, 1787–1801), and many other important works on Biblical studies, most notably *Einleitung in das Alte Testament* (3 vols., 1780–83). (§ 25 n. 1; 26 n. 2)

Elisha ben Abraham (ca. 1500), Jewish Hebraist. He published a work entitled *Magen David* (Constantinople, 1517), in which he defended the theories of *David Kimḥi against the criticism of *Efodi and *David ibn Yaḥya. The work included an introductory ode by *Solomon ben Jacob Almoli. (Note: In the *Encyclopaedia Judaica*, s.v. "Kimḥi, David", he is mistakenly called Abraham b. Elisha.) (§ 14)

Eliyakim ben Abraham of London (Jacob Hart; 1745–1814), British Jewish Kabbalist and grammarian. In addition to works on philosophy and Kabbalah, he wrote two short grammatical works, *Ein ha-Kore* (Berlin, 1803), on vocalization and pronunciation, and *Ein ha-Mishpat* (Rödelheim, 1803), a Hebrew grammar. (§ 41)

Elkanah (13th c. ?), Spanish Jewish Hebraist. He was author of a short grammatical work entitled *Mafteaḥ ha-Dikduk u-Be'ur ha-Nikud*, known today from three manuscripts. The author calls himself *Elkanah ha-Sefaradi*, and notes that the work was written for his brother, Samuel bar Joseph of Rome. Nothing more is known of the author, and the work itself remains unpublished. (§ 13)

Emden, Jacob ben Tzvi (1697–1776), German rabbi, Talmud scholar, and halachic authority. A very prolific writer and a respected scholar, his works include *Luaḥ Eresh* (Altona, 1769), a collection of grammatical notes on the prayers, in which he severely criticized *Solomon Hanau's *Sha'arei Tefillah*. (§ 36)

Erpenius, Thomas (Van Erpe; 1584–1624), Dutch Orientalist. A professor of Oriental languages at Leiden from 1613, he is remembered most for his grammar of Arabic, *Grammatica Arabica* (Leiden, 1613; many subsequent reprints). He also wrote a Hebrew grammar, *Grammatica hebraica generalis* (Leiden, 1627), and a grammar of Aramaic. (§ 21)

Ewald, Georg Heinrich August (1803–75), German Protestant theologian and Semitist. A professor at Göttingen and Tübingen, he advanced the modern study of Hebrew grammar in several ways, and is considered by many the father of Hebrew syntax. He is also notable for having been the teacher of such prominent scholars as Dillmann, Nöldeke, and Wellhausen. SDL cites his *Kritische Grammatik der hebräischen Sprache* (Leipzig, 1827), the first of Ewald's Hebrew grammars. **(Preface; §§ 7 n. 1; 14; 28; 118 n. 1; 121 n. 3; 145)**

Faber, Georg (17th c.), German Christian minister and Hebraist. He wrote two now very rare grammars, the first of which was *Lectionis heb. institutio* (Ansbach, 1608). Sources disagree on the title of the second, which was either *Institutionum heb. gram. libri IV* or *Institutiones grammaticae hebraicae* (Nuremberg, 1626). He may have been a preacher at Gellershausen. **(§ 21)**

Fagius, Paul (Paul Buchelin; 1504–49), German Christian Hebraist. He was a friend and student of *Elijah Levita, whom he asked to supervise his Hebrew press at Isny, the first of its kind in Germany. He translated into Latin Levita's *Tishbi* (Isny, 1541), *Meturgeman* (Isny, 1541), and *Shemot Devarim* (Isny, 1542), in addition to several other Hebrew works. He also authored several original works, including an elementary Hebrew grammar, *Compendiaria Isagoge in linguam Hebraicam* (Kostanz, 1543). In 1544, he became a professor of Hebrew at Strasbourg, and then, in the last year of his life, at Cambridge. **(§ 20)**

Finetti, Bonifazio (1705–1782), Italian Christian theologian. A Dominican priest, he wrote the *Trattato della lingua ebraica e sue affini* (Venice, 1756). This work was intended to be the first of twelve chapters of a larger work, the *Glossologia*. Though he published many other works, mostly on theology, the *Glossologia* never materialized. **(§§ 9 n. 3; 29; 180)**

Finzi, Jacob Levi ben Isaac (Jacob Levita; born ca. 1582), Italian Jew. He wrote a very short (15 folios) compendium on Hebrew grammar, *Divrei Agur* (Venice, 1605). From the preface of this work we learn that he lived in the town of Casale Monferrato, and that he wrote the work at age twenty-three. **(§ 34)**

Foscarini, Marco (1695–1763), Italian literary historian and politician. His work *Della letteratura veneziana* (Padua, 1752) was intended to have eight parts, though only four were completed (some additional material, from his manuscripts, appeared in the 1854 edition). In 1762, he became the 117th

Doge of Venice, though he died after serving less than one year. He was one of the last to hold this title. (**§ 19 n. 1**)

Fourmont, Étienne (1683–1745), French Christian linguist. Though most notably a scholar of Chinese, he had some interest in Hebrew grammar. Among his work on Hebrew is a translation of *Ibn Ezra's commentary on Ecclesiastes. (**§ 9 n. 3**)

Franchi, Guglielmo (died ca. 1600), Italian Hebraist. Born a Jew in Rome, he converted to Christianity and became a Vallombrosan monk. He wrote *Shemesh Leshon ha-Kodesh, Sole della lingua santa* (Bergamo, 1591; several subsequent printings), probably the first grammar of Hebrew written in Italian. He also wrote *Alphabetum hebraicum* (Rome, 1596), a guide to reading Hebrew. (**§ 20**)

Franck, Adolphe (Jacob Franck; 1809–93), French Jewish philosopher and writer. A successful academe and politician, he produced numerous works on philosophy, as well as a Hebrew grammar entitled *Melamed Leshon Ever, Nouvelle méthode pour apprendre la langue Hébraïque* (Paris, 1834). (**§ 29**)

Francis I, Emperor (1768–1835), the last Holy Roman Emperor (1792–1806, under the title Francis II) and emperor of Austria (1804–1835, as Francis I). Though no real friend of the Jews, he approved the opening of the Rabbinical College of Padua in 1829. (**§ 44**)

Gagnier, John (ca. 1670–1740), French Christian Orientalist. A professor of Arabic and Hebrew at Oxford, he contributed information about the holdings at the Bodleian Library to *Wolf's *Bibliotheca Hebraea*. (**§ 25 n. 1**)

Gallicciolli, Giambattista (1733–1806), Italian priest and philologist. A specialist in Hebrew philology, which he had studied with *Rabbi Simone Calimani, he taught Hebrew and Greek in Venice, and was well known and respected as a Hebraist throughout Italy. He had a long-lasting friendship with *G. B. De Rossi, with whom he corresponded frequently on the topic of Hebrew. He wrote, in response to the dissertation of *Giovenale Sacchi, *Dell'antica lezione degli Ebrei e della origine de' punti. Esame di una dissertazione del p. d. Giovenale Sacchi barnabita* (Venice, 1787). In this tractate, he refuted the arguments of Sacchi that the Greek alphabet was derived from the Hebrew, and argued for the antiquity of the vowels points. He left unpublished a compendium of Hebrew grammar that he had written for his students, as well as another work entitled *De philologia Hebraeorum*. (**§ 31**)

Gallo, Giuseppe see Joseph ben Samuel Tsarfati.

Gedaliah ben Joseph ibn Yaḥya (1515–87?), Italian Jewish historian and Talmudist. His single extant work, *Shalshelet ha-Kabbalah* (Venice, 1587; many subsequent editions), is a history of the Jews from the time of Moses until the author's own time. Also included in the work are various tractates on science, and a history of the peoples among whom the Jews dwelt. He made use of many previous works, including *Abraham ben David ha-Levi's *Sefer ha-Kabbalah*. (§ 9)

Génebrard, Gilbert (1535–97), French Benedictine exegete and Orientalist. A professor of Hebrew at the Collège de France, he wrote a number of publications on Hebrew and Jewish history. He also published translations of a number of earlier Jewish works, such as Tractate Sanhedrin of the Babylonian Talmud and a work of *David ben Solomon ibn Yaḥya. (§ 9 n. 1)

Gersonides (Levi ben Gershon; 1288–1344), French Jewish philosopher, exegete, mathematician, and physician. He was the author of a large number of influential works, including commentaries on the Bible and parts of the Talmud, and numerous works on math and astronomy. He is best known, however, as a philosopher. His own philosophy was expounded in his magnum opus, *Sefer Milḥamot Adonai* (1317–29; first published, Riva di Trento, 1560), which also had a long section on astronomy. He also wrote commentaries on the works Averroes and Aristotle, and included much philosophical discussion in his Biblical commentaries. (§ 92)

Gesenius, Wilhelm (1786–1842), German Protestant Semitist and Bible scholar. A professor of theology at Halle, he was probably the most influential Hebraist of the nineteenth century. Versions of his dictionary and grammar are still widely used today. Among his important works are *Hebräisch-deutsches Handwörterbuch über die Schriften des Alten Testaments* (Leipzig, 1810–12; many subsequent editions in German and English; first Latin edition [*Lexicon manuale*], Leipzig, 1833), *Geschichte der hebräische Sprache und Schrift* (Leipzig, 1815), and *Ausführliches grammatisch-kritisches Lehrgebäude der hebräischen Sprache* (Leipzig, 1817) (in some ways superior to his later grammars). His smaller Hebrew grammar, *Hebräische Grammatik* (Halle, 1813), went through many editions—SDL refers to the eleventh (Halle, 1834)—and in greatly revised form remains the standard Hebrew reference grammar today. Also notable is his *Versuch über die maltesische Sprache* (Leipzig, 1810), one of the earliest works on Maltese. (**Preface; §§ 14 n. 2;**

18 n. 2; 25; 26; 52 n. 3; 66 n. 1; 76 n. 2; 112 n. 1; 118 n. 1; 121 n. 3; 125 n. 1; 132; 141; 144 n. 1; 155; 171 n. 1; 182; 197; 198; 199 n. 1; 200)

Ghirondi, Moredchai Samuel (1799–1852), Italian Jewish scholar and biographer. A colleague of SDL at the Rabbinical College of Padua, he was also the chief Rabbi of Padua (1831–52). His major work was the *Toldot Gedolei Yisra'el*, a biographical dictionary of Jewish scholars and Rabbis (Trieste, 1853). (§§ 11 n. 5; 192)

Gikatilla, Moses ben Samuel ha-Cohen ibn (11th c.), Spanish Jewish poet, Biblical commentator, translator, and grammarian. His grammatical works have been lost, but *Ibn Ezra called him "the greatest of grammarians". His Hebrew translations of *Hayyuj survive. He is said to have been the first to recognize that the book of Isaiah (from chapter 40) had a second author. (§ 12)

Glass, Salomon (Glassius; 1593–1656), German Christian Hebraist. A professor of Greek and Hebrew (and later Theology) at Jena, he wrote *Philologia Sacra* (Jena, 1623; several subsequent editions), noted by SDL for its treatment of Hebrew syntax. He also wrote the shorter *Institutiones grammatices hebraeae* (Jena, 1623). (§ 21)

Gousset, Jacques (Jacob Gussetius; 1635–1704), French Protestant theologian and philosopher. A student of *Cappel, and a professor of Greek and theology at Gröningen from 1692, he wrote a Hebrew lexicon entitled *Commentarii linguae ebraicae* (Amsterdam and Utrecht, 1702). The second edition of this work bore the title *Lexicon linguae hebraicae* (Leipzig, 1743). He saw no place for comparative philology in the study of Hebrew, which he saw as "a sun which illuminates itself". This philosophy was refuted by *Schultens in a public discussion the two men held (in 1704) and, later, in print. (§ 67 n. 1)

Grishaber, Reuben Zeligman ben Aharon ha-Levi (Griesshaber, 18th c.), German Jewish Hebraist. He wrote the short treatise *Anaf Ets Avot* (Fürth, 1744), a refutation of *Solomon Hanau's grammatical works. (§ 36)

Guarin, Pierre (1678–1729), French Christian Hebraist. A Benedictine monk, he was the author of the two-volume *Grammatica Hebraica et Chaldaica* (Paris, 1724–26), which he intended (as written in the preface) to prevail over the system of *Masclef; this caused a lifetime quarrel between the two. He also began writing the *Lexicon hebraicum et chaldeo-biblicum* (2 vols., Paris, 1746), which he completed through the letter M. The lexicon was posthumously completed by his colleagues. For a time he taught Hebrew and Greek in Rouens and Reims, but at the time of his death was the librarian of the Abbey at Saint-Germain-des-Prés. **(§ 23)**

Hai ben Sherira Gaon (939–1038), Gaon of Pumbedita. A leading Jewish scholar of his time, he composed a large number of responsa (more than eight hundred) and had a profound influence on halachic laws. SDL notes that he was the author of a lost Arabic grammatical work *(Kitāb) al-Ḥawi* (called in Hebrew *(Ha-)Me'assef)*; fragments have subsequently been discovered and were first published, with Hebrew translation, by A. Harkavy in 1885/86 (see further, § 11). **(§§ 9 n. 1; 11)**

Hanau, Solomon ben Judah ha-Cohen (1687–1746), German Jewish Hebrew grammarian. His Hebrew grammar *Binyan Shelomo* (Frankfurt am Main, 1708) was very critical of the ancient grammarians. Being such a young man at the time of publication, he was forced to write a retraction of his criticism, which was attached to each copy. He wrote several other important works dealing with grammar, vocabulary, and pointing (see above, § 36). Ben-Yehuda attributes Hanau's grammar *Tsohar ha-Tevah* (Berlin, 1733; Dyhernfurth, 1786/87; several other editions) with helping to set him on his course to revive Hebrew as a spoken language. **(§§ 3; 36; 43; 86 n. 2; 194)**

Happel, Wigand (Happellius; 1522–72), German Christian Hebraist. A professor at Marburg, he wrote a Hebrew grammar entitled *Linguae sanctae canones grammatici* (Basel, 1561). This grammar includes some Hebrew correspondence between the author and *Paul Fagius, with whom he had studied. **(§ 20)**

Hartmann, Anton Theodor (1774–1838), German Bible scholar. He studied with *J. G. Eichhorn at Göttingen, then became professor at Rostock, apparently on the recommendation of his former teacher. He published a three volume grammar and dictionary of Mishnaic Hebrew entitled *Thesauri linguae hebraicae e Mischna augendi* (Rostock, 1825–26). **(§ 80 n. 1)**

Ḥayyuj, Judah ben David (ca. 945–1000), Hebrew grammarian. Little is known about his life, but he was born in Fez and came to Cordoba as a young man. One of the most important of the medieval Hebrew grammarians, his contribution to the study of Hebrew grammar was immense. For his works, see above, § 12. **(Preface; §§ 5 n. 1; 11; 12; 13; 15; 195)**

Ḥazzekuni see Hezekiah ben Manoah.

Heidenheim, Wolf (1757–1832), German Jewish exegete, commentator and grammarian. His *Mishpetei Te'amim* (Rödelheim, 1808; reprint Brooklyn 1992/3) was a treatise on the accents according to ancient grammarians. Other works include an edition of the Torah, *Ḥumash Me'or Enayim* (5 vols., Rödelheim, 1818–21), including his own philological notes (*Havanat ha-Mikra*) and the commentary *Ein ha-Kore* by *Jekuthiel ha-Cohen ben Judah; an edition of the book of Esther, *Seder Yemei ha-Purim* (Rödelheim, 1825, also including the work of Jekuthiel); an important Maḥzor with German translation (Rödelheim, 1800–5; many subsequent editions); and an edition of *Ibn Ezra's *Moznayim* (Offenbach, 1791). **(§§ 13 n. 2; 16; 41; 144 n. 4; 198)**

Herbelot, Barthélemy d' (1625–95), French Orientalist. His posthumously published *Bibliothèque orientale* (Paris, 1697) had the subtitle *Dictionaire Universel, contenant generalement tout ce qui regarde la connoissance des peuples de L'Orient*, and went through several subsequent editions. SDL citations may be referring to the edition of 1781–83. **(§ 7 n. 2)**

Hezekiah ben Manoah (13th c.), French Jewish exegete. Around the year 1240, he wrote a commentary on the Torah entitled *Ḥazzekuni*, first printed at Venice in 1524. This commentary, which is heavily influenced by that of Rashi, is generally cited by its title, rather than by its author. **(§ 192)**

Hetzel, (Johann) Wilhelm Friedrich (Hezel; 1754–1824), German Christian Orientalist. First a teacher at Jena, where he had studied, he became a professor of Oriental languages and Biblical literature at Giessen in 1786, and in 1801 at Dorpat. He wrote the *Ausführliche hebräische Sprachlehre* (Halle, 1777) and the pioneering *Geschichte der hebräischen Sprache* (Halle, 1776), as well as grammars of Rabbinic Hebrew, Arabic, and Syriac. **(§ 26)**

Hiller, Matthaeus (1646–1725), German Christian Hebraist and theologian. A professor at Tübingen, he wrote a Hebrew grammar, *Institutiones linguae sanctae* (Tübingen, 1711; 1760), a lexicon, *Leshon Limmudim, sive Lexicon Latino-Hebraicum* (Tübingen, 1688), and several other works on Hebrew and the Bible. Notable also is his *De arcano kethiv et keri*, in which he argues for the antiquity of the pointing, against (as noted on the title page) *Louis Cappel and others. (§ 24)

Hirt, Johann Friedrich (1719–83), German Christian theologian and Orientalist. A professor first at Jena, where he had been a student, and from 1775, at Wittenberg, he wrote a number of works on Hebrew grammar, including *Syntagma observationum philologico-criticarum ad ling. sanctam Veteris Testamenti pertinentium* (Jena, 1771), as well as works on Arabic and Syriac. As SDL notes, Hirt was a follower of *Dantz (who had died less than two decades before Hirt's arrival at Jena); this is clear from another of his works on Hebrew, the hefty *Biblia ebraea analytica … secundum principia ab Danzii instituta* (Jena, 1753; 2nd ed., 1769). (§ 27)

Hitzig, Ferdinand (1807–75), German Protestant Bible Scholar. A student of both *Ewald and *Gesenius, he wrote numerous Biblical commentaries and works on Biblical history. SDL refers to his Isaiah commentary, *Der Prophet Jesaja* (Heidelberg, 1833), in the dedication to which Hitzig credits Ewald with newly founding the science of the Hebrew language. (§ 28)

Höchheimer, Moses ben Ḥayyim ha-Cohen (Hechim, Höchheim; 1750–1835), German rabbi and grammarian. He published an edition of *David Kimḥi's *Michlol* (Fürth, 1792/3; reprint, Jerusalem 1965/6), which included his own annotations and those of *Elijah Levita, as well as a short Hebrew grammar entitled *Safah Berurah* (Fürth, 1790). Hechim was his Hebrew pen-name. (§ 41)

Hoffmann, Andreas Gottlieb (Andrea Teofilo Hoffmann; 1796–1864), German Christian Orientalist and theologian. He studied under *Gesenius at Halle, and became especially drawn to Syriac. He taught for a short while at Halle, but in 1822 became Professor of Theology at Jena. He wrote the *Grammaticae Syriacae libri III* (Halle, 1827), later revised by A. Merx as *Grammatica Syria* (Halle, 1867). An abridged English edition was made by Benjamin Harris Cowper, *The Principles of Syriac Grammar* (London 1858). He is one of the men to whom *Gesenius dedicates the Latin edition of his *Lexicon* (Leipzig, 1833); Hoffmann subsequently emended the second Latin edition of this work (ib., 1847). (§§ 6 n. 1; 43 n. 3; 95 n. 1; 106 n. 1; 109 n. 1; 112 n. 1; 113 n. 1; 114; 125 n. 1; 128 n. 1; 131; 132 n. 1, n. 3; 133; 136 n. 1; 179)

Horace (Quintus Horatius Flaccus; 65–8 BCE), Roman poet. Educated in Rome and Greece, he became a secretary in the Roman treasury under Augustus, who also commissioned literary work from him. SDL twice quotes from his *Art of Poetry* (*Ars Poetica*), also known as the *Epistle to the Pisos* (the third epistle in his second book of epistles). This work was written in 19 or 18 BCE. (§§ 25 fn. 74; 103 n. 1)

Hottinger, Johann Heinrich (1620–67), Swiss Christian Hebraist. Among several other works, he wrote a comparative Hebrew grammar, *Thesaurus Philologicus, seu Clavis scripturae* (Zurich, 1649), as well as *Grammatica quatuor lingarum Hebraicae, Chaldaicae, Syriacae et Arabicae harmonica* (Heidelberg, 1659), and a dictionary, *Etymologicum orientale, sive Lexicon harmonicum heptaglotton* (Frankfurt, 1661). He held a professorship in Zurich, though he also taught for several years in Heidelberg. In 1667, he accepted a position at Leiden, but drowned in a boating accident before his arrival. He is commemorated, along with *Johannes Buxtorf II, on the dedication page of *Alting's *Fundamenta*, from the third (1675) edition on; he had studied with Alting in Leiden. (§ 21)

Ibn Ezra, Abraham (1089–1164), Spanish Jewish grammarian, philosopher, Biblical commentator, astronomer, poet, and translator. In addition to his poetry, his scientific and philosophical treatises, and his very influential Bible commentary, he authored several important grammatical works. The first, *Moznayim*, was written in 1140 and first published in Augsburg, 1521. The second edition of *Moznayim* was published by *Elijah Levita (Venice, 1546), and a later edition included commentary by *Wolf Heidenheim (Offenbach, 1791). *Moznayim* was followed by *Sefat Yeter*, also known as *Yesod Dikduk* (first published, Jerusalem, 1984) and *Tsahot* (1145; first published, Venice, 1546, with *Moznayim*). His final grammatical work, *Safah Berurah*, was completed before 1148 (first published by *Solomon Almoli, Constantinople, 1530). The ideas in his grammars were mostly not original, but his works popularized the ideas of those who preceded him. SDL also refers to Ibn Ezra's *Yesod Mora*, a religious and philosophical work on the Biblical commandments (first published by Solomon Almoli, Constantinople, 1530). (§§ 7 n. 1; 11; 12; 13; 15; 25 n. 1; 36 n. 1; 41; 70 n. 1; 75; 92; 144 n. 2; 158; 171; 192)

Ibn Janaḥ see Jonah ben David ibn Janaḥ.

Imbonati, Carlo Giuseppe (1650?–1696/7), Italian Christian Hebraist. He edited the fourth volume of his colleague *Giulio Bartolocci's *Bibliotheca Magna Rabbinica* (Rome, 1693), and added a fifth volume to the series, *Bibliotheca latino-hebraica* (Rome, 1694). This final volume focused on Christians who wrote on Jews and Judaism. **(§ 29 n. 9)**

Immanuel ben Jekuthiel of Benevento (16th c.), Italian Jewish grammarian and printer. He wrote a work on Hebrew grammar and prosody called *Livyat Hen* (Mantua, 1557; reprint, Jerusalem, 1966/67), and published the first printed edition of the major parts of the Zohar. **(§ 33)**

Immanuel ben Solomon (Immanuel of Rome, Manoello Giudeo; ca. 1261–after 1328), Roman Jewish poet and scholar. He is best known for his poetry, in particular for the collection known as the *Mahbarot*. The final poem in this collection was based heavily on the *Divine Comedy* of *Dante, his contemporary. He also produced an array of scholarly works, including biblical commentaries and an unpublished grammatical work, *Even Bohan*. **(§ 17)**

Isaac ben Samuel ha-Levi (ca. 1580–before 1646), Polish rabbi and grammarian. He wrote a Hebrew grammar entitled *Siah Yitshak* (Prague, 1627/28). In this work he mentions two other grammatical works of his, *Brit ha-Levi*, on compound words, and *Elle Toldot Yitshak*, a commentary on *Rashi. **(§§ 35; 158)**

Jacob ben Hayyim ibn Adonijah (ca. 1470–before 1538), Masorete and printer. A native of Tunis, he eventually settled in Venice, where he found employment with the famed printer, Daniel Bomberg. He is best known for editing the Second Rabbinic Bible (Venice, 1524–25), for which he also supplied the Masoretic notes and wrote a lengthy preface; this preface was translated into English by C. D. Ginsburg (2nd ed., London, 1867; reprint, New York, 1967). Late in his life he converted to Christianity, as had the editor of the First Rabbinic Bible. **(§ 9 n. 3)**

Jacob of Edessa (ca. 633 or 640–708), Syrian Orthodox theologian, grammarian, historian, philosopher, and translator. The author of the first systematic treatment of Syriac grammar, he is still considered one of the greatest Syriac grammarians of all time. In one of his grammatical works, known simply as the 'Syriac Grammar' (once known only from a reference by *Bar Hebraeus until fragments of it were found in the mid-nineteenth century), he invented a unique system of seven symbols to indicate the Syriac vowels. These were intended for illustration of forms and pronunciation only, not for general use. He wrote numerous other important works, including a revision of the Syriac Old Testament., and translated a number of works from Greek into Syriac. (§ 6)

Jahn, Johann (1750–1816), German Catholic Orientalist. A professor at Vienna from 1789–1806, he published many books on Hebrew, Arabic, Aramaic, and Biblical Studies. His works on Hebrew include *Hebräische Sprachlehre für Anfänger* (Vienna, 1792), *Elementarbuch der hebräischen Sprache* (Vienna, 1799), and the more widely known *Grammatica linguae hebraicae* (Vienna, 1809). His introduction to the Hebrew Bible and his book on Biblical archeology were popular enough that they were translated into English. (§§ 5; 6; 25; 27)

Jekuthiel ha-Cohen ben Judah (Yahbi, Zalman Nakdan; 13th c.), Hebrew grammarian. *Elijah Levita calls him the Punctuator of Prague, though he probably lived in the Rhineland. He wrote *Ein ha-Kore*, containing grammatical notes on the Torah, which was published in *Heidenheim's edition of the Torah, *Humash Me'or Enayim* (5 vols., Rödelheim, 1818–21). (§§ 16; 198)

Jerome, Saint (ca. 342–419/20), monk, church father, and translator. After studying Hebrew from Jews in Syria and Palestine, he made a Latin translation of the Bible. Known as the Vulgate, this became the official Bible translation of the Catholic church. In addition, he wrote commentaries, including material he got from Jewish sources. He was canonized in 1767. (§§ 18 n. 2; 19 n. 1)

Jonah ben David ibn Janaḥ (Abu al-Walid, Marwan; early 11th c.), Spanish Jewish grammarian and lexicographer. One of the most influential of the medieval grammarians, his most important work was the *Kitāb al-Tanqīḥ*, translated into Hebrew by *Judah ben Saul ibn Tibbon as *Sefer ha-Dikduk* in 1171. The work consisted of two parts: a grammar entitled *Kitāb al-Luma'* (Hebrew, *Sefer ha-Rikmah*) and a dictionary, *Kitāb al-Uṣūl* (Hebrew, *Sefer ha-Shorashim*). Other works of his, unknown to SDL, are now known, including critiques on the work of *Ḥayyuj, and responses to *Samuel ha-Nagid's criticism of those critiques. (§§ 11; 13; 14; 17; 25; 198)

Joseph Ḥazan ben Judah of Troyes (13th c.), French Jewish Talmudist and ḥazan. It is known from citations in the work *Minḥat Yehudah* (see translator's footnote, § 17) that he was the author of a grammatical work entitled *Sefer Yedidot* and a commentary on Ecclesiastes, both now lost. (§ 17)

Joseph ben Joshua ben Meir ha-Cohen (1496–ca. 1577), Sephardic Jewish historian and physician. A practising physician in Italy, he achieved prominence from his historical works, most notably *Divrei ha-Yamim le-Malchei Tsarfat ve-Malchei Beit Otoman ha-Togar* (Venice, 1534; Amsterdam, 1733). This work is essentially a history of the world from Roman times, seen as a sequence of conflicts between Asia and Europe, and between Islam and Christianity (represented by Turkey and France). SDL edited and annotated the first printed edition of a later work of his, *Emek ha-Bachah* (Vienna, 1852; Krakow, 1895); he also named one of his sons Giuseppe, in honor of this writer. (§ 92)

Joseph ben Samuel ben Isaac (d. 1700), Karaite scholar. A student of Nisan Kukizow, father of *Mordechai ben Nisan, he wrote a grammar entitled *Porat Yosef*, preserved incomplete in a manuscript at Oxford. Some of his prayers and hymns were incorporated into the Karaite prayer book; otherwise, no other works of his have survived. Mordechai consulted with him on his *Dod Mordechai*, and later delivered a funeral oration for him. (§ 17)

Joseph ben Samuel Tsarfati (Giuseppe Gallo; died ca. 1527), Italian Jewish physician. Since his father was a physician to Pope Julius II, for much of his life he enjoyed a great reputation and many privileges. He knew well Hebrew, Aramaic, and Arabic, as well as Latin and Greek, and was a teacher of *Teseo Ambrogio. With his knowledge of Aramaic, he acted as interpreter between Ambrogio and Elia the Syrian. (§ 43 n. 3)

Jost, Isaac Marcus (1793–1860), German Jewish historian and teacher. A correspondent of SDL, Jost had various interests—he wrote a textbook of English and a dictionary of Shakespeare, for example. Much of his work focused on Jewish history, and he published several important works in this field. (§ 9 n. 1)

Judah ben Samuel ibn Bal'am (Abu Zakariya Yaḥya; second half of 11th c.), Spanish Jewish grammarian and commentator. His works, among them *Ta'amei ha-Mikra*, (Paris, 1565), on the Masoretic rules and accents, were all written in Arabic. Like other Spanish grammarians, he applied his knowledge of Arabic to the study of Hebrew. (§ 13)

Judah ben Saul ibn Tibbon (ca. 1120–after 1190), Spanish Jewish physician and translator. A native of Granada who later moved to southern France, he translated numerous important works from Arabic into Hebrew, including the *Sefer ha-Rikmah* and *Sefer ha-Shorashim* of *Jonah ibn Janaḥ, *Judah ha-Levi's *Kuzari*, and *Baḥya ibn Paquda's *Ḥovot ha-Levavot*. Other members of his family became prominent translators, including his son Samuel and grandson Moses. (§ 92)

Judah Eliyakim of London see Eliyakim ben Abraham.

Judah ha-Levi (before 1075–1141), Spanish Jewish poet and philosopher. He was a very prolific poet, and about eight hundred of his Hebrew poems, secular and religious, survive. He is best known, however, for a polemical philosophical work, written in Arabic, that is commonly called the *Kuzari*. This was translated into Hebrew by *Judah ibn Tibbon in the mid-twelfth century, into Latin by *Johannes Buxtorf II (1660), and into Spanish by *Jacob Abendana (1663). The Hebrew version became extremely popular and influential, well into modern times. He was a close friend and colleague of *Abraham ibn Ezra (their children wed), a student of *Isaac Alfasi, and a teacher of *Solomon ibn Parḥon. (§§ 7 n. 1; 13 n. 2; 92)

Judah ibn Quraish (ben Qarish; 9th c.), Hebrew grammarian and lexicographer, living in Algeria. With *Saadiah Gaon, he is considered one of the pioneers of Comparative Semitics. He is well known for a letter he wrote to the Jewish community of Fez after they decided to abolish the reading of the Targum in synagogues. In this letter (simply known as the *risāla* 'letter', though called by *Ibn Ezra both *Sefer ha-Yaḥas* and *Av va-Em*), he discusses the importance of Aramaic for the study of Hebrew. **(Preface; §§ 11 n. 2; 25)**

Judah Leib ben Moses ha-Levi (Edel, Judah Löwe Levita; d. 1827), Polish Jewish Hebraist and Talmudist. In addition to several commentaries and a collection of homilies, he wrote *Safah le-Ne'emanim* (Lvov, 1792/93; reprint, Jerusalem, 2000/01), a short Hebrew grammar for beginners. (§ 41)

Judah Löwe (Leib) ben Zeev (1764–1811), Polish Jewish grammarian and lexicographer. A member of the Haskalah movement, he was among the group that published the journal *Ha-Me'assef*. His best known work is the Hebrew grammar *Talmud Leshon Ivri* (Breslau, 1796), in which he was the first to apply western research methods to the study of Hebrew. As the main source for Hebrew learning in Eastern Europe into the early twentieth century, this work exerted great influence and went through numerous reprints. He also wrote a Hebrew-German German-Hebrew dictionary (with the German in Hebrew characters) called *Otsar ha-Shoreshim* (Vienna, 1807–8; several subsequent editions) and translated the book of Ben Sira into Hebrew (long before portions of the original Hebrew had been discovered). SDL also attributes to him an edition of the prayer *Tefillah Zakah*. (§§ 37 fn. 95; 41; 86 n. 2)

Kalonymus ben David (16th c.), Italian Jewish physician. Known for translating Hebrew works into Latin, he was also the author of the treatise on the accents that appears at the end of Balmes' *Mikne Avram* (Venice, 1523), and probably translated that work into Latin. (Note: The *Jewish Encyclopedia*, in various articles, mistakenly calls him Kalonymus ben Judah.) (§ 17)

Kimhi, David (1160?–1235?), French Jewish grammarian and Biblical commentator. The younger brother of *Moses Kimhi, his Hebrew grammar, *Michlol*, and lexicon, *Sefer ha-Shorashim*, had a major impact in the field of Hebrew philology. His influence on early Christian Hebraists like *Reuchlin, *Pagnini, and *Münster, was also immense. Much of his grammar was not new, but a restructuring of the ideas of *Ibn Janah, *Hayyuj, *Ibn Ezra, and others; however, he made these ideas clearer and more popular. He also wrote important commentaries for many books of the Bible. (§§ 3 n. 4; 9; 12 n. 1; 13; 14; 15; 17; 18; 20 n. 1; 33; 35; 36 n. 1; 41; 43; 92; 125 n. 1; 144; 192; 198; 199)

Kimhi, Joseph (ca. 1105–1170), Spanish (later French) Jewish grammarian, translator, and exegete. Though not as well known as his sons *Moses and *David Kimhi, he nevertheless made several significant contributions to the study of Hebrew grammar, both directly and through the education of his son Moses, on whom he had a great influence. His most important grammatical work was *Sefer ha-Zikkaron* (first published by W. Bacher, Berlin, 1888). He also wrote *Sefer ha-Gilui*, a response to *Menahem ben Saruq's *Mahberet*. He authored numerous exegetical, poetic, and other works, and made translations of Arabic works into Hebrew, including *Bahya ibn Paquda's *Hovot ha-Levavot*. He probably knew *Ibn Ezra, who cites Kimhi in his Bible commentaries. (§§ 13; 192)

Kimḥi, Moses (died ca. 1190), French Jewish grammarian and commentator. The elder brother and teacher of *David Kimḥi, he made a number of influential advances in Hebrew grammar, including the introduction of *pqd* as the paradigmatic verbal root and the traditional arrangement of verbal patterns (qal, piel, pual, hifil, hofal, hitpael). His best known work is *Mahalach Shevilei ha-Da'at* (Pesaro, 1508; Ortona, 1519; several subsequent editions), which was first published with annotations by *Elijah Levita. A Latin translation was published by *Sebastian Münster (Basel, 1531). He also wrote a grammatical work entitled *Sechel Tov* (first published 1894), as well as the lost book *Ha-Taḥboshet*, cited in his brother's *Michlol*. (§§ 13; 18)

Koch, Friedrich Christian (18th c.), German Christian Hebraist. A Hebrew teacher at Jena, he wrote the *Fundamenta linguae Hebraeae suis undique rationibus solide firmata, seu Grammatica Hebraea philosophica* (Jena, 1740), as well as *Praxis seu specimina totius grammatices Hebraeae* (Jena, 1742). (§§ 24; 34)

Kocher, David (Kocherus; 1717–92), Swiss Christian Hebraist. A professor of Hebrew at Bern, he prepared an abridged version of *Schultens' grammar, entitled *Rudimenta Grammaticae hebraeae secundum praecepta Alb. Schultensii* (Zurich, 1766). (§ 25)

Kosegarten, Johann Gottfried Ludwig (1792–1860), German Christian Orientalist and historian. A professor at Jena, and later Greifswald, he wrote a very short work on Hebrew grammar entitled *Linguae hebraicae paradigmata* (Jena, 1822; 2nd ed., 1829). As an Orientalist, he focused more on Arabic, of which he produced a chrestomathy and grammar. He had the distinction of teaching the Arabic alphabet to his famous friend Johann Goethe, for whom he also translated Arabic poetry. From 1835 he focused his scholarly attention almost exclusively on Pomeranian history and related matters. (§ 27)

Köslin, Ḥayyim ben Naphtali (Coeslin; d. 1832), German Jewish grammarian and Talmudist. He published a Hebrew grammar entitled *Maslul* (Hamburg, 1788; Brünn, 1796; at least five additional reprints), which became a very popular textbook for Jewish schools. He also wrote an article called *Be'er Reḥovot*, on the language of the Mishnah, which was printed in *Ha-Me'assef* (1785) and reprinted in *Bikkurei ha-Ittim* (1824–25). (§§ 41; 86)

Kyber, David (1525–53 ?), German botanist and Hebraist. Known more for his botanical work, he was the author of *Yesod ha-Dikduk, De re grammatica hebraeae linguae* and *Hegayon, Meditationes grammaticae ex Threnis Hiermiae desumptae*, published together (Basel, 1552), along with the Hebrew and Latin text of Jeremiah and Lamentations. He also translated sections of the *Sefer Yosippon* into Latin. (§§ 20; 157)

Landau, Moses Israel (1788–1852), Jewish printer, publisher, and lexicographer, living in Prague. His works include *Geist und Sprache der Hebräer nach dem zweyten Tempelbau* (Prague, 1822), which contains a history of language and a chrestomathy of Talmud, Zohar, and Midrashim; a five volume Talmudic dictionary (1819–35); a German translation of the Jewish prayer book, and more. He was also one of the publishers of the journal *Kerem Ḥemed*, to which SDL contributed. As the leader of the Prague Jewish community, he was responsible for bringing in *Solomon Judah Rapoport as head Rabbi. (§ 18 n. 2)

Ledebuhr, Caspar (17th c.), German Christian Hebraist. He wrote the *Shalshelet ha-Mikra, Catena Scripturae* (Leiden, 1647). Intended as a textbook, it is a lengthy treatment of the accentual system of Biblical Hebrew. His work, an important and influential contribution to that field of study, was improved upon by *Wasmuth and *Oesel. He also wrote a Hebrew grammar (Leiden, 1640), though I have not found any copy. (§§ 21; 23; 36)

Lee, Samuel (1783–1852), English linguist and Orientalist. Coming from very humble origins, and mostly self-educated, he became a professor of Arabic at Cambridge, later Regius Professor of Hebrew, and one of the most well-known linguists of his day. He wrote the *Grammar of the Hebrew Language, comprised in a series of lectures* (London, 1827; revised edition, 1844), as well as a Hebrew dictionary, a grammar of Persian, and other works on Arabic and Syriac. He produced editions of the Bible, or portions of the Bible, in Syriac, Malay, Coptic, Arabic, Persian, and Hindi. (§ 29)

Leusden, Johannes (1624–99), Calvinist theologian and Hebraist. Professor of Hebrew and Greek at Utrecht, he published numerous works on Hebrew and Biblical studies. His works include an edition of the Hebrew Bible (Amsterdam, 1661; 2nd ed., 1667), the first (in Hebrew) to be printed with numbered verses. This edition became the standard for generations, remaining the basis of Hebrew Bible editions into the nineteenth century. Also among his works is a short grammar entitled *Synopsis hebracia et chaldaica* (Utrecht, 1667). **(§ 23)**

Levita, Elijah (also Eli, Elias; Elijah Baḥur, Elijah ha-Ashkenazi; 1468/9–1549), German Jewish grammarian, poet, and lexicographer, who settled in Italy. Levita was a hugely influential scholar, not only for his own excellent works, but also because of the fact that he taught or corresponded with several leading Christian scholars. His students included *Sebastian Münster, who translated many of his works into Latin, and the influential Cardinal *Egidio da Viterbo, to whom he dedicated at least two of his books. His own grammatical and lexicographic works include *Sefer ha-Harkavah* (1518), *Ha-Baḥur* (1518), *Masoret ha-Masoret* (Venice, 1538), on the technical terms of the Masorah, and *Shemot Devarim* (Isny, 1542), the first Yiddish-Hebrew dictionary. He also composed secular literature. As SDL points out, he was the first to argue the non-antiquity of the vowel points. **(§§ 3; 7 n. 1; 9 n. 1; 10 n. 1; 14; 15; 18; 20; 32; 36 n. 1; 158; 182; 199)**

Levita, Isaac ben Samuel see Isaac ben Samuel ha-Levi.

Levita, Jacob see Finzi, Jacob Levi ben Isaac.

Levita, Johann Isaac (Johann Isaacs, Johanan Isaac (ha-)Levi; 1515–77), German Hebraist. Born a Jew, he became a rabbi, but then converted to Protestantism (1547), and later Catholicism (1551) in order to serve as a professor of Hebrew at Cologne. He wrote a Hebrew grammar, *Leshon Limmudim, Grammatica hebraea, absolutissima* (4th ed., Antwerp, 1564; 5th ed., Antwerp, 1570). The earlier editions of this work were the *Absolutissomae in hebr. linguam institutiones* (Cologne, 1553; 1554) and *Perfectissima hebraea grammatica* (Cologne, 1557). **(§ 20)**

Loans, Jacob ben Jeḥiel (1440?–1506), German Jewish physician. He was a physician to (Holy Roman) Emperor Frederick III, in whose court he made the acquaintance of *Johann von Reuchlin. He became Reuchlin's first teacher of Hebrew, and is mentioned fondly in the latter's Hebrew grammar. **(§ 19)**

Lolli, Samuel Vita (Lo-ly; 1788–1843), Italian Jewish scholar and teacher. SDL's cousin, lifelong very close friend and correspondent, he was for a time (ca. 1816–19) also SDL's teacher and study partner. Many of the letters between SDL and Lolli appear in the collected Hebrew and Italian letters of SDL (see above, p. xii, fn. 3), as well as in the volume *Devar Shumuel* (ed.

*Vittorio Castiglioni, Krakow, 1895). According to SDL, he wrote an unpublished grammar of Hebrew. (§§ 42; 156 n. 1)

Lombroso, Jacob (Lumbroso; early 17th c.), Italian rabbi and physician. He is best known for the edition of the Bible he published in Venice (1639), in which he included an exhaustive introduction and explanations, as well as Spanish translations of the more difficult passages. (§§ 34; 137)

Lonzano, Abraham ben Raphael de (late 17th–early 18th c.), Hebrew grammarian. He published a short, well-known grammatical work entitled *Kinyan Avraham* (Zolkiew, 1723), from which it appears that he was born in Greece. He later converted to Christianity in Prussia and took the name Wilhelm Heinrich Neumann. (§ 43)

Lonzano, Menaḥem ben Judah (ca. 1550–between 1608 and 1624), Palestinian Jewish Masoretic and midrashic scholar, lexicographer, and kabbalist. He wrote many works, mostly on Midrashic topics. His major work was entitled *Shtei Yadot* (Venice, 1618; reprint, Jerusalem, 1969/70), a collection of essays on various topics, some of which were grammatical. He also authored some lexicographical works, and collaborated with *Jedidiah Norzi on the latter's *Goder Perets* (*Minḥat Shai.*). Little is known about his life. (§§ 14; 34; 121 n. 3)

Löscher, Valentin Ernst (1674–1749), German Protestant theologian. A professor at Wittenberg, he wrote a Hebrew grammar, *De causis linguae Ebraeae libri III* (Frankfurt and Leipzig, 1706), in addition to many theological works. (§ 24)

Löwe, Joel (Joel Bril; 1760–1802), German Jewish Hebraist and Bible commentator. A student of *Isaac Satanow, follower of *Moses Mendelssohn, and editor of the periodical *Ha-Me'assef* (see translator's footnote to § 41), he published numerous commentaries and translations. Perhaps most noteworthy is the introduction and commentary that he wrote for *Mendelssohn's edition of the Psalms (1783). He also wrote a grammatical work entitled *Ammudei ha-Lashon* (Berlin, 1794; Prague, 1803), and contributed to *Eichhorn's *Allgemeine Bibliothek*. (§ 41)

Löwisohn, Solomon (1789–1821), Hungarian Jewish writer. He published two grammatical works, *Be-Olam ha-Neshamot* (Prague, 1811) and *Beit ha-Osef* (Prague, 1812); these were re-published together under the title *Meḥkarei Lashon* (Vilna, 1849). He also wrote a history of the Jews (in German), works on Jewish liturgy, and an important work on Biblical geography. His chief work, *Melitsat Yeshurun* (Vienna, 1816), the first aesthetic interpretation of the Bible in Hebrew, includes the earliest known Hebrew translation of Shakespeare (a passage from Henry IV). (§§ 41; 82 n. 1)

Lowth, Robert (1710–87), Biblical critic and poet. For a time a professor of poetry at Oxford, and bishop of London, Lowth published a series of Latin lectures on biblical poetry, *De sacra poesi Hebraeorum* (Oxford, 1753); subsequent (Latin) editions included a preface and extensive notes by *Johann David Michaëlis. An English edition was published in 1787, under the title *Lectures on the sacred poetry of the Hebrews* (London; several reprints). He was the first modern scholar to formulate the theory of parallelism for Biblical poetry. He is also well known for his translation of the book of Isaiah (London, 1778), and an extremely popular grammar of English (London, 1762; many subsequent reprints). (§ 70 n. 1)

Luzzatto, Moses Ḥayyim (1707–47), Italian Jewish Kabbalist and poet. The brother of SDL's great-grandfather, he is best known for his Kabbalistic and ethical treatises. His *Mesillat Yesharim* became arguably the most influential work on Jewish ethics. SDL makes reference to his poetic works, which include elegies and verse dramas. Some scholars (of this century) have called Moses Luzzatto the first Modern Hebrew writer. (§ 92)

Maimonides (Moses ben Maimon; 1135–1204), Spanish Jewish Rabbinic scholar, commentator, philosopher, and physician. One of the most well-known Jewish scholars of all time, he produced a number of immensely influential works. Among these are his commentary on the Mishnah; *Mishneh Torah*, a colossal work on halachic law, also known as *Yad* (representing 'fourteen', the number of chapters in this work); and his major philosophical work *Moreh Nevukim*, or 'Guide to the Perplexed'. Originally written in Arabic in about 1200, this last work was immediately translated into Hebrew, in consultation with the author, by Samuel ibn Tibbon, son of *Judah ibn Tibbon. (§§ 9; 70 n. 1; 82 n. 1; 92)

Margolioth, Judah Löwe (Leib) ben Asher (1747–1811), Polish rabbi. In addition to several responsa and philosophical works, he wrote the *Iggeret ha-Melitsah u-Mishpat Leshon ha-Kodesh* (Novy Dvor, 1795/96; reprint, Brooklyn, 1992), on Hebrew style. (§ 41)

Marinus, Marcus (Marco Marino; 1541/42–94), Italian Christian Hebraist and censor. He wrote a Hebrew grammar, *Gan Eden, Hortus Eden,*

Grammatica linguae sanctae (Basel, 1580; 2nd ed., Venice, 1585), as well as a lexicon, *Tevat Noah, Arca Noe, Thesaurus linguae sanctae novus* (Venice, 1593). He was the (strict) censor for the Talmud printed at Basel (1578–80; containing notes by Jacob Luzzatto, an ancestor of SDL), which itself was the base for several Talmud editions of the seventeenth and eighteenth centuries. (§ 20)

Martin, Raymund (Raymond Martini; 1220–85), Spanish Dominican friar and anti-Jewish theologian. His main work, *Pugio Fidei* 'The Dagger of Faith', devoted mainly to anti-Jewish polemics, was widely circulated in medieval times. Very proficient in Hebrew, he was an active participant in the (unsuccessful) dispute with *Naḥmanides. (§§ 9 n. 1; 19 n. 1)

Martinez de Cantalapiedra, Martin (b. 1519), Spanish Christian Hebraist. A professor of Hebrew at the University of Salamanca, he wrote the rare *Institutiones in linguam hebraicam et chaldaicam* (Paris, 1548; Salamanca, 1571). (§ 20)

Masclef, François (1662–1728), French priest and Hebraist. He was the author of the *Grammatica hebraica a punctis aliisque inventis massorethicis libera* (Paris, 1716), in which he promoted a bizarre system of reading Hebrew without the vowel points (whose antiquity had been questioned already by *Cappel fifty years earlier). Most subsequent editions (1731, 1743, 1750; not 1781) included a second volume on Chaldean, Syriac, and Samaritan grammar. Masclef's methods were attacked (justifiably) by *Pierre Guarin in the latter's own grammar (1724); Masclef defended himself in a printed letter (1725), and again in the second edition of his own grammar (1731). (§§ 30; 31)

Matthiae, August (1769–1835), German classicist. In addition to many other works, he wrote a Greek grammar, *Ausführliche griechische Grammatik* (Leipzig, 1807; 3rd ed., 1835), which was translated into English and revised by *Edward Valentine Blomfield (*A Copious Greek Grammar*, Cambridge, 1818). (§ 53 n. 1)

Mayer, Wolf (1778–1850), European Jewish scholar and translator (from Prague?). He expanded and improved the Hebrew grammar of *Shalom Cohen, *Torat Leshon Ivrit* (Prague, 1816; six subsequent editions). He also produced a number of bilingual Hebrew-German texts, including prayer books for Purim (Prague, 1835) and Yom Kippur (Prague, 1830), and a collection of fables entitled *Leshon Limmudim* (Prague, 1840). He also edited a Hebrew-German Bible, *Sifrei Kodesh*, (Prague, 1833–37), which included *Mendelssohn's edition of the Torah and the work of several other translators and commentators. (§ 41)

Mayr, George (1564–1623), German Jesuit philologist. Briefly a professor of Greek and Hebrew at Ingolstadt, then a full-time priest in Augsburg, he wrote *Institutiones linguae hebraicae* (Augsburg, 1616). At the time of his death, he was working on a new Hebrew translation of the New Testament. (§ 21)

Meir ben David (late 13th c.), Hebrew grammarian. He wrote the lost work *Hassagat ha-Hassagah*, in which he defended *Ḥayyuj against the criticism of *Ibn Janaḥ. This work is known through two of brief references in *Efodi's *Ma'ase Efod* (pp. 116, 173). (§ 17)

Menaḥem ben Moses Tamar (15th–16th c.), Turkish Jewish poet and commentator. He wrote a lost grammar entitled *Rashei Besamim* (1524), as well as commentaries to several Biblical books and a supercommentary to *Ibn Ezra's commentary on the Torah. (§ 17)

Menaḥem ben Nataniel (11th c. ?), Jewish translator. According to one manuscript of the grammatical work *Horayat ha-Kore* (*Hidāyat al-Qāri*), the author of which was probably *Abu al-Faraj Harun, he translated the work from Arabic into Hebrew. Another manuscript of the Hebrew records the translator as Nataniel ben Meshullam (see translator's footnote, § 13). (§ 13)

Menaḥem ben Saruq (ben Jacob ibn Saruq; 10th c.), Spanish Jewish philologist and lexicographer. He authored a Biblical Hebrew dictionary, written in Hebrew, known as the *Maḥberet*. He refrained from any comparison with Arabic, and the fact that it was written in Hebrew (and not in Arabic) gave it a wider audience among European Jews. It was extensively used by *Rashi, for example. When it was severely criticized by *Dunash ben Labrat, Menaḥem's students came to his defense; one of these was possibly the great *Judah Ḥayyuj, while another, Isaac ibn Gikatilla, was subsequently the teacher of the great *Jonah ibn Janaḥ. (§ 11 n. 2)

Menasseh ben Israel (1604–57), Dutch Sephardic Jewish scholar and printer. Born a Marrano in Madeira, his family returned to Judaism in Holland. He wrote an unpublished grammar, *Safah Berurah*, at the age of seventeen. A leading member of the Jewish community and a prolific writer, he also wrote many other works on Jewish history and customs. In 1626, he founded the first Hebrew press in Amsterdam. (§ 34)

Mendelssohn, Moses (1729–1786), German Jewish philosopher and activist. The most influential Jewish scholar of the eighteenth century and spiritual father of the Jewish Enlightenment, he produced a large body of work during his lifetime. His main contribution to Biblical studies was a German translation of the Pentateuch (in Hebrew characters), which included a Hebrew commentary (1780–83). Contributors to the commentary included such scholars as *Solomon Dubno and *Naphtali Herz Wessely. He also produced a translated Psalter (1783), with commentary by *Joel Löwe. It is also noteworthy in this context that he clashed with the anti-Semitic *Johann David Michaëlis on several occasions. Mendelssohn's Bible translation was meant to serve as a Jewish counterpart to Christian translations, such as that of Michaëlis. (§§ 38; 40; 41; 192)

Messer Leon (Judah ben Jeḥiel; 15th c.), Italian Jewish physician, rabbi, and philosopher. In addition to numerous works on philosophy and rhetoric, he authored an unpublished work on grammar, entitled *Livnat ha-Sappir* (1454). 'Messer' is a traditional title given to physicians, and Leon ('lion') is a common symbol of Judah. (§ 17)

Michaëlis, Christian Benedict (1680–1764), German Christian Orientalist. A professor of theology and Greek and Oriental languages at Halle, and the father of *Johann David Michaëlis, he was the author of a Syriac grammar entitled *Syriasmus, id est, grammatica linguae syriacae* (Halle, 1741). He also wrote numerous dissertations on the Hebrew language. SDL refers to his *Dissertationem philologicam I. Lumina syriaca pro illustrando hebraismo sacro* (Halle, 1756); *Dissertatio, qua soloecismus casuum ab hebraismo sacri codicis depellitur* (Halle, 1739); and *Dissertatio inauguralis philologica, qua soloecismus generis a Syntaxi codicis hebraici depillitur* (Halle, 1739). SDL credits him with bringing the "Schultensian" method to Germany. (§§ 26; 128 n. 1; 132; 133; 199)

Michaëlis, Johann David (1717–91), German Christian Bible scholar and Orientalist. The son of *Christian Benedict Michaëlis, and a professor at Göttingen, his numerous works include a Hebrew grammar, *Hebräische Grammatik* (Halle, 1745; 3rd ed., 1778); a Hebrew Lexicon, *Supplementa ad Lexica hebraica* (Göttingen, 1785–1792); and a Syriac grammar, *Grammatica syriaca* (Halle, 1784). He edited and republished the Syriac portion of *Edmund Castell's *Lexicon Heptaglotton*, as *Lexicon syriacum* (2 vols., Göttingen, 1788). He also authored a thirteen-volume German translation of the Hebrew Bible, with commentary (1769–85), and wrote a preface and extensive notes for *Robert Lowth's *De sacra poesi Hebraeorum* (Göttingen, 1758). **(Preface; §§ 24 fn. 73; 25; 26; 27 fn. 80; 66 n. 1; 70 n. 1; 132 n. 3; 139 n. 1; 141)**

Morais, Sabato (1823–1897), Italian rabbi and Jewish educator. Born in Livorno, Italy, he emigrated to Philadelphia in 1851, where he served as ḥazan to the Sephardic Congregation Mikveh Israel until his death in 1897. He was the principal founder of the Jewish Theological Seminary in New York in 1886, where, until his death, he also served as the president of its faculty and professor of the Bible. In 1887, he became the first Jew to receive an honorary doctor of laws from the University of Pennsylvania. In addition to many other writings, he translated several works of SDL into English, including portions of the *Prolegomeni* and *Ohev Ger*; these were mostly published as serials in Jewish newspapers.

Mordechai ben Nisan (17th–18th c.), Polish Jewish Karaite scholar. He is the author of *Dod Mordechai*, the Hebrew treatise written in response to an inquiry by Leiden professor *Jacob Trigland, in which he defends the antiquity of Karaism. The work was written in 1698/99, and first published in 1714 (Hamburg), with a Latin translation; the Hebrew portion alone was republished in Vienna (1830; reprinted, Jerusalem, 1966), along with another important historical and bibliographical work entitled *Orah Tsaddikim*, by Simḥah Isaac Luzki. For a long time, Mordechai's work remained an important source for the history of Karaism. He also wrote an unpublished Hebrew grammar called *Kelalim Yafim Al ha-Diqduq*. **(§ 17)**

Mordechai Halberstadt of Düsseldorf (d. 1770), German rabbi and grammarian. Though the majority of his work consists of responsa, he refuted *Solomon Hanau's *Sha'arei Tefillah* in a pamphlet entitled *Kontres Hasagot Al Siddur Sha'arei Tefillah* (1738; printed, Prague, 1784). **(§ 36)**

Mori, Raffael (18th c.), Italian Christian Orientalist. A Vallombrosan monk and lecturer of Oriental languages at the Seminary of Florence, he wrote the *Grammatica ebrea ad uso del seminario fiorentino* (Florence, 1787). **(§ 29)**

Morin, Jean (1591–1659), French priest and Bible scholar. He published many works on Bible and theology, of which two notable examples are his *Exercitationes ecclesiasticae* (Paris, 1631) and *Exercitationes biblicae* (Paris, 1633). In these works he sets out to prove the authority of the Samaritan and Greek versions of the Bible, claiming that the Hebrew text had been altered by the Jews. His great interest in Samaritan is evident in other works, in particular his *Opuscula Hebraeo-Samaritica* (Paris, 1639), which included a Samaritan grammar and lexicon. The theories outlined in his *Exercitationes* were attacked by several scholars, notably by *J. H. Hottinger in his *Exercitationes antimorianae* (Zurich, 1644). (§ 155)

Moses ben Shem-Tov ibn Ḥabib (15th–16th c.), Sephardic Hebrew grammarian and poet. Influenced by *Efodi, he wrote in 1484 an unpublished grammatical work entitled *Peraḥ Shoshan*, followed by a smaller work, *Marpe Lashon*. This latter work was published together with his *Darchei No'am*, on Hebrew poetics and versification (Constantinople, 1520?; Venice, 1546; Rödelheim, 1806). The 1806 edition of *Marpe Lashon* and *Darchei No'am* was published by *Wolf Heidenheim. (§ 17)

Moses ben Yom-Tov (Magister Mosseus, Moses (ha-)Nakdan, Moses Ḥazan; d. 1268), London rabbi and grammarian. He is the author of the grammatical work *Darchei Nikud ve-ha-Neginot*, on the rules of punctuation and accentuation, first published in the second Bomberg Rabbinic Bible (Venice, 1524–25). The work was later published separately (Vilna, 1822; Frankfurt am Main, 1854). (§§ 11 n. 5; 15)

Münster, Sebastian (1489–1552), German Christian geographer, cosmographer, and Hebraist. A student of *Pellicanus, he was a contemporary and admirer of *Elijah Levita, with whom he also studied and maintained correspondence. He translated several of Elijah's works into Latin. For example, Levita's *Sefer ha-Baḥur* appeared as *Sefer ha-Dikduk: Grammatica hebraica absolutissima* (Basel, 1525). He also published his own Hebrew grammar, *Opus Grammaticum consummatum ex variis Elianis libris concinnatum* (Basel, 1544; expanded edition, 1549), which draws from the works of Levita and includes a Hebrew version of Tobit. He taught Hebrew at Heidelberg before becoming professor of Hebrew at Basel in 1528. (§§ 18; 19 n. 1; 20; 157; 200)

Naḥmanides (Moses ben Naḥman Gerondi, Ramban; 1194–1270), Spanish Jewish Talmudist, exegete, and physician. Perhaps the greatest religious authority of his time, he left behind a large body of work, mostly on Talmud and Halachah. His last work, a commentary on the Torah, is considered his masterpiece. (§ 192)

Navarra, Menaḥem (Noveira; 18th c.), Italian rabbi and poet. His responsa were inserted into his grandfather Hezekiah Mordechai Basan's *Penei Yitsḥak*, which he published (Mantua, 1744). One of these, *Kero Mikra*, is on grammar. (§ 42)

Neumann, Caspar (1648–1715), German Protestant theologian and minister. After studying theology at Jena, he served as a minister in several places before settling in his hometown of Breslau. There he also taught in the town's two gymnasia, at which he was the first professor of theology. Known also as a Hebraist, he was the author of *Genesis linguae sanctae V. T.* (Nuremberg, 1696), *Exodus linguae sanctae* (Nuremberg, 1697–1700), and *Clavis domus Heber* (Wroclaw, 1712–1715). (§ 24)

Neumann, Moses Samuel (1769–1831), Hungarian Jewish poet and Hebraist. Among his many works, which deal with a variety of topics, he wrote a Hebrew grammar entitled *Ma'agal Yosher* (Prague, 1808; 1816; Vienna, 1831). (§ 41)

Neumark, Judah Löb (Yehudah Leib ben David Neimark; late 17th–early 18th c.), German Jewish printer and Hebraist. The first director of the Jablonski printing press in Berlin (from ca. 1699), he wrote, in Hebrew, a short Hebrew grammar entitled *Shoresh Yehudah* (Frankfurt am Main, 1693). A native of Hanau (where he possibly also worked as a printer before moving to Berlin), he claims in the preface to his grammar that he also wrote a work on the Hebrew accents. (§§ 34; 43)

Nicholas of Lyra (de Lyre; 1270–1340), French Franciscan exegete and theologian. A professor of theology at the Sorbonne, he was the author of the first printed Bible commentary, *Postillae Perpetuae*. This work, written 1322–30, was published in 1471–72 (Rome). He was critical of the state of Biblical studies in his time, asserting that priority should be given to literal interpretation stemming directly from the Hebrew text. His work had tremendous influence; both Wycliffe and Luther, for example, admit their indebtedness to his work. A tradition, dating from the fifteenth century, holds that he was of Jewish descent, but there is no evidence that this is true. (§ 19 n. 1)

Nigri, Petrus (Petrus Niger, Peter Schwartz; 1434–83), Dominican monk, Hebraist, and anti-Jewish writer. Born in Germany, he studied Hebrew in Spain, and subsequently returned to Germany to preach to Jews. His failure to convert Jews led him to write two strongly anti-Jewish works, *Tractatus* *contra perfidos Judaeos* (Esslingen, 1475), in Latin, and *Der Stern Maschiach* (Esslingen, 1477), in German, both among the earliest printed books to contain Hebrew characters. Both works included appendices with a guide to reading Hebrew, along with some grammatical rules. According to SDL, he also wrote a Hebrew grammar, *Rudimenta linguae hebraicae*. If true, this would make it perhaps the earliest Hebrew grammar written in Latin. It was never published, and according to SDL the manuscript is preserved in Paris. Some have suggested that he was a convert from Judaism himself, but this cannot be proven. (**§ 19 n. 1**)

Nold, Christian (Noldius; 1626–83), Danish Christian Hebraist and theologian. A professor of theology at Copenhagen (1664–83), he wrote the massive *Concordantiae Particularum ebraeo-chaldaicarum* (Copenhagen, 1679; Jena, 1734, with revisions and additions by *Johann Tympe). (**§ 24 n. 4**)

Norzi, Jedidiah Solomon ben Abraham (1560–1626), Italian rabbi and exegete. He dedicated much of his career to the critical study of the Bible, traveling abroad extensively in order to search for better manuscripts. He also collaborated with his friend *Menaḥem ben Judah Lonzano. The result of his efforts was the commentary and grammatical work *Goder Perets*, which he completed in 1626. This was later published under the title *Minḥat Shai* (Mantua, 1742). (**§§ 34; 42; 121 n. 3; 144; 195; 196; 199**)

Oesel, Philip (Ouseel; 1671–1724), Dutch Christian Hebraist. A professor at Frankfurt, he made two important studies on the accentual system of Hebrew, in which he updated the ideas of Wasmuth. He published *Introductio in accentuationem hebraeorum metricam* (Leiden, 1714), on the poetic books, followed by *Introductio in accentuationem hebraeorum prosaicam* (Leiden, 1715), on the prose books. (**§§ 23; 36**)

Oliveyra, Solomon de (d. 1708), Dutch Sephardic scholar and Hebraist. An active leader of the Portuguese Jewish community in Amsterdam, he was also the author of a number of grammatical and lexicographic works, including *Yad Lashon, Dal Safatayim: Livro da Gramatica hebrayca et chaldayca* (Amsterdam, 1688/89) and *Sefer Ets Ḥayyim: Thezouro da lingua santa* (Amsterdam, 1682). (**§ 34**)

Opitz, Heinrich (Opitius; 1642–1712), German Christian Orientalist. A professor at Kiel and a colleague of *Matthias Wasmuth, he wrote a Syriac grammar entitled *Syriasmus facilitati et integritati suae restitutus* (Leipzig, 1678;

2nd ed., 1691). He also wrote a Hebrew grammar, a Hebrew and Aramaic Lexicon, and edited an edition of the Hebrew Bible. (§§ 131; 132 n. 1)

Origen (185–253/54), Christian church father and theologian. Long a teacher in his native Alexandria, he relocated to Caesarea in the year 232. He is notable for being the first, or one of the first, Christian scholars to study Hebrew. Of his many works, the most important was his *Hexapla*, an edition of the Hebrew Bible with six parallel columns of text: the Hebrew original, the Hebrew in Greek transliteration, and four Greek versions. The size of this work probably prevented copying, and it was soon lost. What precious little has survived of the *Hexapla* is known through excerpts given by other writers. The column of Greek transcription provides the oldest evidence for Hebrew vocalization, and the fragments that survive are thus quite important for the study of Hebrew. (§ 19 n. 1)

Pagnini, Santes (1470–1536), Italian Hebraist and Biblical scholar. His works include *Institutionum Hebraicarum* (Lyons, 1526) (SDL calls this *Institutiones Gramm. ling. hebraicae*), patterned after David Kimḥi's *Michlol*; *Institutionum hebraicarum abbreviatio* (Lyons, 1528), an abridged version of the 1526 grammar; and a dictionary entitled *Thesaurus linguae sanctae* (Lyons, 1529). He is best known for his Latin translation of the Bible (Old and New Testaments) based on the original texts, the first translation from Hebrew since that of Jerome. His Bible translation was also the first to include verse and chapter numbers, a system which is still in use. (§§ 14; 20)

Pappenheim, Solomon (1740–1814), German rabbi and scholar. He is best known for his three-part book on Hebrew synonyms, *Yeri'ot Shelomo* (part 1, Dyhernfurth, 1784; part 2, Rödelheim, 1811; part 3, Dyhernfurth, 1831). He also began a Hebrew dictionary, *Ḥeshek Shelomo*, of which only one fascicle appeared (Breslau, 1802), and authored numerous works on Jewish customs. (§ 40)

Paradiso, Paolo (Paulus Paradisus; d. 1549 or 1554), Italian Hebraist. A Venetian convert from Judaism to Christianity, he taught at the Collège Royal in Paris, and wrote a short work on Hebrew grammar called *De modo legendi hebraicae* (Venice, 1534). A slightly shorter edition of the same grammar was published in Paris, also in 1534. (§ 20)

Parḥon, Solomon ibn see Solomon ben Abraham ibn Parḥon.

Pasini, Giuseppe (Josephus Pasinus; 1687–1770), Italian priest, Hebraist, and librarian. A professor at the university and gymnasium of Turin, he wrote a Hebrew grammar entitled *Dikduk Leshon ha Kodesh, hoc est Grammatica linguae sanctae institutio* (Padua, 1721; 2nd ed., 1739; several subsequent editions). He was also prefect of the Royal University Library in Turin from 1745–1770, and was largely responsible for the production of the catalogue of manuscripts in that library (Turin, 1749). (§ 29)

Pellicanus, Conrad (1478–1556), German Christian theologian. His grammar, *De modo legendi et intelligendi Hebraea* (written, 1501; published, Basel, 1503; reprinted, Tübingen, 1877) was the first of Hebrew published in a European language, preceding that of *Reuchlin by three years. However, as the much older Reuchlin had helped him learn Hebrew (at Tübingen), Reuchlin can rightly be called the father of Hebrew studies among Christians. He went on to become a professor of Hebrew at Zürich in 1523. (§ 19 n. 1)

Peyron, Vittorio Amedeo (1785–1870), Italian Orientalist. A professor at the University of Turin and a pioneering scholar of Coptic, he amended and added a preface to the second edition of *Caluso's *Prime lezioni di Grammatica ebraica* (Turin, 1826). (§ 29 n. 6)

Pfefferkorn, Johann (born Joseph Pfefferkorn; 1469–after 1521), German convert to Christianity. Baptized in 1505, apparently after spending time in prison, he went on to author a number of anti-Jewish writings. Allied with the Dominicans, he convinced the German emperor Maxmillian to issue an edict, in 1509, ordering the destruction of all Jewish books besides the Old Testament. The edict was soon suspended under the influence of *Johann Reuchlin, leading to a great literary feud between the two men. The controversy weakened the prestige of the Church; it is no coincidence that Luther put forth his theses in 1517, at the very height of this dispute. (§ 19 n. 3)

Postel, Guillaume (1510–81), French Orientalist. Once the official interpreter of the French embassy to the Turkish Sultan Suleiman—during which time he collected Oriental manuscripts for the royal library—he later became professor at the Collège Royal in Paris, where he taught Greek, Arabic, and Hebrew, and held the first chair in Arabic. He wrote a short work on Hebrew entitled *De originibus, seu de hebraicae linguae et gentis antiquitate, deque variarum linguarum affinitate* (Paris, 1538). He also wrote numerous other works, including a very short Arabic grammar, *Grammatica Arabica* (Paris, 1538), the first to be printed in France. A staunch advocate for the unification of all Christian churches, towards the end of his life he was jailed in the Papal prisons in Rome. (§ 20)

Potschka, Juvenalis (18th c.), German Christian monk and Hebraist. A Franciscan friar and lecturer in Bible at the convent in Bamberg, he wrote *Thesaurus linguae sanctae sive phraseologica Hebraica* (Bamberg, 1780). This very rare and unusual work is dedicated to Hebrew phraseology. (§ 27)

Provenzale, David ben Abraham (Provençal; born ca. 1506), Italian rabbi and Hebrew scholar. He is known to have written several commentaries and a grammar, among other works. Of these works, only his commentary to the Mishnaic tractate Avot is extant, though it remains unpublished. In one work, he reportedly attempted to prove that more than two thousand Greek and Latin words derive from Hebrew. *Azariah dei Rossi, in his *Me'or Enayim*, preserves some of his etymologies. (§ 33)

Provenzale, Moses ben Abraham (Provençal; 1503–75), Italian rabbi. Brother of the more well-known *David Provenzale, he wrote a short Hebrew grammar, in verse, entitled *Be-Shem Kadmon* (1535; printed, Venice, 1596/97). He also produced numerous other works, mainly on Maimonides and Talmud, almost all of which remain unpublished. (§ 33)

Quirino, Lauro (15th c.), Italian scholar. A professor at the University of Padua, *Sansovino claims he wrote a Hebrew grammar entitled *Introductio ad linguam sanctam*. If correct, this would be the first grammar written by a Christian scholar, but the work remains otherwise unknown. (§ 19 n. 1)

Raadt, Alhardt de (1645–99), Dutch Hebraist. A follower of the grammatical system of *Alting, he wrote the short treatise entitled *Sugiat ha-Nikud, hoc est De Punctationis hebraicae natura Commentarius* (Leiden, 1671; 1685). (§§ 21; 158)

Rabbenu Tam (R. Jacob ben Meir Tam; 1100–71), French Jewish rabbi and grammarian. A grandson of *Rashi and the younger brother of *Rashbam, who was also his teacher, he was considered the greatest Jewish scholar of his generation. Among his many works are a metric poem on the Hebrew accents, consisting of forty-five strophes rhyming in *-tim*. He also wrote a grammatical work entitled *Sefer ha-Hachra'ot* (published with *Teshuvot Dunash ben Labrat*, by H. Filipowski, London, 1855; reprint, Jerusalem, 1967), which focused on the grammatical disputes between *Menahem ben Saruq and *Dunash ben Labrat. Some scholars suggest that in this work he arrived at the theory of triliteralism independently of *Hayyuj. (§ 11)

Rapoport, Solomon Judah Leib (1790–1867), Galician rabbi, scholar, and pioneer of the Haskalah movement and the modern science of Judaism. A friend and correspondent of SDL, he published numerous articles in the journals *Bikkurei ha-Ittim* and *Kerem Ḥemed*. His most important work was a series of biographies on geonic scholars, originally published in *Bikkurei ha-Ittim*, and later published as *Toledot Gedolei Yisra'el (Yeri'ot Shelomo)* (Warsaw, 1904); an expanded edition was published under the title *Toladot* (Warsaw, 1913; reprint, Jerusalem, 1959/60). (§§ 17 n. 1; 18 n. 2; 25 n. 1)

Rashbam (R. Samuel ben Meir; ca. 1085–ca. 1170), French Jewish commentator. He was taught by his grandfather, *Rashi, and was the teacher of his younger brother, *Rabbenu Tam. He wrote an important commentary to the Bible, though only the portion on the Torah has been preserved nearly complete; his commentaries on other books are known in fragmentary form. (§§ 11; 192)

Rashi (R. Solomon ben Isaac; 1040–1105), French Jewish commentator and teacher. Perhaps the most revered commentator of all time, he wrote a commentary on the entire Bible and Talmud. He also founded a school at Troyes in around 1070. Many well-known scholars came from within Rashi's extended family, most notably his grandsons *Rashbam and *Rabbenu Tam. Rashi often included grammatical discussions in his commentary, and was familiar with the Hebrew (but not Arabic) grammatical works of the Spanish grammarians, in particular *Menaḥem ben Saruq and *Dunash ben Labrat. (§§ 3 n. 1; 11; 15; 17 n. 2; 18 n. 2; 46 n. 4; 92; 192)

Raymond of Pennaforte, Saint (ca. 1190–1275), Spanish Dominican friar. Born into a noble family, and well educated in Barcelona and Bologna, he joined the Dominican order in 1222. He was made Master-General of the order in 1238, but resigned in 1240 to devote himself to the conversion of unbelievers. He was canonized in 1601. (§ 19 n. 1)

Reineccius, Christian (1668–1752), German Christian theologian and Hebraist. A lecturer (*Privatdozent*) at Leipzig, later headmaster of the gymnasium in Weissenfels, he wrote a grammar entitled *Grammatica hebraeochaldaice* (Leipzig, 1704; many subsequent editions), which was an abridgment of the grammar of *Matthias Wasmuth. He compiled two dictionaries, *Lexicon hebraeo-chaldaicum biblicum* (Leipzig, 1733; many subsequent editions) and *Index memorialis* (Leipzig, 1725; 1728; 1735). He also published an edition of the Hebrew Bible with the Masorah, *Biblia hebraica* (Leipzig, 1725; several subsequent editions), and a polyglot Bible, *Biblia sacra quadrilingua* (Leipzig, 1747–51). (**§ 23**)

Reuchlin, Johann von (1455–1522), German Christian humanist. He introduced the study of Greek and Hebrew to Western Europe and was one of the early promoters of the Reformation. He had studied Hebrew with *Jeḥiel Loans in Vienna and *Obadiah Sforno in Rome. His *De Rudimentis Hebraicis* (Pforzheim, 1506; reprint Hildesheim, 1974) was the second (often cited as the first, even by Reuchlin himself) Hebrew grammar published by a Christian; this work greatly surpassed, in quality and in influence, the earlier work of his student *Conrad Pellicanus. He also wrote another grammatical work, *De Accentibus et Orthographia Linguae hebraicae* (Hagenau, 1518). He is also notable for the role he played in the fight against the 1509 ban on Jewish books, putting him in direct conflict with *Pfefferkorn. *Gesenius called him "the father of Hebrew philology among Christians." (**§§ 13; 19; 157; 200**)

Romanelli, Samuel Aaron (1757–1814), Italian Jewish poet and travel writer. A prolific writer and translator of both religious and secular writings, his work included a Hebrew grammar entitled *Grammatica ragionata italiana ed ebraica* (Trieste, 1799). (**§ 42**)

Roorda, Taco (Tacone; 1801–74), Dutch Orientalist and Bible scholar. A professor at Amsterdam, he wrote a Hebrew grammar called *Grammatica hebraea* (2 vols., Leiden, 1831–33), praised by SDL. (**§§ 29; 141 n. 1**)

Rosenmüller, Ernst Friedrich Karl (1768–1835), German Protestant theologian and Orientalist. He wrote many works on the study of the Bible, as well as an Arabic grammar and lexicon. His most important work was the *Scholia in Vetus Testamentum* (Leipzig, 1788–1821), a twenty-four part (eleven-volume) Bible commentary, to which he devoted much of his life, and which formed the basis of much of nineteenth-century Bible exegesis. (**§§ 8; 41; 66 n. 1; 70 n. 1**)

Rossi, Azariah ben Moses dei (ca. 1511–1577/78), Italian Jewish scholar. Deeply affected after experiencing the disastrous earthquake that hit Ferrara in 1571, he decided to write a book. This book became *Me'or Enayim* (Mantua, 1573–75; reprint, Jerusalem, 1969/70; English translation, 2001), a massive chronicle, notable for the plethora of sources quoted. Dei Rossi used a large number of classical and contemporary non-Jewish sources, exhibiting a breadth of learning unusual for a Hebrew author. The book consists of several distinct parts, including a discussion of the 1571 earthquake, a translation of the Letter of Aristeas, and a treatment of Jewish chronology. At one point he incorporates a discussion on the antiquity of the vowel points, in which he vehemently argues against the claims of *Elijah Levita. (§§ 18 n. 2; 33; 78)

Rota, Orazio (18th c.), Italian Christian Hebraist. A Franciscan monk, he wrote a Hebrew grammar entitled *Grammatica della lingua santa* (Venice, 1775), intended primarily for use in seminaries and colleges. (§ 29)

Row, John (ca. 1598–1672), Scottish Christian educator and minister. A lecturer in Hebrew at Aberdeen, he wrote a small (in size, not length) volume on Hebrew grammar entitled *Kitsur ha-Dikduk, Hebraeae linguae institutiones compendiosissimae et facillimae* (Glasgow, 1644), published (and bound) together with a dictionary of a thousand words, *Elef devarim: Chilias Hebraica, seu vocabularium*. In 1652 he was appointed principal of King's College at Aberdeen by Oliver Cromwell, a position which he lost at the Restoration. His father and grandfather (both named John Row) were also accomplished Hebraists; his grandfather is purported to have been the first to publicly teach Hebrew in Scotland. (§ 21)

Saadiah Gaon (882–942), Geonic scholar, philosopher, and Hebrew grammarian. This Egyptian-born scholar, who taught at the Pumbedita and Sura Academies in Babylonia, is considered one of the first, if not the first, Hebrew grammarian. His grammatical works include *Sefer ha-Egron*, a dictionary and grammar written (in Hebrew) at age twenty, and *Sefer Tsahut Leshon ha-Ivrim*; both of these works survive in fragmentary form. He is certainly more well known as a halachist and philosopher, in particular for his *Sefer ha-Emunot ve-ha-De'ot*. This work, originally written in Arabic, was translated into Hebrew by *Judah ibn Tibbon in 1186 (first published, Constantinople, 1562). He also was responsible for the first known translation of the Bible into Arabic, with commentary, which became the standard among Jews in Arab countries. (§§ 11; 92; 192 n. 1)

Sacchi, Giovenale (1726–89), Italian priest and musicologist. A member of the Institute of Bologna and Royal Academy of Mantua, he published mainly on music and the history of music. He wrote *Dell'antica lezione degli Ebrei e della origine de'punti: Dissertazione* (Milan, 1786), in which he advocated a system of reading Hebrew similar to that of *Masclef. His system was criticized by *Giambattista Gallicciolli. (§ 31)

Samson (ha-)Nakdan (13th c.), German Jewish Hebrew grammarian. He wrote the grammatical works *Ḥibbur ha-Konim* and *Mafteaḥ ha-Dikduk*, which remain unpublished. (§ 16)

Samuel ben Ḥophni (d. 1013), Gaon of the Sura academy. Data from the Cairo Genizah documents have forced scholars to revise previous beliefs that Samuel was the last gaon of Sura, and change his believed date of death from 1034 to 1013. A prolific writer, most of his works have been lost, though some have come recently to light from the Genizah. *Jonah ibn Janaḥ counts him among the early grammarians; no grammatical works are extant, and it is likely that his limited work in this field is simply to be found scattered in his Bible commentary. Samuel was the father-in-law of *Hai ben Sherira Gaon. (§ 11)

Samuel ha-Nagid (993–1055/6) Spanish Jewish statesman, grammarian, poet, and scholar. Having risen to the rank of vizier in Granada, he was the most prominent Jew of his time. He used his power to do great good, thus earning him the respect of both Jews (who bestowed upon him the title *Nagid* 'prince') and Muslims alike. He was a pupil of *Ḥayyuj, whom he would later defend fiercely against the criticism of *Jonah ibn Janaḥ. His grammatical works are no longer extant, apart from fragments of two works: *Kitāb al-Istiġnā* (*Sefer ha-Osher*), a Hebrew and Aramaic dictionary, and *Rasā'il al-Rifāq* (*Iggerot ha-Ḥaverim*), in defense of Ḥayyuj. (§§ 11; 13)

Sansovino, Francesco (1521–86), Italian historian and printer. Among his numerous works is *Venezia città nobilissima e singolare* (Venice, 1581; numerous reprints), an encyclopedic description of the city in which he spent most of his life. SDL criticizes the book for its inaccuracy. (§ 19 n. 1)

Sarchi, Phillipe (Francesco Filippo Sarchi, born Samuel Morpurgo; 1764–1829), Italian lawyer and linguist. The son of the Hebraist Elia Morporgo (1740–1830), and part of a well-known Italian family, he left Italy as a young man to study in Vienna. There he converted to Catholicism in 1790, and taught law and the Italian language. In 1807, after fleeing Vienna upon Napoleon's invasion, he probably converted back to Judaism in Italy. Apart from a short stint in London, he lived much of the rest of his life in Paris. He wrote the *Grammaire hébraïque raisonée et comparée* (Paris, 1828; subsequent editions, 1838, 1844), with the assistance of *Abraham de Cologna, as well as *An Essay on hebrew Poetry, ancient and modern* (London, 1824). He also wrote a textbook of Italian in German (1795) and another in French (1823). (§ 42)

Satanow, Isaac ha-Levi (1732/33–1804/5), Polish Jewish scholar and poet. His linguistic works include a short Hebrew grammar, *Siftei Renanot*, *Compendium grammaticae novae linguae sanctae* (Berlin, 1773), a Hebrew-German dictionary, *Sefat Emet* (Berlin, 1787; 2nd ed., Prague, 1803), and *Safah Ehat*, a dictionary of Hebrew homonyms (Berlin, 1784). He also wrote *Mishlei Asaf* (Berlin, 1792–93), a collection of modern proverbs written in the Biblical style, *Va-Ye'tar Yitshak* (Berlin, 1784–85), on Jewish prayer, and an impressive number of other works. (§§ 39; 86 n. 2; 92)

Schickard, Wilhelm (1592–1635), German Christian Orientalist, mathematician, and astronomer. A professor at Tübingen, he wrote numerous works on Hebrew and Judaism, including the *Horologium hebraium* (Tübingen, 1614; 1623; reprinted more than forty times). (§ 21)

Schnurrer, Christian Friedrich (1742–1822), German Protestant Orientalist and theologian. Once a student of *J. D. Michaëlis at Göttingen, he later became Chancellor of the University of Tübingen. He made many contributions to Biblical studies, but his most important were in the field of Arabic. His *Bibliotheca arabica* (Halle, 1811) was a comprehensive bibliography of European works on Arabic language and literature printed between 1505–1810. SDL notes that he published an extract of *Judah ibn Quraish's *Risāla* in *Eichhorn's *Allgemeine Bibliothek* (vol. 6, Leipzig, 1792). (§ 25 n. 1)

Schroeder, Nicolaus Wilhelm (1721–1798), German Christian Orientalist. A professor at Gröningen, he published a grammar based on that of *Schultens, with the same title, *Institutiones ad fundamenta linguae hebraeae* (Gröningen, 1766; many subsequent editions). He published several other works on the Bible, Arabic, and Aramaic. (§ 25)

Schultens, Albert (1686–1750), Dutch Christian Orientalist. A professor at Franeker (1713–29), then at Leiden (1729–50), he was the first modern scholar to make scientific use of Arabic in the study of Hebrew. He wrote the influential *Institutiones ad fundamenta linguae hebraeae* (Leiden, 1737; 2nd eds. [sic!], 1743, 1756), in addition to other works on grammar and Biblical commentary. In 1704, at the age of just eighteen, he had a public discussion with *Jacques Gousset, who saw no value in comparing Hebrew with Arabic and Aramaic; he also refuted Gousset's theories in print. **(Preface; §§ 24; 25; 26; 29; 34; 118 n. 1; 121 n. 1, n. 3; 152; 153)**

Sennert, Andreas (Sennertus; 1606–89), German Christian Orientalist. A professor of Oriental languages at Wittenberg, his many grammatical works include *Hypotyposis harmonica linguarum Orientalium Chald., Syr. et Arab. cum matre Hebraea* (Wittenberg, 1653; 2nd ed., 1655); *Centuria canonum philologicorum* (Wittenberg, 1657; 3rd ed., 1665); *Arabismus, hoc est, præcepta Arabicæ linguæ, in harmoniam ad Ebræa* (Wittenberg, 1558). **(§ 21)**

Sforno, Obadiah ben Jacob (ca. 1475–1550), Italian Jewish exegete, philosopher, and physician. While studying medicine in Rome, he was recommended as a Hebrew tutor to *Reuchlin, who wanted to better learn the language; this he did from 1498–1500. He wrote commentaries to much of the Bible, as well as an unpublished grammar (apparently unknown to SDL) entitled *Dikduk Leshon Ivri*, Hebrew translations of Euclid, a work on Aristotelian philosophy (which he opposed), and a number of other works. **(§§ 19; 192)**

Shalom ha-Cohen see Cohen, Shalom ben Jacob.

Shem-Tov ben Abraham ibn Gaon (1283?–after 1330), Kabbalist and halachic scholar. Born in Spain, he worked mainly in Safed. He is the author of the work *Migdal Oz*, an important commentary on Maimonides' *Mishne Torah*, for which he is best known. In the past, this work was erroneously attributed by SDL and others to *Yom-Tov ben Abraham Ishbili (see § 9, note 1). **(§ 9 fn. 10)**

Simon, Richard (1638–1721), French Catholic priest. He had a strong interest in the religion of the Jews, whom he befriended and defended. His work *Histoire critique du Vieux Testament*, Paris, 1678 (reprinted, Rotterdam, 1685), essentially the first work of its kind, was harshly criticized; practically the entire 1678 printing was burned. **(§§ 11 n. 1; 34; 57 n. 1)**

Simonis, Johann (1698–1768), German Christian Hebraist. A professor of Church history at Halle, where he had been a student of *C. B. Michaëlis (and thus of the "Schultensian" school), his many grammatical works include *Arcanum formarum nominum liguae hebraicae* (Halle, 1735), *Introductio Grammatico-critica in linguam hebraicam* (Halle, 1753), *Onomasticum veteris Testamenti* (Halle, 1741), and *Analysis et explicatio lectionum Masorethicarum Kethibban et Krijan vulgo dictarum* (Halle, 1752; 3rd ed., Halle, 1824). He also wrote a popular dictionary entitled *Lexicon manuale hebraicum et chaldaicum* (Halle, 1756; 1771), which was reprinted with emendations and additions by *Eichhorn (Halle, 1793) and then by *Georg B. Winer (Leipzig, 1828), as well as a much smaller dictionary entitled *Dictionarium Veteris Testamenti Hebraeo-Chaldaicum* (Halle, 1752; 1766; English edition by C. Seager, London, 1832). He also published an important edition of the Hebrew Bible, *Biblia Hebraica manualia* (Halle, 1752; 2nd ed., 1767), which became the basis for several nineteenth-century editions. (§§ 26; 144 n. 3)

Sisti, Gennaro (18th c.), Italian Christian philologist. A teacher of Greek at the University of Naples, later at the Seminary of Calvi, and a member of the Vatican library, he wrote *Lingua santa da apprendersi anche in quattro lezioni* (Venice, 1747; 2nd ed., Naples, 1777), as well as the earlier *Epitome hebraicae linguae* (Naples, 1741). (§§ 29; 158)

Solomon ben Aaron of Troki (died ca. 1745), Karaite scholar. A native of Troki, near Vilna, he is said to have written two grammatical works, *Ḥanoch la-Na'ar* and *Rach ve-Tov*. It is unclear if these works were ever published. He also wrote several other works, of which his best known was probably *Appiryon Asah Lo*, a treatise on Karaism and how it differs from Rabbinism, written at the request of two Swedish scholars (first published by A. Neubauer, Leipzig, 1866). He was also apparently a relative of *Mordechai ben Nisan. (§ 17)

Solomon ben Abba Mari (ha-)Yarḥi (Lunel; late 14th c.), French Jewish grammarian. A scholar from the French town of Lunel, whence his Hebraized name *Yarḥi*, he wrote an unpublished Hebrew grammar entitled *Leshon Limmudim*. In this work he was the first to set the number of Hebrew verbal patterns (*binyanim*) at seven. Many scholars, such as *Johann C. Wolf, have confused Solomon Yarḥi with *Rashi; this is because Rabbi Solomon Yarḥi is abbreviated in Hebrew as רש״י, which, unpointed, is easily read as *Rashi*. (§ 17)

Solomon ben Abraham ibn Parḥon (12th c.), Spanish Jewish lexicographer and philologist. A student of *Abraham ibn Ezra and *Judah ha-Levi, his only extant work is a lexicon of Biblical Hebrew entitled *Maḥberet He-Aruch*, written in 1160 or 1161 (see further § 113, note 2). The lexicon is based heavily on the work of *Ibn Janaḥ and *Ḥayyuj (*Judah ibn Tibbon, Ibn Janaḥ's translator, unfairly called it a plagiarism), but it contains very valuable original material as well. The introduction also preserves one quarter of a grammatical poem by *Solomon ibn Gabirol. (§§ 11; 13; 15; 144 n. 4)

Solomon ben Melech (16th c.), Moroccan Jewish commentator. He wrote a Bible commentary, including much analysis of grammar, entitled *Michlal Yofi* (Constantinople, 1549). His analysis was based heavily on the grammatical theories of *David Kimḥi. A second edition, with annotations, was put out by *Jacob Abendana and his brother Isaac (Amsterdam, 1660/61; 1684/85; reprint, Jerusalem, 1969/70). (Note: *Jewish Encyclopedia* has a cross-reference to an entry "Solomon ibn Melek", but the entry itself is missing.) (§ 33)

Solomon ben Moses Chelm (1717–1778), Polish rabbi, grammarian, and mathematician. A rabbi in Lemberg, later in Salonika, he wrote, among many other works, *Sha'arei Ne'imah* (Frankfurt an der Oder, 1776/77), a treatise on the accents of the poetic books, edited and annotated by his student *Solomon Dubno. This work was reprinted many times as an addendum to *Judah ben Zeev's *Talmud Leshon Ivri*. (§ 37)

Solomon ibn Gabirol (ca. 1020–ca. 1058), Spanish Jewish poet and philosopher. A prolific and influential poet, he wrote a grammatical poem at the age of nineteen, which, according to Ibn Ezra (in *Moznayim*), consisted of four hundred verses. Most of this poem, which is often called *(He-)Anak*, has been lost, but about a quarter of it is preserved in the preface to *Solomon ibn Parḥon's *Maḥberet he-Aruch* (written about 1160). (§ 11)

Sonnenfels, Aloys von (Perlin Lipmann, Aloys Wiener; died ca. 1770), German Semitist. Born Perlin Lipmann, son of the chief Rabbi of Brandenburg, he and his children (though not his wife) converted to Catholicism sometime in the late 1730s. He changed his name to Aloys Wiener, and later moved to Vienna, where he taught Semitic languages at the university and acted as court interpreter to Maria Theresa. In 1746 he was granted the noble name Sonnenfels. He published a Hebrew grammar in Latin and German, entitled *Even Bohan, Lapus Lydius, Prüfstein* (Vienna, 1757), in which (according to SDL) he blatantly plagiarized the theories of *Hanau. Despite his apostasy, he (and his influential son Joseph) remained sympathetic to the Jewish cause. (§ 36)

Spinoza, Benedict (Baruch; 1632–77), Dutch Jewish philosopher and Bible critic. Though famed for his philosophy, which in his lifetime led to excommunication from the Jewish community, he also had an interest in the

Hebrew language. Included in the publication of his posthumous works (*Opera Posthuma*) was the *Compendium grammatices linguae hebraeae* (Amsterdam, 1677; English translation, New York, 1962; French translation, Paris, 1968). (§§ 34; 70 n. 1)

Storr, Gottlieb Christian (1746–1805), German Christian theologian. A professor of theology at Tübingen, and a colleague of *Schnurrer, he wrote the *Observationes ad analogiam et syntaxim hebraicam pertinentes* (Tübingen, 1779). The majority of the rest of his large body of scholarship is on theology and exegesis, in particular of the New Testament. (§ 26)

Süsskind, Alexander ben Samuel (Alexander Süsskind ben Samuel; late 17th–early 18th c.), German Jewish grammarian and kabbalist. He wrote a grammatical work entitled *Derech ha-Kodesh* (Köthen, 1717/18), appended to which is a treatise on the accents written in Judeo-German. He also wrote several unpublished theological and kabbalistic works. (§ 34)

Tiboni, Pietro Emilio (1799–1876), Italian priest and scholar. A professor at the seminary of Brescia (where there is today a street named for him), he wrote *Anthologia hebraica* (Padua, 1833), noted by SDL for its fine glossary. In 1852, his political activism, coupled with his historical-critical approach to Bible teaching, caused the Bishop to remove him from his chair at the seminary. He had correspondence with SDL, some of which can be found in the collection of SDL's Italian letters (see above, p. xii, fn. 3). (§ 29)

Tiraboschi, Girolamo (1731–94), Italian literary historian. Often called the first historian of Italian literature, his *Storia della letteratura italiana* (1771–82; many subsequent editions) traces Italian literature from the time of the Etruscans through the seventeenth century. (§ 19 n. 1)

Trigland, Jacob (1652–1705), Dutch Christian theologian and Hebraist. A professor at Leiden, he wrote the *Diatribe de secta Karaeorum* (1703), on the history and supposed antiquity of the Karaites. The work *Dod Mordechai*, by *Mordechai ben Nisan, for a long time the chief source for the history of Karaism, was written in response to four questions posed by Trigland; Mordechai also supported the antiquity of the Karaites. (§ 4 n. 1)

Troki, Solomon see Solomon ben Aaron of Troki.

Tympe, Johann Gottfried (1699–1758), German Christian Hebraist. A professor of Oriental languages at Jena, where he had studied with *Johann

Dantz, he published a revised and enlarged edition of *Christian Nold's *Concordantiae Particularum Ebraeo Chaldaicarum* (Jena, 1734). He also put out a revised edition of Dantz's *Turgeman, sive, Interpres ebraeo-chaldaeus* (Jena, 1755). Simon Benedict Tympe, presumably Johann's brother, assisted with the second edition of the *Concordantiae Particularum*. (§ 24)

Uberti, Fazio degli (ca. 1310–ca. 1370), Italian author and poet. He wrote the allegorical poem *Dittamondo* (ca. 1346–67, first published 1447), in imitation of *Dante's *Divine Comedy*. In the poem, Fazio is guided across Europe, Africa, and Asia by the geographer Solinus. In a sense the *Dittamondo* provides an earthly parallel to the *Divine Comedy*. (§ 101)

Vater, Johann Severin (1771–1826), German Christian Orientalist and Slavicist. A professor mainly at Halle, he authored the *Hebräsiche Sprachlehre* (Leipzig, 1797); the second edition appeared as the two-part *Grammatik der hebräischen Sprache* (Leipzig, 1807), and an 1814 edition appeared again as *Hebräische Sprachlehre*. He also wrote the *Handbuch der Hebräischen, Syrischen, Chaldäischen und Arabischen Grammatik* (Leipzig, 1802; 2nd ed., 1817). (§ 26)

Vico, Giambattista (1668–1744), Italian philosopher and historian. A professor of rhetoric at Naples for most of his career, his most important work was the *Scienza Nuova* (Naples, 1725; 3rd ed., 1744; many subsequent reprints). This work, which was much more popular in the century after it was published, was an early forerunner of what today is designated cultural anthropology. (§ 102 n. 1)

Vita della Volta, Samuel (1771–1853), Italian Jewish physician and Hebraist. A regular contributor to the periodical *Kerem Ḥemed*, he also (according to SDL) published the preface of *Jedidiah Norzi's *Minḥat Shai* (Pisa, 1819). (§ 34)

Wasmuth, Matthias (1625–88), German theologian and Hebraist. A professor of theology at Kiel, and a colleague of *Heinrich Opitz, he published *Hebraismus facilitati et integritati restitutus* (Kiel, 1666) as well as *Institutio methodica accentuationis hebraeae* (Rostock, 1664). He had studied Hebrew with *Johannes Buxtorf II at Basel. (§§ 23; 34; 36; 182)

Wessely, Naphtali Herz (Hartwig) (1725–1805), German Jewish Hebraist, poet, and pioneer of the Haskalah movement. His philological works include the two-volume *Gan Na'ul* (also called *Levanon*) (Amsterdam, 1765; Lemberg, 1806; Vienna, 1829), on Hebrew synonyms and roots; *Yein Levanon* (Berlin, 1775), on the Mishnaic tractate Avot; *Ruaḥ Ḥen* (Berlin,

1780), on the Wisdom of Solomon; and a commentary to Leviticus, which appeared in the Pentateuch edition of *Moses Mendelssohn. (§§ 40; 192)

Winer, Georg Benedikt (1789–1858), German Protestant theologian and Bible scholar. In addition to many works on Biblical studies (mainly pertaining to the New Testament), and grammars of Biblical, Targumic, and Talmudic Aramaic, he produced an enlarged (third) edition of *Simonis' *Lexicon manuale hebraicum et chaldaicum* (Leipzig, 1828). (§ 26 n. 2)

Wolf, Johann Christoph (1683–1739), German Christian Hebraist and bibliographer. An avid collector of Hebrew books and manuscripts, he produced a monumental work on Jewish literature entitled *Bibliotheca Hebraea* (4 vols., Hamburg and Leipzig, 1715–33), totaling roughly 5000 pages. For over 150 years after its publication, the work was a chief source of knowledge among Christians for post-Biblical Jewish literature. (§§ 14; 17; 18 n. 3; 29 n. 9; 34 n. 2; 36 n. 1; 43)

Worms, Asher Anshel (1695–1759), German Jewish physician, mathematician, and Hebraist. He wrote numerous works on mathematics and other sciences, as well as on Hebrew literature and grammar. Most importantly among the latter was his posthumously published *Seyag le-Torah* (Frankfurt am Main, 1766), on the Masorah and the Masoretes. Worms held that the Masoretes did not invent the vowel points, but rather only transcribed them. (§ 10 n. 1)

Yarḥi, Solomon see Solomon ben Abba Mari (ha-)Yarḥi.

Yom-Tov ben Abraham Ishbili (ca. 1250–1330), Spanish Jewish Talmudist. A native of Seville (hence the name Ishbili), he is best known for his novellae to the Talmud. Scholars (including SDL) formerly attributed to him the work *Migdal Oz*, the true author of which is *Shem-Tov ben Abraham ibn Gaon. (§ 9 n. 1)

Zacuto, Abraham ben Samuel (ca. 1450–after 1515), Spanish Jewish historian and astronomer. Well known in Spain for his knowledge of astronomy, he wrote numerous astronomical treatises. His own astrolabes (the first made of metal) and astronomical tables were used by the explorers Vasco da Gama and Columbus. After the expulsion from Spain, then from Portugal, he settled in Tunis, where in 1504 he wrote *Sefer ha-Yuḥasin*, a history of the Jews from creation to the year 1500 (first published, Constantinople, 1566; several subsequent reprints). (§ 11 n. 4)

Zamora, Alfonso de (ca. 1475–ca. 1544), Spanish Marrano Hebraist. First a professor of Hebrew at Salamanca, he subsequently occupied the first chair of Hebrew at the University of Alcalà de Henares. He wrote a grammatical work entitled *Introductiones artis grammaticae hebraicae* (Alcalà de Henares, 1526), a lexicon, *Vocabularium primitivorum hebraicorum* (1515?), and contributed greatly to the Complutensian Polyglott Bible (1514–17). (§ 20)

Zarka, Joseph (Zarko; 14th–15th c.), Sephardic Hebrew grammarian and poet. A pupil of *Efodi, he composed a grammatical work entitled *Rav Pe'alim* in 1429, and a Hebrew dictionary, modeled after *David Kimḥi's *Sefer ha-Shorashim*, entitled *Ba'al ha-Lashon*. These remain unpublished. (§ 17)

Zunz, Leopold (1794–1886), German Jewish historian. Considered one of the founders of the modern study of Judaism as a science, his *Gottesdienstlichen Vorträge der Juden* (Berlin, 1832) is one of the most important Jewish books of the nineteenth century. In it, the historical evolution of Hebrew literature was presented for the first time. (§ 18 n. 2)

Printed in the United States
48176LVS00004B/17